# ANATOMY *of* HOSTILITY

## The US-Soviet Rivalry in Perspective

# ANATOMY *of* HOSTILITY

## The US-Soviet Rivalry in Perspective

## Miroslav Nincic

*New York University*

HARCOURT BRACE JOVANOVICH, PUBLISHERS

San Diego   New York   Chicago   Austin   Washington, D.C.
London   Sydney   Tokyo   Toronto

ISBN: 0-15-502712-3
Library of Congress Catalog Card Number: 88-82144
Printed in the United States of America

Map: Maryland CartoGraphics

*To My Mother*

◆　　　◆　　　◆　　　◆　　　◆

*"We find it almost as difficult as the communists to believe that anyone could think ill of us, since we are as persuaded as they that our society is so essentially virtuous that only malice could prompt criticism of any of our actions . . ."*

Reinhold Niebuhr, *The Irony of American History*

# Preface

This book examines the political, social, and economic circumstances that underlie and shape the course of US-Soviet relations. The subject may seem exhausted but, surprisingly, it is not: the matter of what molds the hostility between the superpowers typically is relegated to a set of questions to which the answers appear so evident as to require no further elaboration. Although excellent histories of the Cold War and of the period of détente have been published, and specific facets of superpower interaction have been studied extensively, there have been astonishingly few efforts at furnishing an overall framework for understanding the basis for the state of relations between the two countries.

Historical overviews of US Soviet relations are certainly valuable, but they reflect the specific focus of the historian's task. Historiography seeks to establish the facts and, although each author brings an implicit explanatory perspective to the work, its central aim is not to provide a *conceptual* framework for understanding US-Soviet interactions. There also is a specialized body of work that focuses on narrower issues in Soviet-American relations—studies of the economic aspects of the Cold War and détente, of superpower rivalry in certain geographic regions, analyses of specific aspects of the two nations' interaction (e.g., technological exchanges), and so forth. These generally are useful contributions to an understanding of how the United States and the Soviet Union deal with each other; they are, however, by virtue of the goals they set for themselves, appropriately biased contributions.

This book seeks to go beyond the available literature by providing a general framework for explaining the hostile rivalry that, for several decades, has dominated the superpowers and has molded the fulcrum around which a substantial part of world politics has revolved. The central aim is to fashion an integrated view of the causes of the hostility, and of the ups and downs it experiences. The theme carried through the book is that US-Soviet relations are shaped largely by forces generated from within the two societies rather than by credible conflicts of interest between them. It is not infrequently recognized that the tone of US–Soviet relations is determined partly by domestic drives; nevertheless, there have been few efforts at translating an understanding of these pressures into a theory of the superpower rivalry. Yet the building blocks for such an approach are available, and this is the primary goal of this book.

I would like to thank Drake Bush and Robert C. Miller of Harcourt Brace Jovanovich for encouragement and assistance. Donna Klick, Alexander Yanov, and Christer Jönsson, University of Lund, Sweden, read the entire manuscript and offered constructive comment. Allison Astorino was my conscientious research assistant during the early phases of the project.

Miroslav Nincic

# Contents

## CHAPTER FIVE
♦ ♦ ♦ ♦ ♦

# Russia's American Policy and the Structure of Soviet Politics    183

## CHAPTER SIX
♦ ♦ ♦ ♦ ♦

# The Implications    237

# CHAPTER ONE

◆ ◆ ◆ ◆ ◆

# The Issue in Focus

Alexis de Tocqueville observed in 1835:

> There are at the present time two great nations in the world, which started from different points, but seem to tend toward the same end. I allude to the Russians and the Americans. . . . All other nations seem to have nearly reached their natural limits, and they have only to maintain their power; but these are still in the act of growth. . . . Their starting-point is different and their courses are not the same; yet each of them seems marked out by the will of Heaven to sway the destinies of half the globe.[1]

With remarkable prescience, de Tocqueville described the international system of the second half of the twentieth century. He was not able to predict, however, that the "two great nations" would come to be linked by a uniquely perilous relationship whose causes and character we do not yet fully understand.

The depth and duration of US-Soviet hostility marks a major discontinuity for the foreign relations of both countries. America's history had been pockmarked with rivalries, but they were generally of limited scope and intensity. (From the US perspective, even the two world wars were limited conflicts fought on foreign soil.) These episodes amounted to no more than occasional blemishes on a past that had been devoted primarily to meeting internal challenges, and sustained and bitter rivalries generally did not intrude on the nation's idyllic existence. This condition changed in the aftermath of World War II, as waging the East-West hostility became a major national priority; for the first time US society was galvanized around an assumption of permanent foreign threat.

While the United States has remained uninvolved with the outside world during the greater part of its history, Russia's past has included an almost unbroken sequence of invasions and counterinvasions, of suffering imposed and suffering absorbed. Nevertheless, many of Russia's earlier rivalries were part of a complex pattern of enmities and friendships, and of shifting international loyalties. An adversary on one issue was often a potential ally on another issue, and, before the Cold War, few antagonisms involved a near-total focus of national effort. Although the wars of resistance to Napoleon and against the German invasions of the twentieth century were obvious exceptions, on all three occasions the hostility was limited to the duration of the fighting, and it assumed the possibility of a victor and a vanquished. The antagonism with the United States—which seems to revolve around fundamental issues—that is of a theoretically indefinite duration and that carries even graver perils than Russia's earlier hostilities, is not a mere continuation of that country's troubled past.

The significance of the hostility between the superpowers flows from its actual and potential consequences, the most dramatic of which is the threat of mutual annihilation. If nuclear war should occur, it would be distinguished from all previous conflicts by the fact that total recovery may not be merely a matter of time and effort—it may simply never occur. What applies to the nation may apply to the individual as well. As political scientist Michael Mandlebaum has pointed out, the destruction caused by all previous wars had a finite aspect in that even if individuals within the nation perished, they could at least expect to endure in the symbolic sense that some of the things they had created, or some of the people they had affected, would survive. In other words, *symbolic* immortality of a sort could be assumed. Not so with nuclear war. Nuclear weapons, unlike the instruments of conventional warfare, have the power to destroy even that which previously could have guaranteed symbolic immortality, ensuring, for the first time in human history, total destruction.[2]

Nuclear peril is the most dramatic result of Soviet-American antagonism; a second, if less-widely recognized, consequence is its impact upon the two superpowers' societies. In their own ways, both countries have adapted domestically to the task of confronting each other, and the results generally have been harmful. Although the possibility of nuclear holocaust is real but remote, domestic costs are a permanent and pernicious consequence of the rivalry.

Hostility toward the Soviet Union is reflected in US

governmental structure, and in the balance of power between the various bureaucracies of which it is composed.
Most significantly, the Department of Defense, the network
of intelligence agencies, and those portions of the State Department involved in US-Soviet relations have carved out a
privileged position at the pinnacle of the government's bureaucratic hierarchy. These interests play a preeminent role
in shaping national priorities and, since they are called upon
to assess the very threats upon which their power and resources depend, the nation's Soviet policy acquires a self-
perpetuating momentum. As the Cold War has come to
permeate internal politics as well as foreign policy, it is mirrored in the country's domestic beliefs and practices. For
example, the East-West antagonism has narrowed the scope
of acceptable political discourse within the United States by
increasing the fear of being associated with communist
and left-wing positions. Thus, dialogue on purely domestic matters is more constrained than it might otherwise
have been.[3]

Russian society has been organized to facilitate military
action since its origins in Muscovy in the fifteenth century.
Much more so than in the United States, political values and
institutions have been molded by the assumption of a hostile
outside world. Even so, the Cold War has both solidified
Russia's established political practices and exacerbated some
of its more paranoid and repressive manifestations. In order
to maximize the country's capacity for disciplined response
to the perceived US threat, the distinction between internal
and external enemies has been explicitly blurred, the dominance of the national security bureaucracy has become more
pronounced than ever before, and the traditionally narrow
scope of permitted political discourse has been narrowed
further by the perceived need to wage a grim international
struggle.

Societal mobilization for mutual hostility has been expressed in national economic priorities as well. In the United
States, a substantial portion of economic activity has been
placed in the service of the Cold War. Between 1955 and

1986, defense spending has averaged more than seven percent of gross national product (GNP) and more than one-third of total federal outlays. In the early 1980s, some five million people owed their employment, directly or indirectly, to military programs.[4] The Cold War's impact on the US economy also is felt in the hold it exercises on technological innovation, as sectors of the economy linked to the military enterprise—microelectronics, aeronautics, advanced metallurgy—have enjoyed priority access to the nation's investment resources and scientific talent.[5] All this has entailed certain costs for American society. Overall employment suffers from the fact that the military dollar is not as efficient at job creation as are many other forms of public or private spending.[6] The fiscal burden of the arms race is felt by individuals, and places additional limits on the ability of private consumption to fuel continued economic growth. The biased pattern of investment may not be the principal reason for the sluggish pace of growth in US productivity since the seventies, but its role cannot be discounted.

Given the slimmer economic foundation on which the USSR must sustain its own military effort, the cost of competition is even greater for the Soviet Union. Russia's military spending is roughly equivalent in absolute size to that of the United States, yet because its gross national product is only half as large, its defense burden is twice as onerous in relative terms. Low productivity—probably the single greatest obstacle to accelerated Soviet economic growth—is partly attributable to the defense sector's near-monopoly on the nation's best scientific and engineering talent, as well as on available investment funds. Because the continued legitimacy of any regime depends largely on its economic performance, and since Soviet economic growth regularly has fallen short of official promises, the military rivalry may aggravate the internal threats to the leadership's position.

Thus both sides have been led to accept unprecedented dangers, and significant political and economic costs, for the purpose of confronting each other in a Cold War that has waxed and waned, but never really abated, over more than four decades. The fact that these costs and risks have been tolerated requires explaining in and of itself; however, several paradoxes compound the challenge.

To begin with, neither the United States nor the Soviet Union can claim to be any more secure today than 5, 10, or even 20 years ago. Although this is generally if vaguely understood, the full extent of the paradox does not seem to strike most people. This fact may reflect what one might call the "fallacy of the last step," whereby both nations believe that their security demands they take at least one more step to bolster their power—typically defined as military capacity—and assume that the competition will be frozen at that point. Both nations feel that they will derive continuous benefits from that last step (e.g., the security of an antimissile defense system), but forget that it will simply call forth a countermove by the adversary (who also might think of this as its final move), thus bringing matters back to the starting point. Although this is probably an accurate description of the action–reaction process that sustains the rivalry, one is left to wonder why neither side sees the fallacy or, if so, why it fails to act accordingly? In principle, both countries could have agreed to stabilize their investment in confrontation at levels considerably below those presently attained, at no loss to their relative security.

Another paradox is that, despite their commitment to hostility, both sides make major and continuous efforts to maintain their rivalry within safe bounds. Rarely have belligerence and prudence been taken so far at the same time. At the simplest level, both the United States and the Soviet Union have developed a variety of complex technological safeguards to avoid the accidental or unauthorized use of nuclear weapons.[7] Beyond that, each side has avoided activities that could lead to a military clash on those occasions when they have been embroiled in international crises. For example, during the several crises in the Middle East, both countries took extraordinary precautions to avoid being drawn into conflict by their respective clients. In recognition of the risks of a military clash caused by the frequent entanglements of their navies within narrow bodies of water, the superpowers have signed an agreement to help prevent dangerous incidents involving their ships or aircraft on or over the high seas. The Hot Line agreement of 1963 provided for a direct and virtually immediate link between the White House and the Kremlin. In 1984, the Hot Line was improved through the capability to transmit whole pages of text, photographs, and graphic material (such as maps of respective military positions). It now links military headquarters as well as the two nations' leaders. And in 1987, the two sides agreed to establish a joint crisis control center where, during a crisis, experts from both sides could exchange the sort of information that would prevent either side from misinterpreting the other's intentions.

Each side also demonstrates its self-restraint through an unwillingness to threaten geopolitical interests that the other considers vital. For example, the United States has never been prepared to challenge Soviet interests in Eastern Europe. Although the US government complained about the establishment of Soviet satellites on Russia's European borders, it has never taken meaningful steps to "roll back" Moscow's presence in this part of the world. The repression of the Hungarian uprising of 1956 evoked nothing more than routine US condemnation, and the invasion of Czechoslovakia in 1968 brought a response approximately as limp. Although Washington protested more forcefully the imposition of martial law in Poland in 1981, it never challenged the basic fact of Soviet control over that country. Similarly, the volume of US assistance to the Afghan rebels fighting the Russian invaders suggested that it was designed to make a political point rather than to alter the fact of Soviet military occupation.

The Soviet Union has been at least as circumspect with regard to the US sphere of interest and toward countries in whose future the United States has claimed to possess a vital stake. For example, Moscow has never entertained serious ambitions vis-à-vis Western Europe, and it took no more than token steps to challenge US intervention in Vietnam. Moreover, Moscow has been very prudent in pressing whatever advantage it may have enjoyed in Nicaragua during the eighties. In only two cases—Korea in 1950 and Cuba in 1962—did the Kremlin act in a seemingly incautious manner, perhaps misreading US signals on both occasions. Stalin almost surely condoned North Korea's attack on South Korea in 1950, but this followed both the withdrawal of US troops from South Korea in 1949 and, more significantly, Secretary of State Dean Acheson's January 12, 1950 speech describing America's security perimeter in a manner that excluded the Koreas. Similarly, Khrushchev's decision to install nuclear missiles in Cuba followed the failed and half-hearted US effort to overthrow Fidel Castro in the 1961 Bay of Pigs invasion. The Kremlin may have believed, understandably, that the United States lacked the will to challenge Soviet interests in Cuba.

In 1972 the superpowers signed the Basic Principles Agreement, conceived of as a charter for prudent relations. It states that ideological and social differences should be the object of peaceful negotiations, and it specifies that "both sides recognize that efforts to obtain unilateral advantages at the expense of the other, directly or indirectly, are inconsistent with these objectives."[8] The agreement, however, is too vague to furnish meaningful guidelines to either superpower as to its permissible behavior toward the other; nevertheless, even in the absence of an explicit code of conduct, neither side has been willing to threaten positions that the other unambiguously has proclaimed as vital to its geopolitical interests.

Although both political systems produce a bias toward assertive external behavior (Chapters 4 and 5), each generally has discouraged policies that are rabidly belligerent or gratuitously provocative toward the other side. Extreme Soviet hardliners, from Lavrenty Beria to Aleksandr Shelepin, generally have not managed to get their hands on the levers of foreign policy. The Cold War rhetoric of John Foster Dulles was not matched in its anticommunist fervor by his policies. And Ronald Reagan's pugnacious pronouncements during the early years of his administration were not translated into comparably bellicose policies.[9]

Nothing demonstrates the paradoxical quality of

US-Soviet relations more clearly than the concept of nuclear deterrence, for here incalculable destructive power is acquired professedly for the sole purpose of ensuring that it shall never be used. In 1946 one of America's most prominent strategic theorists explained: "Thus far, the chief purpose of our military establishment has been to win wars. From now on, its chief purpose must be to avert them. It can have almost no other useful purpose."[10] And at the level of official nuclear doctrine, this has been a central assumption ever since. US and Soviet strategic thinking has differed in several ways, but both countries have emphasized repeatedly the deterrent (i.e., war-avoiding) function of strategic arms. The only exceptions were the allusions, at the beginning of the Reagan presidency, to a war-fighting rather than a deterrent role for U.S. nuclear weapons; however, the hostile domestic reaction to this shift of emphasis caused the administration to revert to a more traditional justification for its expanding nuclear arsenal.

Inasmuch as neither side wishes to employ force against the other, why has force been so relentlessly acquired? If the superpowers have led themselves into a hostility whose dangers are abundantly clear, why has this course been chosen? Considering the substantial economic, and perhaps sociopolitical, cost, the choice is especially puzzling.

## ACCOUNTING FOR THE RIVALRY

There are various approaches to accounting for the nature of US-Soviet relations, but three have dominated our thinking. The first approach attributes the mutual antagonism to innate characteristics of the Soviet Union or Soviet Communism, and traces the rivalry, indeed most international problems, to Russia's aggressiveness and expansionism. Though this approach has several variants displaying different levels of sophistication, all are linked by the belief that the fault lies exclusively with the other side. The second (game-theoretic) approach seeks the source of international rivalries in the structure of the interaction, or "game," by which the two countries are linked. The nature of the game is such that even perfectly rational social entities behave in an uncooperative, and even confrontational, manner toward each other, although both may understand that they would do better to overcome the rivalry and cooperate. The third approach is associated with the theory of "political realism," and accounts for the antagonism in terms of a drive deemed proper to all nation states—the drive for power. According to this perspective, if any two nations emerge as more powerful than any other nation, but are of roughly comparable strength to each other, rivalry and hostility between them necessarily ensues. Each approach may seem appealing, even compelling, to some observers, but each explanation of the rivalry is flawed or substantially incomplete.

## The Demonological View

According to this view—which may be the oldest and most widely held of the three—it is because the USSR behaves as it does that superpower relations have taken the course that they have, such behavior springing from what the Soviet Union is: from features that are part of the essence of the country or of its regime. The crux of the belief is that the Soviet Union is evil, and so it is not surprising that the United States cannot get along with it.

This is not an unusual way of perceiving other nations, especially those considered adversaries. The approach probably stems from an inclination to characterize others in a way that is both simple and meaningful, and that does not demand too much in terms of analytic exertion. This inclination implies that nations often will be grouped into simple and clear-cut categories, no distinction being easier to grasp than that which separates "good" and "bad" nations. It also implies that assignment to either category should be based on properties as simple and meaningful as the categories themselves, properties that can be ascribed to the nation's essence and that, in terms of one's own culture, unambiguously denote goodness or badness. Accordingly, badness—

typically a negation of what one's own society is thought to stand for—is broadly generalizable in that badness can account for most aspects of the other nation's behavior. This perspective is captured in Ronald Reagan's description of the Soviet Union as "the focus of evil in the modern world . . . an evil empire." A shorthand way of identifying this approach is to term it the *demonological* view of the adversary.

The Soviet Union has its own demonological perceptions as well. Although official thinking in Moscow has become more flexible and sophisticated than in earlier decades, vestiges of oversimplified, and at times grotesquely biased, views of the United States can still be found. Generally, such views share the conviction that US foreign policy is dictated by the financial community acting in greedy pursuit of its self-interest, and that the main sources of trouble in the world derive from the conspiracies of rapacious capitalists.[11]

For those Americans who subscribe to the demonological view of East–West relations, Soviet evil has several facets. Its external expression is ruthless aggression and relentless expansionism, a drive for global domination and a conviction that, no matter how violent the methods may be, the end justifies the means. The ultimate goal, it is usually assumed, is a world of nations subservient to Moscow and whose politics are patterned on the Soviet model. According to Richard Pipes, a Harvard historian and leading exponent of this view: "The end objective of Soviet global policy is, of course, a world from which private property in the means of production has been banished and the constituent states are, with minor exceptions, copies of the Soviet state."[12]

The roots of the Soviet Union's international behavior are sometimes sought in properties of the Russian nation but, more frequently, in the nature of Soviet Communism. John Foster Dulles, Eisenhower's secretary of state and one of the most implacable cold warriors in US history, exemplified the demonological view especially clearly. On one occasion Dulles explained: "Soviet Communism starts with an atheistic, Godless premise. Everything else flows from that premise."[13] In another context his depiction of Soviet politics seemed to be based on a literal reading of George Orwell's *Animal Farm*. According to Dulles, Soviet ideology

> believes that human beings are nothing more than somewhat superior animals . . . and that the best kind of a world is that world which is organized as a well-managed farm is organized, where certain animals are taken out to pasture, and they are fed and brought back and milked, and they are given a barn as shelter over their heads.[14]

The foreign policy implications of this view of an ideal political organization were evident to Dulles: "I do not see how, as long as Soviet Communism holds those views, there can be any permanent reconciliation. . . . This is an irreconcilable conflict."[15]

The demonological view of the Soviet Union is rooted in a variety of beliefs and needs. It flows partly from the conviction that a nation which stands for values that run counter to so much of what the United States stands for also must be a nation with predatory international ambitions, and certainly a country that wishes America nothing but ill. Thus the approach may repose on a striving for perceptual consistency (a matter further explored in Chapter 3). At times, demonological assessments of Soviet foreign policy are based on Moscow's behavior in the years immediately following World War II, especially the hegemony it established over much of Eastern and Central Europe, and its disturbing behavior vis-à-vis Turkey and Iran.[16] At times too, extreme and uncritical hostility toward the Soviet Union may serve the purpose of bolstering one's commitment to the values for which the United States stands. In fact, a willingness to grant Russia the benefit of the doubt on any issue is sometimes interpreted as a rebuff to America's own values, institutions, and policies. Although there is nothing astonishing about this—a link between the solidarity within a group and its hostility toward another group has been established[17]— still, a commitment to one's own country seems an insufficient foundation upon which to interpret the behavior of another nation.

The demonological perspective often seeks to emphasize its claims with telling analogies. If the adversary is considered irremediably evil, the most apt analogy is of another nation that was, at one time or another, considered equally vile. The example of Nazi Germany is most frequently pressed into service. The Committee on the Present Danger, which lobbied vigorously against détente in the late seventies, observed that in the years before 1939

> the world order, partly restored at Versailles in 1919, fell apart under the hammer blows of Adolph Hitler. Today a similar process is taking place as the Soviet Union pursues a program of expansionism even more ambitious than that of Hitler, claiming the sanction of scientific Socialism for designs in the ancient mold of conquest and predation.[18]

The concept of *appeasement,* used to denote an insufficiently assertive policy toward the Soviet Union, has its roots in the democratic West's failure to confront Hitler in the years preceding World War II (the "Munich syndrome"). Such analogies may seem compelling, but represent a risky form of reasoning. Analogies can help make a point, but frequently are misused. By stressing certain differences while ignoring others, analogies can bias the analysis in an insidious manner;[19] moreover, analogy itself can prove nothing. As historian David H. Fischer has explained:

> Analogical inference itself is powerless to . . . *prove* (emphasis added) that because A and B are alike in respect to X, they are therefore alike in respect to Y. Proof requires either inductive evidence that Y exists in both cases, or else a sound deductive argument for the coexistence of X and Y.[20]

That the demonological view relies on inadequate standards of proof and more often draws on an ideological than empirical source does not necessarily invalidate its conclusions. Correct conclusions sometimes are reached by inadequate methods, and much of Chapter 2 focuses on examining the claim that the Soviet Union is an aggressively expansionist nation. At the moment, however, all that can be said is that, on the evidential basis it provides, the demonological view fails to make its case.

## The Game-Theoretic View

A very different perspective comes from what is known as "game theory." For moral judgments and Manichaean interpretations of the world, game theory substitutes assumptions of rationality; it demonstrates, with mathematical rigor, how certain forms of behavior are predictable and how apparently irrational outcomes can be produced by perfectly rational actions.[21] As the term is used here, a "game" does not connote frivolity and amusement. Though chess or bridge bear an abstract relation to the games of social scientists, the latter "games" refer specifically to situations of interdependent decision making in which the players maintain rational control over their moves and where outcomes are determined not only by one's own moves, but by the moves of the other players as well. The United States and the Soviet Union, for example, can be viewed as two nations that play a variety of games with each other, and with other nations as well. And if the structure of the game is understood properly, the nature of their relations can be explained as well.

There are, it seems, two major advantages to viewing social interaction in terms of games. First, games make the options available to the players, and the anticipated outcomes ("payoffs") of the various combinations of their joint decisions, explicit and unambiguous. By so doing, game theory lays bare the elemental structure of the decisions faced by the players. Second, game theory often demonstrates how outcomes that are suboptimal, indeed apparently irrational, from the perspective of the players can be the product of decisions that, taken individually, are quite rational. As a leading game theorist in political science observes in a book devoted exclusively to the superpower rivalry:

> The *apparent* irrationality of such conflict stems . . . more from the intractable choices that players face in the "superpower games" than from the actions the players take that may, on occasion, appear irrational. . . . Because the games they find themselves embroiled in make conciliatory choices extremely problematic, their play frequently leads to pernicious conflict.[22]

Given that Soviet-American relations are fraught with paradoxes, the game-theoretic approach may furnish some of the answers and insights we seek. The game in terms of which US-Soviet relations are usually described is the "prisoner's dilemma"—a game that pervades political life and to which social scientists have devoted much attention.[23] It embodies a pervasive paradox of social existence: the tendency to accept the costs and risks of a confrontational relationship though all players understand that they would be better off if they behaved cooperatively toward one another.

The prisoner's dilemma most often is illustrated by some variant of the following story. Two suspects are arrested for armed robbery and murder. The prosecutor in charge of the case, though convinced of their guilt, lacks sufficient evidence to obtain a conviction without a confession from at least one of the prisoners. The prosecutor keeps the two suspects isolated from each other, and approaches them in turn with the following proposition:

"If you agree to confess before the other prisoner confesses, and to testify against him, you will be set free and receive a handsome reward. Of course, the other prisoner will almost certainly be sentenced to death. But you should know that my assistant is making the same proposition to the other suspect and, if he confesses before you do, he will get his freedom and the reward, while you will surely be sentenced to death."

"But," asks the first prisoner, "suppose we both confess at the same time?"

"Then," says the prosecutor, "I will see that you both get sentenced to ten years in jail, though I will not seek the death penalty for either of you."

"What if neither of us confesses?" continues the prisoner. "In that case," responds the prosecutor, "I will have to set you both free for lack of evidence, but neither of you will get the reward I mentioned."

The offer being made to both prisoners, they are left to think about what they should do.

To illustrate the choices and outcomes available to the prisoners (X and Y), a game matrix (or "payoff" matrix) usually is provided. Each player may confess or refuse to confess. A refusal is a cooperative move vis-à-vis the other player (C); a confession is a noncooperative move, usually termed a "defection" (D).

## The Prisoner's Dilemma Payoff Matrix

**X**

|  |  | C | D |
|---|---|---|---|
| **Y** | **C** | +1(R) <br> +1(R) | +20(T) <br> −20(S) |
|  | **D** | −20(S) <br> +20(T) | −10(P) <br> −10(P) |

The four possible outcomes are represented in the four cells of the matrix. The numbers roughly depict the expected benefits or losses, to each player, from each course of action.[24] From X's perspective, there are four possibilities. If he cooperates by refusing to confess, one of two things will happen. The other prisoner may cooperate as well, in which case they both go free but neither gets the money (an outcome depicted by a reward of +1 to both players). If the other prisoner defects by confessing, X will get the death penalty (−20) whereas Y will go free with the reward (+20). If X decides to defect, he again faces two possible outcomes. Y may rashly cooperate, in which case X gets his freedom and the money (+20) whereas his partner in crime gets the electric chair (−20). But if Y also decides to defect by confessing, they both get the lower, ten-year penalty (−10, −10).

Several things are now apparent. Each prisoner is tempted (T) to defect while hoping the other will cooperate, making the latter a saint or a sucker (S). At the same time, a situation where both get the reward (R) for mutual cooperation is much preferred to a situation where both must accept the punishment (P) for simultaneous defection. (The numbers in the cells are illustrative only; the only requirement is that 'T' be preferred to R which is preferred to P which, in turn, is preferred to S).[25]

Unable to communicate with each other (and possibly not willing to trust each other even if they could), each player must do what seems best for him regardless of what the other player does. Unfortunately, this dilemma drives both players to mutual defection if they are rational. Player X knows that if player Y cooperates, the best thing for X to do is to defect (entitling X to the T payoff); however, if Y defects, it certainly is in X's interest to defect as well (since P is much preferred to S). Thus, no matter what Y does it is rational for X to defect. The same being true of Y, both players defect—placing themselves in the (P, P) situation and depriving themselves of the reward of mutual cooperation (R, R). In other words, both players land themselves in a suboptimal situation.

As long as the players' interests are, or are thought to be, partly incompatible and as long as they cannot communicate effectively (either they lack the means to communicate or they do not trust each other's promises), a prisoner's dilemma is likely to occur, and the temptation not to cooperate will dominate the urge to do so. In many respects this is an excellent description of US–Soviet rivalry. In particular, the arms race is often considered a typical prisoner's dilemma,[26] and can be illustrated by a comparable payoff matrix.

In this game, disarming is the equivalent of cooperation whereas continued arming is the equivalent of defection. Each side would consider itself best off if it continued to arm while the other disarmed (T), and each would consider itself worse off if it disarmed unilaterally (S). At the same time, both countries would do better by disarming simultaneously (R), thus saving the economic expense of inexorable military growth. Nevertheless, given their mutual distrust, both

## The Arms Race as a Prisoner's Dilemma

**United States**

| | Disarm | Arm |
|---|---|---|

<table>
<tr><td rowspan="2">Soviet Union</td><td>Disarm</td><td>R      R</td><td>S     T</td></tr>
<tr><td>Arm</td><td>T     S</td><td>P     P</td></tr>
</table>

(where $T > R > P > S$)

countries choose the suboptimal course of proceeding with (continuing) the arms race (P).

The same game structure seems to apply to other central aspects of superpower competition: it has been applied to the process of nuclear deterrence,[27] and it may be applied to various nonmilitary aspects of the rivalry as well. For example, both nations may wish to acquire an additional strategic foothold in the Third World by enlisting a previously nonaligned nation as an ally. Since the attempt to do so may entail a variety of costs (the foreign aid required to purchase the nation's friendship, the costs of establishing military facilities abroad, and so forth), it would be in both superpowers' interests to agree to forego such competition. Yet each would be worse off if the other managed to acquire Third World allies and, not trusting the other's restraint, each felt compelled to pursue the competition—with all its costs and risks. Consequently, we can explain the superpowers' repeated decisions to compete when both would do better if they cooperated.

The game-theoretic perspective thus sheds light on an important paradox of US-Soviet relations and, possibly, on its underlying dynamics. As an explanation of the hostility, however, it does not go far enough, for it takes as given much that requires explanation. The game-theoretic perspective assumes that the interests of the two sides are largely incompatible, or at least that they are perceived as such. Why else, in the arms race example, would either side care whether the other acquired more weapons? The perspective also assumes that the sides cannot communicate effectively their intentions to each other, even when acting in good faith (because of mutual distrust and, possibly, because of mutual misperceptions). Thus, game theory begs several basic issues instead of analyzing them. It states why some situation will lead to an undesirable outcome but not why the situation was created in the first place.

What are the US and Soviet interests that are assumed to be in conflict, and are they indeed incompatible? Were such interests less incompatible at the height of détente in 1972, or during the thaw in Soviet-American hostility in the late eighties than, say, during the surges of hostility in the early fifties and late seventies? If there is too much mutual suspicion to allow for effective communication, why is this so? Inasmuch as the quality of relations has shifted, has distrust also experienced ebbs and flows? These, and many other, issues are central to understanding both the origins and the subsequent course of superpower rivalry, yet game theory has little, if anything, to say about them. The structure of the game is assumed, but never accounted for.

By analogy, if we saw two cars driving at breakneck speed toward each other though a single-lane tunnel, we could confidently predict their collision. The structure of the situation—the inability of either car to avoid the other and a speed that precluded stopping in time—would account for the crash. However, can we really understand why the crash occurred without knowing why a tunnel with only one lane was built and, especially, how two cars could have driven headlong toward each other under the circumstances?

### Realpolitik

Realpolitik, or "political realism," partakes of what may be called "grand theory." Grand theory is based on a few sweepingly bold assertions from which a large number of specific implications are derived. So powerful do its assumptions seem that virtually nothing escapes their explanatory net, and variations of the theory generally consist of minor twists on a single, central theme. The proposition that lies at the heart of political realism is that the behavior of nations stems from an overriding impulse: the drive for *power*. Everything else about international politics flows from this simple and inescapable fact. An implication is that any two countries that become more powerful than all others, yet roughly equal to each other, inevitably will experience a mutually competitive and hostile relationship.

Although the scholarship of international relations has seen several variants of political realism from Thucydides and Machiavelli to Kissinger,[28] its most comprehensive, articulate, and influential modern statement was provided by Hans J. Morgenthau in his *Politics Among Nations,* first published in 1948. Statesmen, according to Morgenthau, "think and act in terms of interest defined as power. The aspiration for power being the distinguishing element of international politics, as of all politics, international politics is of necessity power politics."[29] This is not surprising since the drive to "dominate" has the status of an "elemental biosocial drive" that is "common to all men."[30]

It seems then, in Morgenthau's view, that power is an end in itself (although he does at times also view power as a means to an end). But the potential for circular reasoning is evident here, and many realists are aware of this. For example, Kenneth Waltz, who defines his approach to international politics as "neo-realism,"[31] explicitly maintains that the only ultimate end of nation states is security, whereas power is "a means not an end." Yet because of the essential anarchy of the international system—which unlike the domestic systems of nation states lacks a common set of behavioral norms or the means of enforcing collective decisions—security ultimately depends on power; hence power is pervasively sought by nation states.

Whatever their differences may be, realists share the conviction that the international system tends to establish a rough equilibrium of power among its various members. In Morgenthau's words:

The aspiration for power on the part of several nations, each trying either to maintain or overthrow the status quo, leads of necessity to a configuration that is called the balance of power and to policies that aim at preserving it.[32]

This is only natural, for it follows from the essence of international politics. Although sought by every nation, power is relative since any country's position in this respect depends on the power possessed by others. Thus, each nation is driven both to enhance its own power directly and to ensure that no *other* nation or group of nations becomes too powerful. Under the circumstances, the tendency is for a rough balance of power to be established among the various members of the international system. Waltz heartily endorses this view; in fact, he points out that the achievement of balance may be attained even if it is not the explicit goal of all states: "Balances of power tend to form whether some or all states consciously aim to establish and maintain a balance, or whether some or all states aim for universal domination."[33]

The search for equilibria is as common in the social sciences as it is in the physical sciences, and it may correspond as much to an intellectual need to discover order as to a pervasive characteristic of the real world. In political thinking, moreover, a balance of power generally means that no unit within a system will be able to totally dominate the others. A balance of power is thus considered normatively desirable, as in the American constitutional principle of "checks and balances." In international politics, power equilibrium is the only reliable guarantee of peace and of the independence of nation states. As Morgenthau again observes:

International peace and order are a function of the balance of power—that is, of an approximately equal distribution of power among several nations or a combination of nations, preventing anyone of them from gaining the upper hand over the others. It is this approximate, tenuous equilibrium that provides whatever peace and order exists in the world of nation states.[34]

A special case emerges when two nations acquire a clear preponderance of power: a world in which bipolarity has replaced multipolarity. When this occurs

> a bipolar political system has an inherent tendency to trans-form itself into a two-bloc system. With the flexibility of the multipolar system gone and their allies firmly within their re-spective orbits, the two superpowers can increase their strength in terms of prestige, territory, population, and natural resources only by drawing the uncommitted nations into their orbits.[35]

This is where the pressure toward hostility and confronta-tion arises, since any increase in either side's power is achievable only at the other's expense. If the military capac-ity of the two superpowers is sufficiently great and if it is somewhat evenly balanced, outright warfare may be avoided by mutual deterrence;[36] but this condition does not preclude permanent hostility at a level of intensity just below that of armed conflict.

The differences between political realism and the first two perspectives discussed are clear. Unlike the demono-logical view, political realism does not divide the world into nations that are either virtuous or evil. It does not seek the sources of nations' foreign policy in their ideological convic-tions or in their political and economic arrangements. All nations, political realism maintains, behave similarly under similar circumstances: each nation is driven by the same motivational pressure—the drive for power. Political real-ism is not incompatible with game-theoretic approaches to international politics, but its focus is different. Generally it is not concerned with formal models of how nations or their leaders rationally choose among several courses of action, but is concerned with how various distributions of power emerge as a result of nations' security concerns and with what the consequences of these distributions may be, espe-cially for international peace.

Although it sheds important light on the nature of world politics, the realist outlook is flawed in important respects. In addition, there are too many questions about the Soviet-

American rivalry that political realism does not, or cannot, usefully address. To begin with, the central assumptions underlying political realism may not be as compelling as its proponents claim. Particularly troubling issues arise if power is considered an end in itself; if so, it is difficult not to assume, along with Morgenthau, that the drive for power is an "elemental biosocial drive." However, this is an assumption for which there is no credible empirical evidence.[37] Moreover, even if it were proven that individuals really are propelled by such a drive, it would remain to be demonstrated that the motivational properties of individuals can be projected onto nation states: organizations erected around norms, customs, institutions, and procedures that bear little resemblance to the "biosocial" makeup of individuals.

Realists may seek to circumvent this problem by claiming that nations behave *as if* they were motivated by innate power drives, but even this claim is questionable. Much of what states pursue in international affairs concerns such goals as domestic economic welfare or international prestige. Although attainments in such areas may be convertible ultimately into national power, this is usually not their basic purpose. And, if one maintains that pursuit of power must be all-pervasive since so many national attainments can be converted somehow into increased power, then political realism is reduced to limp tautology.

One also must ask to what extent the principal predictions of political realism are borne out in fact. Does the international system tend to gravitate toward an equilibrium of power?[38] The experience of numerous empires suggests, at least on a regional level, that such has not been the case. And whether or not it has been true on a global level depends on how one chooses to measure power. It also depends on how unhurriedly this equilibrium can occur without invalidating the theory; for example, by most criteria the world of the interwar period witnessed several decades of unmatched US power. Most importantly, it has never been proven that two particularly powerful nations inevitably must be locked in mutual rivalry. The most obvious counterexample involves Great Britain and the United States at the beginning of the twentieth century. As the first nation to benefit from the industrial revolution and as the possessor of the largest empire on earth—including at its peak 360 million people and 12 million square miles of territory— Great Britain enjoyed global supremacy throughout most of the nineteenth century. On the other hand, the United States enjoyed an abundance of natural resources, the benefits of massive immigration, and an enormous and surging industrial base. The gap between the two nations narrowed and, by the time of World War I, the United States had surpassed England as the most powerful nation on earth. Yet no conflict, or even apparent hostility, marred relations between the two countries. In fact the friendship between America and Britain was very strong at a time when the former was overtaking the latter.

The belief that power is pursued as an end in itself yields tautology instead of explanation. We are on much firmer ground by stating that power is desired as a means to an end, for this view accords with the international system's main feature: its relative anarchy. In the absence of international (global) government or internationally recognized rules of conduct, each nation ultimately must rely on self-help to protect its interests. Accordingly, such nations must seek power to ensure they will prevail when other nations' objectives clash with their own or when, for whatever reason, other nations behave in a predatory manner. Yet, this view restricts the applicability of realpolitik concepts. As John W. Burton pointed out more than 20 years ago: "One suspects that the greater proportion of everyday human and inter-State relationships requires no exercise of power, not even the exercise of persuasion."[39] Further according to Burton:

> The assumption that politics is the pursuit of power is meaningful where . . . there is an objective difference to be resolved. It is also meaningful, though not so strikingly inevitable, where a subjective clash of interests emerges due to false perceptions or lack of communication.[40]

This is exactly the point. Power is pursued, and used, for the purpose of overcoming another nation's resistance when interests collide or when, for other reasons, nations are driven to confrontation; nevertheless, antagonism is a routine expectation between certain nations but not between others. The United States and the Soviet Union, India and Pakistan, and Greece and Turkey are examples of nations that constantly worry about each other's power. The United States and Great Britain, Denmark and Sweden, Bulgaria and Paraguay, all provide the opposite example. Moreover, there are countries that have worried about each other's power at certain times in history but not at others. France and Germany exhibited such concerns during their many decades of hostility—they no longer do. The United States and China did so at one time—not anymore.

Merely stating that superpowers are driven to hostility by seeking power at each other's expense is not particularly enlightening. The more meaningful question is *why* they should do so? Is it because each side has objectives that can be attained only by harming the other side's interests? Is it because superpowers experience what Burton calls a "subjective clash of interests" due to false perceptions or faulty communication? Is it, perhaps, because hostility satisfies some internal need for one or both sides? These are not questions that the analytical equipment of political realism is suited to answer. Nor can political realism explain why US-Soviet rivalry has experienced the shifts that it has since the onset of the Cold War, during which time phases of improvement and deterioration have succeeded each other in quasi-cyclical progression. As long as it treats power as a means and not as an end, political realism provides important insights into the character of international politics and often accounts for existing configurations of international power. But political realism depicts the world with so broad a brush and takes for granted so much that requires explanation, that its utility falls far short of the claims made on its behalf.

The perspectives thus far surveyed do not account adequately for the origins of the rivalry nor can they explain credibly its subsequent development. What is needed is an approach with greater explanatory power, an approach that will identify the mechanisms which drive US-Soviet rivalry along its sinuous path and that will suggest useful clues to policies capable of placing relations on a more genuinely co-operative course.

## SHARPENING THE FOCUS

If none of the established approaches to looking at US-Soviet hostility provides an adequate explanation of its causes, where are we to turn for more productive insights? As a point of departure, we must recognize that hostility between countries can flow from one, or both, of two sources.[41] To begin with, countries may be linked by incompatible overall interests or incompatible specific goals. When this is the case, the basis for hostility is a given. Although one may wish to probe more deeply to discern why these incompatibilities exist, this is not essential if the sole aim is to account for the hostility. It may be interesting to trace the roots of Argentina's and Britain's simultaneous claim to the Falkland Islands (the Malvinas, if one prefers), but it is enough to know that the issue exists for the hostility to be accounted for. Once such antagonisms emerge, both sides may seek to enhance their power in order to prevail; however, the struggle for power should not be confused with the incompatibility that made its pursuit seem necessary. Britain and Argentina may vie for international support regarding their respective designs on the Falklands, but the competition for friends and allies is a consequence of their hostility, not its cause. The incompatible goal must be pursued as an end in *itself* to be a cause of antagonism; nevertheless, there are many instances of international antagonisms that cannot be traced to objective conflicts, and other sources of hostility must be assumed to exist.

When compelling conflicts of interest cannot be found, the usual recourse is to assume that hostility is the product of psychological mechanisms. Warped perceptions of the other side, irrational distrust, and aggressive instincts at times have been assigned primary responsibility for international antagonism,[42] and it may be that the problems separating the two superpowers are of this nature. For example, the distrust and inadequate communication that form a large part of the *dilemma* in the Prisoner's Dilemma could be rooted in mechanisms less logical than psychological. Similarly, psychologically based antagonism could impel nations to pursue power in order to protect interests that are as yet unthreatened. Psychological explanations must be given their due, but take care not to go too far in this direction. Foreign policy behavior is the product of a variety of institutional and social forces, and analogies between individuals and nation states require considerable caution.

A premise of this book is that foreign policies are grounded in national political systems, and that the key to their explanation must be sought in their domestic roots.[43] Even as committed a disciple of realpolitik as Kenneth Waltz has recognized that "structurally, we can describe and understand the pressures states are subject to. We cannot predict how they will react to the pressures without knowledge of their internal predispositions."[44] Waltz himself, however, does little to enlighten us on these internal predispositions. Of the three perspectives on US-Soviet tension surveyed, only the demonological seeks the sources of the rivalry in the other superpower's domestic properties. But, as we have seen, this approach rests on a foundation that is more emotional than empirical, and provides a callow and drastically oversimplified view of East–West relations.

Arguably, the surest way to understand any nation's foreign policy is to examine its *political reward structure*. Each political system creates a pattern of expectations regarding the governmental activities that will be recompensed or punished, and the probability that its leadership will undertake certain forms of behavior is shaped accordingly. A Swedish administration, for example, is more likely to be chastised for failing to provide for the destitute than is a US administration; a French administration is less likely to encounter political trouble at home for encouraging trade with the Soviet Union than is an American administration. Accordingly, one is more likely to encounter ambitious social programs in Sweden and more active East–West trade in France than in the United States.

If an unambiguous conflict of interest exists, hostility between nations is explicable directly. Misperceptions between nations also may help us grasp why they sometimes fail to get along. Even domestic politics may explain why incompatible goals are pursued or why faulty perceptions are allowed to persist. But the need to probe political reward structures is especially strong when neither authentic conflicts of interest nor credible psychological drives can be found. By understanding a country's political reward structure, one is in a far better position to account for predictable tilts in its foreign policy than by relying on the assumption of an invariant power drive, on a mechanistic conception of rationality, or on a demonological view of that country's character. Although there have been few efforts to establish systematic links between political systems and their foreign policies (which must be counted as a failure of modern political science), it is difficult to understand the course of Soviet-American hostility, and international relations more generally, if such connections are not made. The second half of the book attempts to establish just such links.

Political reward structures are comprised of three strands—interests, beliefs, and power—that, when interwoven, define the essence of political life and chart the course governments are most likely to pursue. Politics is the organized pursuit of *interests;* policy is the result of such pursuit. Interests can, broadly speaking, originate at two levels. They can originate within the state, mainly within governmental institutions that promote the policies from which their own organizational interests stand most to benefit, or they can originate outside of the state's organizational contours, within interest groups and the public at large (i.e., within civil society). Patterns of interests at both levels represent the first component of the political reward structure. The second component derives from the structure of *beliefs and values* in the society. People do not act exclusively on the basis of vested interests but also are driven by relatively abstract principles they seek to have embodied in governmental policy. Sometimes these principles are straightforward rationalizations of parochial interests, but not always, and examples of individuals or groups acting in apparent defiance of what would most benefit them occasionally are encountered. The third component of a political reward structure is the distribution of power within the political system. In other words, groups with no power are not in a position to threaten significant punishment when governments do not act in accordance with their interests and beliefs nor to offer meaningful rewards when they do. In US political science, the study of power usually ranks above the study of interests, and considerably above the structure of beliefs. Yet all three jointly constitute a political reward structure that accounts for predictable patterns in the way in which most nations react to international events.

In practice, however, it is not enough to pinpoint mechanisms that tilt a superpower's policies toward confrontation rather than cooperation; it is also necessary to identify the forces that account for changes these policies sometimes experience. Although the United States and the Soviet Union have been inclined to act toward each other in a generally hostile fashion, their attitudes have shifted, with the confrontational component of their policies more pronounced at certain times than at others. If shifts in either side's policies toward the other are not merely reactions to the other's behavior—and we shall see that they often are not—then how are these fluctuations to be explained? The clues provided in this regard by the three models just surveyed are rough at best and of limited use. Yet an examination, often subtle, of the changes in patterns of interest, values, and power—in the components of political reward structures—offers far more sensitive and accurate predictions of the directions in which Soviet-American relations are likely to move.

## A NOTE OF EXPLANATION

The book seeks to account for the rivalry between the superpowers, but the accounting is not intended to be exhaustive: many facets of the rivalry are neglected. Nevertheless, the book focuses on mechanisms that represent the core of the antagonism, the intention being to clarify our under-standing of the hostility by discarding explanations that have not served us well and by suggesting a few that promise to be more helpful. The ultimate aim is to demonstrate "the range of possible alternatives and the potentiality for effective action."[45]

The last point is particularly important because the strongest justification for the social sciences is that they stand to make the world a better place. Although the social scientist's ultimate goal is to be useful, there must be a judicious linking of research and policy. All too often, writings with a policy bent seem designed to develop a rationale for a course of action that, because it is rooted in emotional or ideological convictions, actually has molded the analysis and predetermined its conclusions. Apologetics that masquerades as analysis is at least as insidious as outright propaganda; fortunately however, professional academics generally have been unwilling to permit their discipline to be subverted in this manner. More often academics are guilty of the opposite failing: an inability to place their work in a context that makes the work relevant. Their aim may be "pure" theory or a demonstration of methodological dexterity, but the end product often lacks meaningful connection with the world it purports to account for. And sometimes its only apparent function is to perpetuate itself by providing a foil for academic debate and readings for a captive student audience.

Social science should be neither a vehicle for proselytizing nor a socially irrelevant exercise in academic pomposity; it must seek useful knowledge, but will fail if policy preferences are permitted to intrude upon and to guide the analysis itself. Whatever ultimate usefulness social science might have in guiding policy depends, above all, on the quality of the analytical work that precedes the policy recommendations. The analyst's first task is to identify and account for the causal mechanisms behind the phenomenon sought to be understood. Policy recommendations may flow naturally from this enterprise, but should be secondary to the task of understanding.

Nevertheless, the probability that useful conclusions will be reached increases significantly under two circumstances. First, and most obviously, one must deal with problems of substantive import; in other words, questions should be studied because they involve significant problems—not because they are conveniently researchable. Second, the analysis should be cast at a level at which relevant levers of change can be found. Beyond a certain level of abstraction, the ability to formulate recommendations that have concrete meaning is lost and one is left with vague platitudes (world government, goodwill among men). But at too specific a level of analysis one loses the ability to make suggestions encompassing enough to place a meaningful dent in the reality one is seeking to change.

Beyond this, it is important to place analysis in an adequate historical context. Political scientists often shun too pronounced a reliance on history—largely, perhaps, for fear of being deemed "descriptive" rather than analytical, of being thought of as storytellers rather than scientists. Yet by shunning history they deprive themselves of much of the explanatory benefits gained by analyzing the present against the backdrop of its past, and by illuminating both continuities and discontinuities in the phenomena they wish to understand. Apart from the fact that adequate description of a phenomenon generally must precede the search for its causes,[46] attentiveness to historical context furnishes two major benefits.

First, history provides at least a rough illustration of the range of possibilities, thereby allowing us to overcome the myopia that comes with an unwillingness to think in time. For instance, it would be easy to forget that Europe was once a particularly war-prone region if our observations were founded merely on the last few decades. And if this fact were forgotten, the conditions that might reignite conflict in this part of the world could be neglected by anyone contemplating Europe's future. In the early fifties, many observers of Sino-Soviet relations would have found it difficult to believe that the two communist countries could ever be anything but allies; yet, since the sixties, their relations have been extraordinarily venomous. On the other hand, some-one observing US-Russian relations at the time of America's Civil War would have found it difficult to conceive that they could ever be anything but warm and mutually supportive; subsequent history, however, has demonstrated otherwise. Thus a long-term perspective provides a better idea of what is feasible, and is especially valuable when the phenomenon we wish to understand has a cyclical quality: the shorter the period over which we examine it, the more likely we are to extrapolate unjustifiably from the present into the future and to assume that the current state of affairs is the natural state of affairs.

A historical perspective is essential for a second reason as well: it enables us to establish whether or not two phe-nomena jointly vary across time, and thus to discover rela-tions of cause and effect. If one phenomenon is to be another's cause, it is necessary, though not sufficient, that the occur-rence of the former be associated with the occurrence of the latter. If, for example, excessive government spending causes inflation, one would expect instances of exceptionally large public outlays to precede or appear in tandem with evidence of surging price levels.

Although an absence of covariation suggests that no causal association exists, its presence does not prove causation: two phenomena can jointly vary because they are connected si-multaneously to some third force, rather than in direct re-sponse to each other. The fact that high-crime neighborhoods in many US cities often are inhabited by nonwhites does not mean that there is a causal relation between race and crime. Since these also are neighborhoods of great poverty, the ap-propriate inference is that destitution accounts for the inci-dence of crime. Still, covariation is a necessary condition of cause, and usually its first clue. To establish a basis for ex-plaining US-Soviet relations it is imperative that we give potential covariations sufficient opportunity to manifest themselves; in turn, this requires that the history of relations be traced through a sufficiently long period of time.

Chapters 4 and 5 examine the structure of domestic po-litical rewards and punishments that have molded the course of US-Soviet rivalry, and identify common patterns between the superpowers in this regard. Accordingly, these are core chapters. But before analyzing the connection between domestic politics and US-Soviet relations, it is useful to address two assumptions that pervade our thinking and that, directly or indirectly, characterize the three models surveyed in this chapter: (a) that there are objective conflicts of interest between the superpowers and (b) that the rivalry is somehow driven by psychological mechanisms. Chapters 2 and 3 undertake this task. Finally, Chapter 6 discusses the policy conclusions yielded by the view of superpower relations developed in this book.

## NOTES

1. Alexis de Tocqueville, *Democracy in America*, I (New York: Alfred A. Knopf, 1945), p. 343.

2. Michael Mandelbaum, "The Bomb, Dread, and Eternity," *International Security*, Fall 1980, pp. 3–24.

3. One of the few books to discuss the domestic political effects of US-Soviet rivalry is Bernard A. Weisberger, *Cold War, Cold Peace* (New York: Houghton Mifflin, 1984).

4. *Statistical Abstract of the United States: 1987* (Washington, DC: Bureau of the Census, 1987) and Robert W. Degrasse Jr., *Military Expansion, Economic Decline: The Impact of Military Spending on U.S. Economic Performance* (Armonk, NY: Sharp, 1983).

5. See Lloyd J. Dumas, "Military Spending and Economic Decay," in Lloyd J. Dumas, *The Political Economy of Arms Reduction* (Boulder, CO: Westview Press, 1982), pp. 1–26.

6. This is discussed in Miroslav Nincic, *The Arms Race: The Political Economy of Military Growth* (New York: Praeger, 1982), Chapter 3.

7. Many such safeguards are described in Paul Bracken, *The Command and Control of Nuclear Forces* (New Haven: Yale University Press, 1983).

8. See Alexander L. George, "The Basic Principles Agreement of 1972: Origins and Expectations," in Alexander L. George, ed., *Managing U.S.-Soviet Rivalry* (Boulder, CO: Westview, 1983), pp. 107–108.

9. For an explanation of why more extreme foreign policy positions rarely prevail in the United States, see Miroslav Nincic, "The United States, the Soviet Union, and the Politics of Opposites," *World Politics*, July 1988, pp. 452–475.

10. Bernard Brodie, *The Absolute Weapon* (New York: Harcourt Brace Jovanovich, 1946), p. 52.

11. For the views of selected Soviet demonologists, see Chapter 6.

12. Richard Pipes, *Survival Is Not Enough* (New York: Simon and Schuster, 1950), p. 176.

13. John Foster Dulles, *War and Peace* (New York: Macmillan, 1950), p. 8.

14. "Nomination of John Foster Dulles," U.S. Senate, Committee on Foreign Relations, 83rd Congress, 1st Session (Washington, DC, 1953), p. 10.

15. Same as 14, p. 11.

16. Soviet behavior during this period is discussed in more detail in Chapter 4.

17. See Dorwin Cartwright, "The Nature of Group Cohesiveness," in Dorwin Cartwright and Alvin Zander, eds., *Group Dynamics*, 3d edition (New York: Harper and Row, 1968); Lewis Coser, *The Functions of Social Conflict* (New York: Free Press, 1956); Robert L. Hamblin, "Group Integration During a Crisis," *Human Relations*, February 1958, pp. 67–76; Arthur Stein, "Conflict and Cohesion: A Review of the Literature," *Journal of Conflict Resolution*, March 1976, pp. 143–172.

18. The Committee on the Present Danger, *Alerting America: The Papers of the Committee on the Present Danger* (Washington, DC: Pergamon-Brassey's, 1986), p. 175. See also Les K. Adler and Thomas G. Perterson, "Red Fascism: The Merger of Nazi Germany and Soviet Russia in the American Image of Totalitarianism, 1930s–1950s," *American Historical Review*, April 1970.

19. For illustrations, see Ernest R. May, *Lessons of the Past* (New York: Oxford University Press, 1973).

20. David H. Fischer, *Historians' Fallacies: Toward A Logic of Historical Thought* (New York: Harper and Row, 1970), p. 259.

21. The pioneering work in game theory is John von Neumann and Oscar Morgenstern, *Game Theory and Economic Behavior*, 3d edition (Princeton, NJ: Princeton University Press, 1953). A nontechnical survey is Morton D. Davis, *Game Theory: A Nontechnical Introduction*, revised edition (New York: Basic Books, 1983). For an interesting survey of some applications of game theory to political life, see Steven J. Brams, *Paradoxes in Politics: An Introduction to the Nonobvious in Political Science* (New York: Free Press, 1976). See also Duncan Snidal, "The Game Theory of International Politics," *World Politics*, October 1985, pp. 1–24.

22. Steven J. Brams, *Superpower Games: Applying Game Theory to Superpower Conflict* (New Haven: Yale University Press, 1985), p. xi.

23. For some applications of game theory to international relations, see Robert Axelrod, *The Evolution of Cooperation* (New York: Basic Books, 1984); Malvern Lumsden, "The Cyprus Conflict as a Prisoner's Dilemma," *Journal of Conflict Resolution*, XVII, 1973, pp. 7–32; Glenn H. Snyder and Paul Diesing, *Conflict Among Nations: Bargaining, Decision Making, and System Structure in International Crises* (Princeton NJ:

Princeton University Press, 1977); Harrison R. Wagner, "The Theory of Games and the Problem of International Cooperation," *American Political Science Review*, June 1983, pp. 330–346.

24. The numbers themselves are not central here and are supplied for illustration only. All that is required is that the conditions in note 25 be met.

25. For there to be a Prisoner's Dilemma, the payoffs must be ranked in the following order: T>R>P>S. It is also assumed that CC>(DC+CD)/2; this ensures that mutual cooperation is preferred to an even chance of being the exploiter or the exploited.

26. See, for example, Steven J. Brams, *Superpower Games*, Ch. 3; Steven J. Brams, Morton D. Davis, and Philip D. Straffin Jr., "The Geometry of the Arms Race," *International Studies Quarterly*, December 1979, pp. 567–588; George W. Downs, David M. Rocke, and Randolph M. Siverson, "Arms Race and Cooperation," *World Politics*, October 1985, pp. 118–146.

27. Frank C. Zagare, *The Dynamics of Deterrence* (Chicago: University of Chicago Press, 1987).

28. For a recent overview of the various strands of political realism, see Robert G. Gilpin, "The Richness of the Tradition of Political Realism," in Robert O. Keohane, ed., *Neorealism and Its Critics* (New York: Columbia University Press, 1986), pp. 301–322.

29. Hans J. Morgenthau, *Politics Among Nations: The Struggle for Power and Peace*, 6th edition, revised by Kenneth W. Thompson (New York: Alfred A. Knopf, 1985), p. 37.

30. Same as 29, p. 37.

31. Kenneth N. Waltz, *Theory of International Politics* (Reading, MA: Addison-Wesley, 1979). See also Robert O. Keohane, "Realism, Neorealism, and the Study of World Politics," in Keohane, ed., *Neorealism and Its Critics*, p. 1–27.

32. Same as 29, p. 187.

33. Same as 31, p. 119. For a brief survey of the balance of power in international history, see Martin Wight, "The Balance of Power and International Order," in Alan James, ed., *The Bases of International Order* (London: Oxford University Press, 1973).

34. Same as 29, p. 388.

35. Same as 29, p. 377.

36. See especially Kenneth N. Waltz, "The Stability of a Bipolar World," *Daedalus*, Summer 1964.

37. The best empirical treatment of the power drive is David G. Winter, *The Power Motive* (New York: The Free Press, 1973).

38. For excellent critiques of balance of power theories, see Inis L. Claude Jr., *Power and International Relations* (New York: Random House, 1962), Ch. 3 and Dina A. Zinnes, "An Analytical Study of the Balance of Power Theories," *Journal of Peace Research*, III, 1967, pp. 270–288.

For a critique with a somewhat different bent, see Richard K. Ashley, "Political Realism and Human Interests," *International Studies Quarterly*, June 1981, pp. 204–237.

39. John W. Burton, *International Relations: A General Theory* (Cambridge: Cambridge University Press, 1967), p. 49.

40. Same as 39, p. 46.

41. See Miroslav Nincic, "Understanding International Conflict: Some Theoretical Gaps," *Journal of Peace Research*, XVIX, 1982; Miroslav Nincic, *United States Foreign Policy: Choices and Tradeoffs* (Washington, DC: Congressional Quarterly Press, 1988), Ch. 7.

42. The pyschological aspect of the superpower rivalry is discussed in Chapter 3.

43. There is very little useful literature that systematically examines the domestic political roots of foreign policy. The only exception is the literature on bureaucratic influences on foreign policy and the body of theory attributing foreign policy, especially imperialism and militarism, to domestic economic needs. These are useful but narrow approaches; where appropriate, they are discussed in greater detail in Chapter 4.

44. Same as 31, p. 71.

45. Barrington Moore Jr., *Political Power and Social Theory* (New York: Harper, 1962), p. 159.

46. A useful discussion of the relation between description and explanation is William G. Runciman, *A Treatise on Social Theory*, I (Cambridge: Cambridge University Press), Chs. 3 and 4.

# CHAPTER TWO

◆ ◆ ◆ ◆ ◆

# Conflicts of Interest: Objective or Derivative?

**A**lthough objective conflicts of interest do not *necessarily* undergird international rivalry, their presence is usually assumed where relations are as bitterly
confrontational as those that have linked the United States
and the Soviet Union. Adherents of the demonological view
consider conflicts of interests between the superpowers obvious and ineradicable, but such conflicts are implicit in the
other two approaches as well. Unilateral defection (T) is so
tempting in a Prisoner's Dilemma precisely because there is
an assumed conflict of interest between the players. A similar conclusion applies to the realpolitik view, for if power
is considered a means of prevailing in a confrontation rather
than an end in itself, there is probably a reason for the confrontation.

Though many consider it apparent that the two sides'
needs are somehow incompatible, the precise reasons are
rarely articulated, at least not in a systematic fashion. What
we must search for, as a first order of business, is evidence
of *objective conflicts of interest* (i.e., evidence of situations where
one of the superpowers would be objectively better off only
as a consequence of making the other objectively worse off).
For example, the appropriation by one country of a section
of borderland would imply a direct loss for a neighboring
country that coveted the same section of land.

It is important to distinguish *objective* conflicts of interest
from those that are *derivative* in nature. The former involve
incompatible pursuits that, in and of themselves, would suffice to pit two sides against each other; the latter assume that
an objective conflict of interest already exists (which assumption may or may not be correct) and usually involve a
contest over the *means* required to pursue the conflict (i.e.,
over the sources of power). If, as a result of their contest
over land, the adversaries sought the diplomatic support of
other countries, they would experience further a derivative
conflict of interest over friends and allies (which are in limited supply and where one side's acquisition is, in principle,
the other's loss). It is derivative because, had the parties not
already been quarreling over something, the contest for supporters would have been unnecessary. Although derivative

conflicts of interest may further fuel a rivalry, they cannot be its primary cause. And if derivative conflicts do not repose on a plausible foundation of objective conflicts, one must ask how they are in fact sustained.

Historically, three sorts of activities have produced objective conflicts of interest between countries: the quest for territorial expansion, the competitive promotion of religious or political beliefs, and the pursuit of economic gain. Such conflicts can occur simultaneously and can amplify each other, but they involve different objectives and each is assumed to affect Soviet-American relations.

## TERRITORIAL CONTENTION AND US-SOVIET RELATIONS

Territorial quarrels traditionally have been a major source of international conflict.[1] The larger the territory encompassed by the nation state, the greater its potential power, prestige, and wealth. Thus, for many nations expansion has been a significant goal at various times in their history. France, Sweden, Germany, Spain, Portugal, Japan, and China, for example, have had histories marked by vigorous bouts of imperialism and expansion. Even US history, despite the nation's quasi-insular character, has been marked by territorial conflict: the 1835 war with Mexico over Texas is one example, and fighting with American Indians surely was rooted in conflicts over land.

East–West hostility often is thought to have a territorial source. The assumption is that Russia is bent on constant aggrandizement; that, like an expanding inkblot, it is driven to spread itself over an ever-larger surface. This inclination is thought to affect crucial American interests and must, in this view, be checked by firm counterpressure: diplomatic if possible, military if necessary. Richard Pipes maintains that "in the history of Russia, expansion is not a phase but a constant."[2] And according to Richard Nixon, "Most of the obstacles to peace today result from the Soviet Union's expansionist policies."[3] These are important claims and they are, in the United States at least, widely shared. As such assertions presumably are grounded in a reading of Russia's history, it is useful to survey the record for the lessons it might teach and for the inferences that may be drawn concerning US-Soviet relations. This survey is necessary because the Cold War accounts for a small portion of Russia's international history—and it is useful to judge allegations of Soviet expansionism during the recent period against the longer measure of its overall national experience.[4]

## RUSSIAN EXPANSIONISM: AN AMBIGUOUS RECORD

Encompassing 8.6-millon square miles, the Soviet Union is the largest nation on earth. It stretches through most of the northern half of the Eurasian land mass and across eleven time zones. Russia is more than twice as large as second-ranked Canada (3.8-million square miles) and dwarfs the 3-million square miles covered by the United States (although its population is not substantially greater). The Russian nation was not born to this territory—its current spread is the product of many centuries of steady expansion. Other countries have had histories of territorial growth, but rarely has this growth been as pronounced as in the case of what is now the Soviet Union. The implications, however, are not as obvious as they are often taken to be.

### Before the Twentieth Century

The origins of modern Russia usually are traced to the city and principality of Kiev at the time of the early Middle Ages, when the Russians assimilated Eastern Orthodox Christianity, absorbed the cultural influence of the Byzantine Empire, and waged virtually continuous warfare against Asian nomadic tribes. The Kievian period ended in the thirteenth century under the blows of invasions by Tatar Mongols (under the descendants of Ghengis Khan), who conquered the Russian principalities and turned them into tribute-paying puppet states.

Resistance gained momentum under the leadership of Russian princes in the northern city (duchy) of Muscovy (Moscow) and, by the middle of the fifteenth century, Mongol domination was overthrown and Muscovy emerged as the capital of a Russian state. This state was forged in warfare and organized to facilitate mobilization for military purposes—which included territorial expansion. Under Ivan the Great (1462–1505), the Muscovite state absorbed the far-larger neighboring city of Novgorod, effecting a fourfold increase of its area. In the sixteenth century, Russia's domination extended over non-Russian peoples as well, as Ivan the Terrible (1533–1584) captured the Tatar kingdoms of Kazan and Astrakhan and extended his rule across the Urals into Siberia. By the sixteenth century, Russia was launched firmly on its outward drive and did not relent in subsequent centuries.

Czar Mihail, who acquired the Russian throne in 1613, led Russia to victory over Poland and expanded its domination into new areas of Europe and Northern Asia. This pattern of lateral expansion characterized the next three centuries. Peter the Great (1689–1725), the first Russian monarch to exhibit genuine interest in Western Europe, moved the capital westward—from Moscow to what was later named Saint Petersburg—and introduced the Russian army to Western military techniques and equipment (which proved most useful in subsequent wars). In 1695 Peter was battling the Turks and, a few years later, fighting with Sweden. By 1721 he had pressed Russia's western frontiers into the Baltic region. A further surge of expansion occurred during the reign of Catherine the Great (1762–1796) who, by seizing Crimea from the Turks in 1783, placed Russia firmly on the Black Sea. She too pushed expansion westward by acquiring what is now Byelorussia, the remainder of Latvia, and the Ukraine. Russia was steadily claiming an ever-larger territory.

The Russian nineteenth century opened with the reign

of Alexander I and with repeated efforts to fend off Napoleonic expansion that, by 1808, had placed much of Europe under French control. Although Russia suffered several early defeats at Napoleon's hands, the French emperor was wary of prolonging the war on hostile soil, and both rulers were anxious for a truce. By the terms of the peace of Tilsit, they agreed to divide Europe between them—giving Russia the Danubian provinces and Finland. But Tilsit, like the pact signed more than 120 years later between Stalin and Hitler, merely postponed an inevitable clash. In 1812, tired of the truce, Napoleon launched a vast army of 600,000 troops against Russia.

Napoleon's forces were successful on the initial offensive. As the Czar's army retreated, the French penetrated as far as Moscow, which the Russians preferred to evacuate and burn rather than leave to the invading forces. The torching of Moscow before Napoleon's armies was an enormous blow to a nation substantially inured to invasions, counterinvasions, and suffering. "After this wound, all others are trifling," declared the Czar. But the French had driven deeply into a vast and inhospitable land, their resupply lines were strained or nonexistent, and the Russian winter was fast upon them. The tide changed rapidly as the Czar's forces launched guerrilla actions against Napoleon's tattered and freezing troops, which were being decimated further by hunger and desertions. As Napoleon's retreating forces approached the Polish border, Russian armies followed, inflicting final and crushing defeats on the invaders (60,000 returned alive). The French were repelled but at enormous human, economic, and psychological costs.

Following the Napoleonic era, Russian expansion again turned toward Asia and, by 1828, what are now the Transcaucasian republics (Georgia, Armenia, and Azerbaijan) were acquired from Turkey and Persia. Russia continued its eastward drive, leading to the seizure of China's Maritime Province, including the present port of Vladivostok. When Alexander II died in 1881, Russia controlled nearly 8-million square miles (i.e., over ninety percent of its present territorial spread). Russia encompassed an area some 13,000 times larger than the 600-square-mile principality of Muscovy in the fourteenth century.

It is easy to draw ominous conclusions about the expansionist inclinations suggested by Russia's history; however, prior to the twentieth century growth was generally deemed a major power's prerogative, even its mission. And Russia was hardly different in this regard than, say, France, Sweden, or Japan. Though the entire stretch of Russia's history is sometimes invoked as proof of its inevitable drive to expand, its behavior in the present century, especially following the Bolshevik Revolution, has produced even stronger allegations regarding its ultimate intentions.[5]

## The Twentieth Century

In many ways the twentieth century has been the most traumatic period in Russia's history, and has imbued Soviet leaders with much of their obsession with foreign invasion and secure borders. In 1904, without declaring war, Japan's superior naval forces struck in the Pacific region, routing the Russians and seizing Port Arthur and southern Manchuria. Although a humiliating experience, it was negligible compared to the costs and suffering occasioned by World War I—the first of two major incursions from the west in this century.

When Austria attacked Serbia in retribution for Archduke Franz Ferdinand's assassination by a Serbian nationalist in June 1914, Russia prepared to defend her fellow Slavs. As Germany's lot was linked to Austria's, the Kaiser declared war on the Czar. Industrially backward Russia was no match for the German military machine, a disadvantage compounded by the military ineptitude of Nicholas II. Russia suffered enormous casualties, and German forces pushed back the country's borders almost as far as its western boundary of the eighteenth century. The suffering, and the total loss of faith in the government, accelerated the maturing of revolutionary forces.

In February 1917, the Old Regime was overthrown and replaced by a provisional republican government that, it was hoped by many (including most Americans), would provide stable democratic government to a country which had never known anything but autocratic rule. Within eight months, however, continued privations and successful Bolshevik agitation led to the Provisional Government's collapse and to the beginning of Communist rule.

Exhausted by the war and confident that capitalist treaties would soon be repudiated by a vast proletarian uprising in Germany, the new rulers agreed to the draconian peace terms of the Brest-Litovsk Treaty. The Germans occupied large portions of Russia, including most of the Ukraine and parts of the Caucasus; Poland, Finland, and the Baltic States were to pass under German control. Ultimately Germany's defeat made Brest-Litovsk irrelevant, but Russia felt it had learned another painful lesson regarding the costs of weakness.

These lessons were impressed on the Russians even more deeply by World War II. German and Russian collision—for the second time in several decades—was largely the result of Hitler's racial hatred toward the Slavs and his determination to procure additional "living space" *(lebensraum)* for the German people at the expense of Russia and Poland. Before the war ended at least 20 million Russians had died, and the nation resolved that foreign aggression would never happen again. On June 22, 1941, Germany and its Axis allies launched 190 divisions across the Soviet border in Operation Barbarossa. The Red Army, badly positioned for a defense in depth, was quickly encircled; nearly 2 million Soviet prisoners were taken in the first six months of the campaign (most of whom starved to death during the following winter). German troops had reached and besieged Leningrad (as Saint Petersburg had been renamed) and, by November, had reached Moscow's suburbs. But the Russian winter again enveloped the invader and, during the winter of 1941–1942, the Red Army managed to push back the Germans from Moscow, though the siege of Leningrad was not yet broken and the Germans still occupied the Ukraine. In the summer of 1942 Hitler launched a second offensive through the south and at Stalingrad. But, like Moscow, the city held (though virtually every

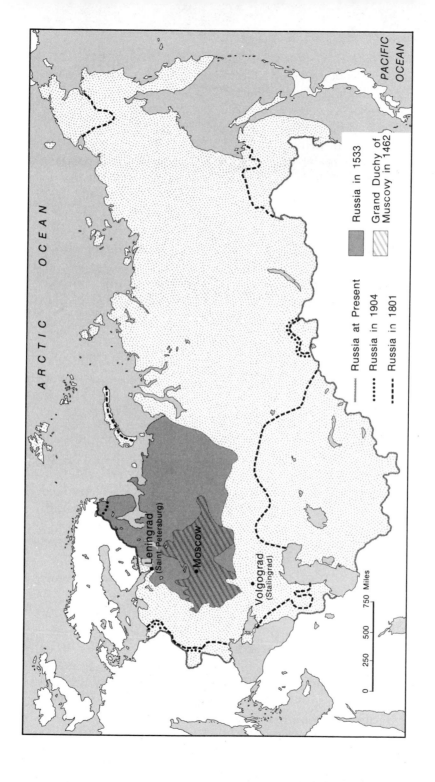

PACIFIC OCEAN

ARCTIC OCEAN

Leningrad
(Saint Petersburg)

• Moscow

Volgograd
(Stalingrad)

Russia at Present
——— Russia in 1904
········· Russia in 1801
– – – Russia in 1533

Russia in 1533

Grand Duchy of
Muscovy in 1462

Miles
0    250    500    750

structure was destroyed by German bombardment) and, early in 1943, Stalingrad was liberated. That same year the Red Army began its counteroffensive, progressively repelling the invaders and liberating the occupied territories.

The siege of Leningrad was broken in the winter of 1944, and as Soviet forces drove westward of their own frontiers in pursuit of Hitler's armies, they penetrated into the Baltic regions. By the spring of that year Soviet forces crossed into Poland and Rumania, and it became apparent that most of eastern and southeastern Europe would be liberated by the Red Army. As part of Russia's reward for her war effort and contribution to the defeat of Nazism, the Soviet Union emerged from World War II with a western frontier pushed farther outward than ever before. The country had indeed grown since the days of Muscovy.

## THE IMPLICATIONS FOR US-SOVIET HOSTILITY

As with autocracy, expansion has been a dominant fact of Russian history. The fact, however, is less meaningful than the interpretations we place on it. What should concern us most here are the implications to be drawn for *conflicts of interest* between superpowers. Russia's past often is invoked as proof of inexorable aggressiveness, and the Soviets can, it is sometimes said, be expected to continue their nation's outward drive. This position is central to the demonological view. Many Americans would heartily endorse Karl Marx's remark that "[Russia's] methods, its tactics, its maneuvers may change, but the guiding star of this policy—world hegemony—will never change."[6] Under the circumstances, it frequently is held that no country can ever feel quite safe, and that the United States must expect its interests to be trampled upon. The first consideration then is whether history requires that Russia be considered, fundamentally and inevitably, an aggressive nation, a nation eager to spread its rule by foreign conquest? Though many endorse this view, the situation is too complex to be captured by a simple formula.

## An Aggressively Expansionist Nation?

Russia is certainly not the only great power to engage in a major effort at territorial aggrandizement. Its growth often coincided with the expansion of the European empires: Portugal, Spain, the Netherlands, France, and Great Britain. Russian imperialism was simply more stubborn and, in the long run, much more successful. As one would surmise, however, its circumstances were rather different from those of other major powers.

A long and tragic history has taught the Russians that national existence is closely molded by warfare. Centuries of repelling foreign invaders seemed to prove, time and again, that national survival depends on military strength and centralized government. Russian history legitimized offensive military action—partly for economic purposes (as in the quest for furs and arable land) but usually for the greater power, glory, and, especially, security of the realm. A militarized and autocratic society, one that views the use of force as acceptable and legitimate, also is likely to regard expansion as part of the natural order of things. In addition, a variety of conditions further facilitated Russia's outward drive.

The vast area of eastern Europe and northern Asia now occupied by the Soviet Union presented few natural barriers to movements of troops and populations (which helps explain both the frequent incursions Russia had to fend off and its own expansive temptations). As George Kennan observed, "Behind Russia's stubborn expansion lies only the age-old sense of insecurity of a sedentary people reared on an exposed plain in the neighborhood of fierce nomadic peoples."[7] In addition to the absence of major natural barriers, the ethnic and cultural problems of absorbing new peoples usually were manageable. As Russia moved into immediately adjacent areas, the populations typically were not much different from the neighbors to which they became politically attached. And the country's own multiethnic character even further facilitated assimilation—Russian and local aristocracies mixed without much difficulty, and there was a fair amount of racial mingling. Thus neither major geographical obstacles nor significant ethnic discontinuities impeded territorial spread, and contiguous colonization became part of the pattern of Russian history.

Although much of the expansion was offensive (especially toward the south and east) and some of it motivated by the drive for warm-water ports, much of the expansion also was, from the very beginning, defensive. For example, defense against the Tatars, who burned Moscow in 1571 (and menaced it again 20 years later) required taking the offensive against them. Similarly, when fighting against Swedish invasions, the Russians gained extra territories through successful counteroffensives.

It is significant that the most costly and traumatic aggressions to which Russia fell victim occurred, from a historical perspective, quite recently—in the nineteenth and twentieth centuries. These are the aggressions that are most deeply imprinted on the nation's psyche, and their lessons matter most to Soviet leaders. In each case an enemy from the West penetrated deeply into Russian heartland and, though ultimately routed, exacted an immense toll in blood and treasure. In each instance, especially in the case of the Nazi invasion, it was decided that engaging the enemy in depth was too costly and that the major line of defense had to be pushed forward. Pressing the borders farther and farther outward seemed best to serve national security. The policy was partly preemptive (occupying a territory from which attack might be launched), but also made it easier to defeat an enemy before it penetrated too deeply into Russian territory.

At each stage Russian behavior was shaped by the lessons of its earlier experience, as well as by the political, ethnic, and geographical circumstances of the area over which the nation's history unfolded. Although the historical record is complex, it yields nothing so simple as a conclusion of congenital aggressivity or of an ineluctable drive for world domination.

Concerns may nevertheless linger. After all, why might the same sort of conditions that accounted for Russia's past history of expansion not also fuel a drive for conquest today? And if so, would Soviet expansionary urges not conflict, very objectively, with US interests? Left at that, the reasoning is unacceptable. Simple extrapolations will not do. Many of the circumstances (e.g., geographical and ethnic continuity) that facilitated prior bouts of territorial growth have few current parallels. And the administrative obstacles to ruling an expanded territory might, by themselves, deter any thought of further growth. But because doubts naturally persist, our purpose is to discover whether objective conflicts of interest, stemming from assumed territorial expansionism, can explain the state of US-Soviet relations—an endeavor requiring that we narrow the focus of our inquiry.

The obvious task is to identify those parts of the world in which both superpowers appear to have a direct and significant interest. We might then ask how likely it is that the USSR would be tempted to grab that region, through some form of conquest, to America's objective detriment.

### Arenas of Potential Conflict

At the most direct level, there is no territorial contention between the superpowers. Neither nation seeks, nor has ever sought, territorial aggrandizement at the other's expense. With the exception of Alaska (later sold to the United States), Soviet pretensions have never transcended Eurasian limits and, plainly, the United States has never laid claim to Soviet land nor is it ever likely to do so. Although the two countries are separated by the Bering Straits (a mere 26 miles of water) and are located on separate sides of the Arctic, there are no mutually contiguous areas, either land or narrow seas, endowed with sufficient people or resources to serve as likely arenas of confrontation.

Although there are no direct clashes of territorial objectives between the two countries, *indirect,* yet objective, conflicts may nevertheless exist. One side (presumably the Soviet Union) may wish to expand into areas the United States does not regard as part of its territorial preserve, but in which it nevertheless has a real interest (perhaps a significant commercial or a deep cultural attachment) that would suffer if the region were to be absorbed by Russia. Thus the territorial issue might be one (from the American side at least) of *turf* rather than of land. Is this a more plausible source of confrontation, and, if so, to which parts of the world does it refer?

Geopoliticians often divide the vast Eurasian landmass into two parts with distinct strategic significance. Its center, loosely speaking, is the area occupied by the Soviet Union and denominated the "heartland." Although throughout European and Asian history numerous struggles have centered on this area, the key to global power has been identified more recently as the control of the Eurasian "rimland." This is the tier of states—from Maritime Europe, to the Middle East, to southern Asia, to eastern Asia—that encircle the heartland. In the opinion of the late Nicholas Spykman,[8] the countries of the rimland—because of their substantial and relatively advanced populations, abundant natural resources, and valuable geostrategic position—are the key to world power. Spykman maintained that "who controls the rimland rules Eurasia; who rules Eurasia controls the destinies of the world."[9] And Spykman urged the United States to impose its influence on the rimland or, at the very least, to prevent control of the rimland by the Soviet Union. Whether or not one agrees with Spykman's perspective, it is within the rimland that the two superpowers' interests are most often thought to clash, and it is in this part of the world that the bulk of US efforts at containment have been directed.

WESTERN EUROPE    Within the rimland, Western Europe is often regarded as the top prize in the superpowers' contest. Its nations have been America's leading trading partners and, as the primary early source of emigration to the United States, the natural object of American emotional attachment. In addition, Western European nations provide the finest example, outside the United States, of the viability of political democracy, and the two regions buttress each other through mutual example. The tangible and intangible benefits to the United States of an independent Western Europe thus transcend the East–West rivalry, and we must ask whether Russian territorial pretensions in this part of the world can help us understand the hostility of US-Soviet relations.

As Cold War attitudes and perceptions congealed after World War II, the United States feared a massive Soviet thrust into Western Europe. At its simplest level, the image was of direct territorial conquest and of a Western Europe incorporated into the Soviet realm. At a more complex level, the Soviets were thought ready to force servile Communist governments upon European democracies, transforming them into replicas of Russia's Eastern European satellites. The Kremlin's pressure on Turkey, the fear of Communist influence in Greece, as well as the Soviet presence in East Germany and behavior in Poland (where the Allies believed they had extracted a promise of free elections from Stalin), intensified the West's concerns. The Prague Coup in 1948, abetted by the presence of Russian troops on Czech borders, sealed the fate of one of the rare Central European countries to have had a prewar history of genuine democracy. Why, it was asked, should the Soviets stop there rather than pursue their westward push as far as possible? Averell Harriman warned of a "barbarian invasion of Europe,"[10] and many US statesmen shared his fears.

Indeed, additional expansion might have appealed to Stalin and his lieutenants. On the one hand, the Soviet Union had suffered enormously from the war and was determined to avoid future aggression by pushing its line of defense as far outward as possible. Moreover, the Kremlin was not convinced that Germany, once recovered, could be trusted, believing that the West yearned for Soviet demise. Thus, might it not have wished to move its borders even farther westward, or at least to add another Communist puppet state or two to its western buffer region?

Possibly. On the other hand, Russia already had accomplished much in the way of improving its security toward the West. Thus, it is doubtful whether the price of additional expansion would have outweighed, from its own point of view, the marginal benefits to be gained. The costs of subduing, occupying, and administering a Western European country would have vastly exceeded the costs of maintaining existing Soviet satellites in subservient status. And, quite apart from considerations of motivation, one wonders how a war-devastated Russia could have borne the military costs of conquering a significant part of Western Europe. It may be argued that the Russians had demonstrated their capacity to absorb enormous costs in wartime, but it would be a mistake to equate the costs a nation will endure to stop and expel an invader with the costs it will accept to conduct unprovoked aggression abroad. Even at the height of the Cold War, some of the most vocal proponents of containment appeared to doubt that the Soviets contemplated military conquest in Western Europe. In 1949, Dulles himself declared that "I do not know of any responsible official, military or civilian, in this government or any government, who believes that the Soviet government now plans conquest by open military means."[11]

The situation has not changed much in subsequent decades. Although the Soviet Union is more powerful now than in the early years of the Cold War, the Western European nations also are far more capable of defending themselves today than they once were. Moreover, Moscow has had such difficulty holding its own bloc together as to make the notion that it contemplates stretching its empire yet further almost absurd. The effort in keeping a Poland or Czechoslovakia in line, substantial though it has been at times, would be dwarfed by the difficulty in keeping West Germany, France, or even Greece in colonial or satellite status. This does not mean that there are no circumstances in which the Soviets would not make a military move into Western Europe. However, most such situations assume an actual *armed conflict* with the West, or at least the clear imminence of hostilities—in which case Soviet military doctrine seems to call explicitly for a preemptive westward drive.[12]

But perhaps we are focusing too closely on Western Europe. After all, most of America's military activities in recent decades have involved other parts of the Eurasian rimland, especially eastern Asia and the region of the

Middle East and the Persian Gulf. Is any territorially based conflict of interest with the Soviet Union at issue here?

OTHER AREAS OF THE RIMLAND   The United States sent its troops to Korea in 1950 and, 15 years after that war ended, sent more than five-hundred thousand Americans to fight in Vietnam. In both cases the rationale was to prevent Russian (as well as Chinese) expansion into these areas but, whatever else may have been behind the decisions to intervene, *territorial* incompatibilities were not a consideration.

Kim Il Sung's decision to launch his forces against South Korea met no objection from the Kremlin, but probably was made without its active encouragement.[13] Additionally, the area was one that, just before the invasion, had been excluded by Secretary of State Acheson from the US defense perimeter. Indeed, at the time it was not obvious that the United States had any significant interests in Korea independent of its Cold War objectives. That Washington felt compelled to intervene was rooted primarily in its fear that the area would come under Moscow's and Beijing's orbit, thus providing US adversaries with a symbolic victory as well as a modest geostrategic gain. The reasoning may have been perfectly understandable, but it reflected at most a *derivative* conflict of interest: had there been no Cold War, the area would not have merited much attention. The Korean War in fact led to a temporary intensification of East–West hostility, but that fact does not help explain its origins. A remarkably similar case can be made concerning US intervention in Vietnam. The argument for dispatching troops to this remote land flowed from the domino theory, the notion that one country's shift to communism would make it much more probable that the contiguous country would do likewise and so forth. And as Southeast Asia's value to the United States was defined almost exclusively by its effect on the Cold War balance, the calculus again was linked to a preexisting rivalry.

The part of the Eurasian rimland that has evoked most US concern is the region abutting the Persian Gulf. The area's oil reserves make it a valuable prize for either superpower, and the fear has been that Russia might try to seize it by force. With the invasion of Afghanistan, the Soviet military position was enhanced in the area, and the creation of the US Rapid Deployment Force (later renamed US Central Command) was specifically intended to deter a USSR thrust into the region. Do these events reflect a conflict of local territorial aspirations? To some extent they do. Problems in this region did undermine US-Soviet relations in the early eighties and, because of the oil factor, America's interest in this area may be partly independent of its rivalry with the Soviets—qualifying the situation as one of objective conflict of interest. Nonetheless, one should not overstate either Soviet interest in Persian Gulf oil or US dependence on this petroleum source.

As the Rapid Deployment Force was acquiring full operational capability in 1983, the United States depended on the Persian Gulf for only ten percent of its domestic oil consumption,[14] and oil competes with natural gas, coal, and nuclear power as a source of domestically consumed energy. Hence US reliance on oil from the Gulf area is really quite marginal. Many of America's industrialized allies are much more dependent on oil imports from the Persian Gulf region. Some 40 percent of the oil consumed by Western European nations comes from the Persian Gulf; in Japan's case the figure hovers around 60 percent. Western oil dependence is expected to increase during the 1990s,[15] but is not likely to reach the levels of the mid-seventies. In any case, it is unlikely that Soviet thirst for foreign petroleum would cause it to grab the Persian Gulf oilfields (and turn off the spigot for the West). There may be some grounds for an objective conflict of interest here, but not much. If the two superpowers view each other's presence in the region with misgivings, it is mainly because each fears the other may attempt outright military *denial* of petroleum access. The aggressor's aim here would be to weaken his adversary, not to satisfy his own oil needs. This is a very different matter and, plainly, assumes a high degree of preexisting hostility. In any case, because concern with the Persian Gulf dates from the late seventies, several decades after initiation of the Cold War, it cannot therefore provide an independent explanation of its causes or of its course.

WATERWAYS   We have not managed as yet to find much in the way of credible conflicts of territorial interest, but our focus may have been misdirected. Perhaps the territory in question consists not of land but of *waterways*. To some extent geostrategic perspectives have moved from a heavy preoccupation with the Eurasian rimland to a concern with maritime control, particularly control of major sea lanes of communication. Mastery of the seas, rather than dominance on the Eurasian landmass, has, by this perspective, emerged as the key to world control and superpower security.[16] America's quasi-insular position, the role that long-distance force projection plays in its military calculations, and the growing importance of international trade to its economy has created obvious vulnerabilities. Accordingly, certain analysts fear that the Soviet Union might try to weaken the United States by disrupting its principal sea lanes of communication—a threat that obviously would increase if East–West relations deteriorated yet further or if hostilities appeared imminent. In addition, Moscow's increasing investment, during the seventies and eighties, in the expansion of its naval force has heightened concerns.

Whatever the merits of the arguments stressing seapower over landpower, the need for maritime access and freedom of navigation cannot be a source of objective conflict of interest between the superpowers: the volume of international shipping is hardly such that there is an insufficiency of navigable water to accomodate US and Soviet needs. Whatever presumed conflict of interest may be assigned to control of the major sea lanes of communication, it is evident that this is, at the very most, another case of derivative antagonism: one that *assumes* some preexisting hostility and that stems from the need to acquire a relative advantage over the other nation.

Not only is there no discernible US-Soviet territorial competition (in the sense of each wanting to appropriate the same piece of land), but there are very few instances where one side has a territorial objective that threatens the other's nonterritorial interests in the same part of the world. Something of this sort could be identified only in the area of the Persian Gulf, and even there the rivalry is more derivative than objective. In any case, the notion of a contest for control of foreign oil emerged in the mid-seventies—three decades after the postwar deterioration of US-Soviet relations. A cause can precede the event it accounts for, or the two can occur pretty much simultaneously, but a cause cannot follow its own consequence by several decades. Similarly, an objective conflict of interest can account for a derivative conflict of interest, but the causal arrow logically cannot be reversed.

## IDEOLOGICAL CONFLICTS OF INTEREST

Although many might agree that US-Soviet rivalry is not driven by quarrels which, directly or indirectly, involve land, it seems axiomatic that the conflict has deep ideological roots. In numerous crucial ways the two belief systems are based on incompatible premises, and their practical expressions, as witnessed in the political institutions and practices of the two nations, are quite antithetical.

Marxism assumes that political and economic transformations revolve around social classes; liberal democracy views individuals as the driving force of society. Marxist ideology is inspired by a faith in the immutability of certain laws of political and socioeconomic development, most prominent among which is the notion of a class struggle pitting exploiter against exploited. American belief systems are permeated by the notion of a harmony of interests between the various segments of society, and of their mutual interdependence in the quest for prosperity and welfare. Marxism, especially as modified by Leninism, insists on the role of revolutionary force in effecting necessary social transitions; American ideology places its faith in consensus and nonviolence.

At a more practical level, the differences are just as stark.

The Soviet-style political system is designed to absorb as much of society as possible into a powerful state; the US model of democracy is founded on the belief that a political organization should limit the power of the state. One system raises individual liberty to the pinnacle of values it professes to defend; the other system willingly sacrifices liberty for equality, together with material and national security. Most disturbingly from the American perspective, Marxism traditionally has proclaimed as its ultimate goal the abolition of capitalism and, at least at the rhetorical level, Soviet leaders have claimed that their nation stands at the helm of a historical process culminating in capitalism's destruction—a victory of admittedly uncertain date and to be achieved by generally unspecified mechanisms. Americans, on the other hand, rarely hide their desire to see communism disappear from those countries in which it has taken root.

Under the circumstances it is scarcely astonishing that many people, even outside the ranks of demonologists, are convinced that the rivalry springs from clashing ideologies: the rivalry should be viewed as a duel between democracy and totalitarianism, religion and atheism, free enterprise and state-run economies—in short, between goals and values that are fundamentally incompatible.

The introduction of ideological goals into the analysis makes it somewhat easier to argue the case for Soviet expansionism and for the existence of authentic East–West conflicts of interest. No longer must we demonstrate Russian territorial ambitions, or even that Moscow seeks direct political control of foreign nations. All we need to show is that the Soviet Union is intent on exporting its particular belief system, together with the political institutions and practices that embody these beliefs. Similarly, it may be assumed that America too is intent on promoting the spread of its political system and the principles from which it stems. Consequently, Soviet and US interests clash.

If what we have in mind are objective conflicts of interest, the promotion of ideology should be desired as *an end in itself*—not simply as a means toward a Cold War advantage. Moreover, if one side's gain is to be the other side's loss, either of two conditions must be met. First, one or both superpowers should strive to bring down the other's political order. The Soviet Union might seek, through its efforts, to engineer the collapse of capitalism and democracy in America; the United States might attempt to undermine communism within Russia. In other words, either or both should be engaged in ideologically based subversion. Second, an objective conflict of interest could occur if the two superpowers were vying for ideological converts, at each other's expense, from within the ranks of other nations. As the number of potential converts is limited, an acquisition by one superpower would be deemed a loss by the other. The question then is whether either situation characterizes the US-Soviet rivalry.

### Direct Political Subversion?

Although representatives of the demonological view would argue otherwise, there is little evidence to suggest that either superpower is intent on bringing about the downfall of the other's system.

Attempted Russian subversion of US values and institutions was conceivable in the immediate aftermath of the Bolshevik Revolution, and to a lesser extent during the early 1930s when the Soviets expended modest efforts at exporting revolution. Their major instrument for this purpose was the Comintern, the Russian-led international organization of Communist parties whose purpose, according to Leon Trotsky, was to "facilitate and hasten the victory of the Communist revolution throughout the world."[17] If Moscow's ambition was to export revolution, it has failed miserably. The only two brief Communist grabs for power occurred in 1919—in Germany with the Spartacist League and in Hungary under Bela Kun—and both were quickly defeated. Moreover, no Soviet-sponsored organization has ever managed to inject itself into American politics to any meaningful extent. Nevertheless, this does not mean that Soviet subversion has not been feared. In 1919, shocked by the Bolshevik victory in Russia and rattled by a series of major strikes, the US Government lashed out at real or suspected American leftists. The guiding hand behind the repression was that of Attorney General A. Mitchell Palmer, assisted by J. Edgar Hoover, chief of the Justice Department's General Intelligence Division.[18] But the raids and arrests of the Great Red Scare unearthed no significant evidence of Soviet subversion; nor, for that matter, did the witch-hunts of the McCarthy era.

As Americans have worried about Russian attempts to export Communism to the United States, so has the Kremlin feared US attempts to strangle it within the USSR itself. Probably nothing aroused such fears more than the military intervention of American, British, French, and Japanese forces against the Bolsheviks soon after they came to power. Two units, some 10,000 troops, were dispatched by President Woodrow Wilson to Russia, and US forces remained on Russian territory until 1920.[19] Although American troops did not participate extensively in combat, and though their presence did little to influence the actual course of events, the West's intervention was the most direct step ever taken by either side to destroy the other's political system. Still, many decades have elapsed since then, and no major campaigns of political subversion—as opposed to propaganda and espionage—have been undertaken of late.

Although Glasnost may falter—and the Kremlin may once again justify internal repression by the need to combat foreign "class enemies"—and McCarthyism may occasionally reappear in the United States, the stability of both systems is established firmly. It seems unlikely that either superpower expects to undermine successfully the other's political structure, or that either is devoting much effort to so vain a hope.

### A Struggle for Converts?

The second form of ideological conflict, a competition for third-party converts, is a more plausible source of antagonism. Russians feel that the United States is bent on undermining socialism wherever it appears in the world; many

Americans are convinced that it is a matter of high Kremlin priority to promote, through subversion or coercion, the international spread of its own political principles. Bringing other nations into their respective ideological fold is the assumed objective of both superpowers, and conflicts of interest are the natural outcome. Plainly there is something to this, but just how much of a role does competition for political converts and allies really play in US-Soviet rivalry? The best answer is to question where such ideological clashes have happened or could occur. Three theaters of confrontation spring to mind: the industrialized West, Eastern Europe, and the Third World.

### The Western Democracies

It is difficult to believe that Moscow entertains any serious hope of drawing the industrialized democracies into its ideological orbit. It cannot fail to have impressed itself on the Kremlin that Western societies are inhospitable to the values and practices for which it stands. Though Lenin and his lieutenants firmly expected several capitalist democracies, Germany in particular, to be swept up in a vast revolutionary uprising during or immediately following World War I, such hopes were soon dashed and have never really been revived.

Although a number of western democracies have spawned communist parties, for the most part such parties do not represent significant political forces within their respective societies. Only the communist parties of Italy and France have played meaningful roles in national politics. The Italian Communist Party (PCI), the largest in Europe, at times has been considered a potential aspirant to power, and produced at least one major and charismatic leader in the person of the late Enrico Berlinguer. Nevertheless, and despite the expectations of its supporters and opponents, it has never managed to propel itself into national government. Most importantly, the Italian communists' fealty to Moscow has not been apparent. In fact, since the PCI embraced the doctrines of Eurocommunism, it has distanced itself from the Soviet Union. The Italian communists condemned the invasions of Czechoslovakia in 1968 and of Afghanistan in 1980, and firmly opposed the introduction of martial law in Poland. In addition, Berlinguer explicitly criticized the repressive character of the Soviet system. So it is easy to conclude that the Kremlin would be at least as unhappy as Washington if the PCI did manage to come to power. The French Communist Party has been much less willing than its Italian counterpart to reject Moscow's tutelage; on the other hand, it has never really had its hands on the levers of power. With the apparent hope of buying labor peace for its programs, the Mitterrand government initially granted four minor cabinet posts to communists; yet it is significant that this same government pursued a far more pro-American foreign policy than had its right-wing predecessors. The French communists have never managed to acquire a significant share of power at the national level, and shrinking domestic support has eroded even their slimmest hopes.

Apart from Italy and France, communist influence in the industrialized West has never been significant and, even where it has been felt, its influence rarely has been put at Moscow's service. Most importantly, the electorate of most western nations has shown little or no sympathy for Soviet-type political systems.

Responsible Russian officials in recent decades cannot have failed to appreciate the vitality of industrialized capitalist societies and the firm public support their political systems enjoy. Fundamentally, Soviet leaders are realists; even if allowances are made for wishful thinking, they have a fairly accurate picture of political trends in the world they live in. A central part of being a realist is guiding one's activities by reasonable estimates of likely costs and benefits. The Kremlin does not tend to invest heavily in virtually hopeless projects, and we must assume that conversion of western democracies to Soviet-style Communism *is* regarded as such.

### Eastern Europe

For decades Moscow's Eastern European allies have been a recognized part of the Soviet bloc; yet it is in this part of the world that the origins of US-Soviet hostility can be most plausibly linked to conflicting ideological designs.[20] As the Russians pursued Nazi armies into central and southeastern Europe, it became obvious that the Soviet Union would have a say in the political future of the liberated countries—just how much a say was initially uncertain. In the Declaration of Liberated Europe, Moscow had led the West to believe that it would permit free elections and national self-determination in the areas occupied by the Red Army, but the promise was never kept. Rather, Stalin followed a pattern of establishing coalition governments in which the key ministries of defense and the interior (police) were held by Communists. Control of the instruments of coercion eventually allowed the Kremlin's ideological allies to subvert the democratic process and turn their countries into Soviet satellites.

When this occurred in Hungary, Bulgaria, and Rumania, the West's objections were not overly strenuous—after all, these countries had never meant much to the United States or Britain, and Soviet domination did seem consistent with what was agreed upon at Yalta. Soviet control of Poland and Czechoslovakia, however, was much less acceptable. Both countries had strong prewar cultural and commercial links with the West and, though Slavic, were not natural Soviet clients.

Historically, Poland and Russia had been enemies rather than friends, and the prospects for democracy in Poland seemed good after the war. In addition, the Polish people's devout Catholicism made their integration into the Soviet orbit an awkward prospect. Finally, millions of US voters of Polish extraction presumably were not eager to see the "Old Country" disappear behind the iron curtain. Nor was Czechoslovakia viewed as a natural Soviet satellite. Its citizens tended to regard themselves primarily as westerners, and Czechoslovakia was the only Eastern European country with a prewar tradition of political democracy. The prospect of integrating Czechoslovakia and Poland into the Soviet orbit was regarded by the West as a major ideological loss.

Differences over Poland's future provided one of the first

causes of East–West acrimony following World War II. As pointed out, the West had interpreted the Declaration of Liberated Europe to imply that the main ingredients of the country's political life would be free elections and a coalition government. Though Roosevelt and Churchill understood Stalin's concern that Poland should not have an anti-Soviet government, neither felt that this *had* to mean the exclusion of all non-Communists from power. Moscow disagreed, and established a "provisional" Communist government in the city of Lublin. By 1947 the country was turned into a typical Soviet satellite.

Hope for democracy in Czechoslovakia did not die as quickly. Though Stalin had established a basis for his influence in that country during the war, Soviet control initially was not complete. In the elections of 1946, communists won 37 percent of the popular vote and entered into a coalition government in which Klement Gottwald, the party leader, held the premiership. Nevertheless, President Eduard Benes and Foreign Minister Jan Masaryk (son of Czechoslovakia's founder Thomas Masaryk), neither of whom were communists, resisted total Soviet domination for several years. By 1947—attracted by the prospect of US economic aid— the Czech government expressed an interest in closer ties with the West, a possibility that the Kremlin and Gottwald were determined to prevent. Under Moscow's pressure (Soviet tanks were massed along the Czech border), the non-Communist members of the government were forced to resign in what became known as the Prague Coup. Several weeks later the world learned that Masaryk had "fallen" to his death from his bedroom window. Truman, comparing the Prague Coup to the situation faced by the West at the time of Hitler's seizure of Czechoslovakia, observed that it "sent a shock wave throughout the civilized world."[21]

Soviet motivations were clear with regard to Poland and Czechoslovakia: both were sought as buffers against the West, and against German recidivism in particular. The Russians could not forget that twice within three decades Poland had provided the corridor through which Germans had invaded their country. And Czechoslovakia's dismemberment by the

1938 Munich agreement was seen as an attempt by the West to facilitate Hitler's designs on Russia. Thus from the Soviet perspective, fear of future invasions required the incorporation of both countries into its protective ring of satellites, ideological objectives being incidental to this security concern. For the West, and especially the United States, ideology was the major issue, and the absorption of Poland and Czechoslovakia into the Soviet orbit was seen as a powerful blow to democracy. The Kremlin, however, interpreted US opposition to its designs in Eastern Europe as proof positive of Washington's unwillingness to grant the Soviet Union the secure buffer zone that, from its viewpoint, history had entitled it to claim.

The ideological issue should nevertheless be kept in perspective. Although partially responsible for initiating the Cold War, competition over Eastern Europe had little to do with its subsequent course. The West has substantially accepted that these countries do belong in the Soviet orbit and that, lamentable though it is, this outcome should be regarded as the logical manifestation of postwar bipolarity. Neither the 1956 invasion of Hungary nor the crushing of Czechoslovakia's modest attempts at liberalization in 1968 evoked much US opposition. This exemplifies the stability that political realism imputes to bipolarity: it was felt, on both occasions, that Russia's actions within Eastern Europe should be accepted as a matter of realpolitik, and as the price to be paid for Moscow's expected circumspection outside its own bloc.

The only apparent exception to this passive acquiescence occurred in 1981. American anger at the "internal invasion" of Poland, through the imposition of martial law, was as authentic as US sympathy for the challenge directed at the Communist monopoly of power by the Solidarity movement. Although ideology was therefore not irrelevant, it is difficult to disentangle purely ideological feelings from the Reagan Administration's less lofty desire to score international propaganda points against the Kremlin. Moreover, the contrast between the strong US response to repression in Poland and its mild reaction to the invasions of Hungary and Czechoslovakia was probably rooted in the absence of a significant body of American voters of Czech or Hungarian ancestry: ethnic Poles are not only numerous but concentrated in a number of electorally powerful urban areas.

## The Third World

Richard Pipes has observed that the ultimate aim of Soviet grand strategy is "the elimination, worldwide of private ownership of the means of production and the 'bourgeois' order which rests upon it, and its replacement with what Lenin called a 'worldwide republic of Soviets.' "[22] An aim that, according to Pipes, is directed principally at the Third World. Certainly the developing world has provided numerous arenas of East–West competition, and both sides have couched their economic and military assistance, as well as occasional military interventions, in terms of high-minded political principles. It is nevertheless revealing that, although rivalry over the Third World has molded the course of US–Soviet relations, ideology has been an evanescent component of the competition.

There is no denying that several Russian clients, such as Vietnam or Cuba, have adopted a political system not radically different from the Soviet Union's. Although in developing nations communism typically has been brought to power by domestic forces, ideological affinity has made dependence on Moscow easier to ensure. Occasionally too, Russia has assisted radical or Marxist Third-World movements that have not managed to overthrow the existing order. Nevertheless, Soviet sympathies and support have been guided more closely by *geostrategic opportunism* (i.e., by the pursuit of power) than by ideological kinship. The Kremlin has invariably abandoned its ideological bedfellows when forced to choose between support for a local communist movement and the promotion of other diplomatic or security objectives.

Soviet priorities in the Cold War became apparent at a very early stage. For example, when fighting broke out in Greece between communists and the British-backed royalist government following World War II, Russia (apparently in keeping with its interpretation of the Yalta accords) left the communists to their fate. Similarly, the Communist Party of India was disgruntled when Khrushchev, as part of his campaign to secure the sympathies of the Third World, decided to court Jawaharlal Nehru, India's non-Marxist Prime Minister. Khrushchev informed the Indian Communists that, if forced to choose between them and the Nehru government, he certainly would opt for the latter. Nor have the Soviets been reluctant to seek improved relations with regimes engaged in the active persecution of local communists when this promised to strengthen their hand in the East–West rivalry. Iraq, although communists languished in its jails, was easily able to enlist Russian support and assistance. Egypt's Gamal Abdel Nasser received one of the highest Soviet decorations, the Golden Star of a Hero of the Soviet Union, even though he had outlawed Egypt's Communist Party and ruthlessly persecuted its members. In a more recent and unblushingly open display of opportunism, the Kremlin threw its support behind Ferdinand Marcos of the Philippines, at a time when even the United States had withdrawn its support from this spectacularly corrupt dictator whose main claim to American sympathy had been his staunch anticommunism.

Exporting communism to the Third World clearly is not a very high Soviet priority; rather, it is systematically subordinated to a pragmatic pursuit of its rivalry with the United States.[23]

Should one assume that the United States cares more about promoting its own political values and practices abroad than does the Soviet Union? The record suggests otherwise. To begin with, many (perhaps most) of America's Third-World allies and clients over the decades can hardly have been considered models of democratic virtue. In fact, the United States has numbered among its friends an extremely unsavory set of right-wing dictatorships: from Marcos in the Philippines, to Pinochet in Chile, to Mobutu in Zaire. It might be suggested that in the developing regions anticommunism rather than political freedom is the wellspring of US foreign policy, but this would not fit the evidence either. Not only has the People's Republic of China—the most populous communist nation in the world—become America's quasi-ally, but cordial relations exist with other nominally Marxist nations as well.

Following Marshal Tito's rupture with Stalin in 1948, Yugoslavia gravitated toward the West and, though officially nonaligned, has been both a recipient of US assistance and frequent critic of Soviet policy. By many standards, Belgrade's relations with Washington have been better than those it maintains with Moscow. Similarly, the professed Marxism of Zimbabwe's leadership has not been an obstacle to its cordial relations with the United States (or to its distrust of the Soviet Union). America's leading objective in the Third World is neither to promote democracy nor to defend capitalism, but simply to pursue, as successfully as possible, its competition with the Soviet Union. To some extent then, it could be argued that the competition is its own leading cause.

The primacy of the derivative conflict of interest was amply apparent in the Horn of Africa in the late seventies. The Soviet Union initially had military ties with Somalia, a Marxist state upon whose naval facilities at Berbera Moscow had cast its eye and with which the Russians signed a Treaty of Friendship in 1974. America's sympathies were with Ethiopia whose nonaligned, but on the whole pro-Western, Emperor Haile Selassie had reigned for several decades. The Ethiopian monarch was deposed that year, and the country's new leaders espoused the rhetoric of revolutionary Marxism. Relations between the two neighbors took a violent turn in 1977 when Somali forces invaded the Ogaden region in an attempt to wrest this area from Ethiopia. The latter sought Russian help and, though linked by treaty to the former, Moscow apparently decided that Ethiopia was the bigger prize. The Soviets airlifted military supplies and Cuban troops to their new ally while, undeterred by the proclaimed Marxism of its leader Siad Barre, the United States made successful overtures to Somalia. US support for a nominally Marxist regime, against another government of similar persuasion, was a further example of superpower confrontation unconnected to any sense of ideological mission. (In any event, the decision paid off as Russian facilities at Berbera were turned over to the United States). In a further manifestation of its readiness to support a nominally Marxist movement opposing the Soviet Union, the United States consistently has aided the forces of Jonas Savimbi in Angola against the country's Soviet- and Cuban-supported government.

This is not to suggest that neither the United States nor the Soviet Union has a sense of ideological commitment, and would not prefer to support politically compatible as well as strategically useful clients. But simply that the pursuit of an advantage over the other superpower has been, virtually from the start, far more important than the promotion of a political philosophy.[24] Each side occasionally may feel uncomfortable with the political complexion of its friends and allies but, as long as they are thought to be assets in the East–West struggle, such discomfort is borne with considerable fortitude.

## PLACING IDEOLOGY IN PERSPECTIVE

Opposing-belief systems can mar relations even without generating incompatible goals—by producing intolerance and dislike, by coloring mutual perceptions (matter discussed in Chapter 3)—yet objective conflicts of ideological interest provide but a partial explanation for the state of US-Soviet relations. Although colliding aspirations for the political future of Poland and Czechoslovakia did contribute to the onset of the Cold War, competing ideological pursuits in Eastern Europe have not significantly shaped its subsequent path. And although each side would prefer that Third-World countries embrace its own political values, each side has been quite willing to befriend countries of opposite political stripe when diplomatic or strategic benefit was in the offing. Quite simply, the rivalry has outrun whatever ideological foundation it may once have had.

During the past several decades there has been a common belief that Soviet foreign policy is driven by messianic Marxism, by a determination to spearhead the international drive for Communism. Assuming that it serves no purpose other than that proclaimed by Russian leaders, the Kremlin's own rhetoric is invoked as evidence; by doing so we fail to place Soviet ideology in its proper context.

We have seen that the Kremlin is unwilling to subordinate the pursuit of a traditional conception of its national interest to the claims of ideological consistency. In fact, ideological consistency does not seem to be a major Soviet concern at any level, for the precepts of Marxism-Leninism are used more often to justify decisions made on bureaucratic, pragmatic, or nationalistic grounds than to inform and guide national behavior. Ideology is at the service of the regime, rather than the other way around.

It is almost universally reported that the average Soviet citizen cares little about the pronouncements of Marx, Engels, or Lenin and is cynical about the Kremlin's own use of ideological slogans.[25] It is also unlikely that top Soviet leaders are avid readers of the Marxist prophets or alert to the nuances of their regime's holy writ. As Seweryn Bialer points out, Mikhail Suslov, the late Party ideologue, was probably the last Politburo member to have read even the first volume of Karl Marx's *Capital* or some of Lenin's more complex works.[26]

One cannot claim that Soviet ideology has no functions other than to provide a convenient and malleable set of slogans with which to rationalize a variety of policies, but its actual functions are not those that most Americans have in mind. While Marxism-Leninism does not provide the Kremlin with an actual guide for concrete decisions, it does provide a set of broad themes that form a basic structure for justifying the *existence* of the Communist regime rather than for justifying its specific policies. The legitimizing value of such abstract principles as the "struggle against exploitation," "classless society," "anti-imperialism," and so forth, provides a buffer against the unflattering judgments often made concerning the regime's mediocre performance regarding more immediate and worldly goals. The roughly hewn version of Marxism embraced by the Kremlin also provides the comforting conviction that, present failures and frustrations notwithstanding, history is ultimately on the USSR's side—a belief which also may explain the apparent patience and long-term perspective that characterizes Soviet policy. But it is a major and tenuous leap to the conclusion that the Soviet leaders have a single-minded obsession with communizing the world.

If anything, the appearance of other major centers of communism would probably be viewed by Moscow more as a threat than a benefit. Although the conversion of a dependent Third-World country to some variant of Leninism might facilitate the consolidation of Soviet control (e.g., as in Vietnam or Ethiopia), the emergence of another communist nation of any stature could present an unwelcome challenge to the Soviet Union.

The Soviet Union's pursuit of international leadership often is justified by the major and transcendental principles for which it is supposed to stand, but this rationale could be undermined quickly by the existence of other credible (perhaps more credible) centers of Marxism. The rift between Russia and China was largely the product of their rival claims to ideological orthodoxy. And the breach between Stalin and Tito flowed from the Soviet dictator's anger at Yugoslav pretensions to leading a Balkan federation of communist nations. A communist France, Germany, even India or Brazil, would probably be viewed as an intolerable challenge to Soviet primacy within the international Marxist movement and as a blow to its international position.

As we have seen, the United States also is less concerned with promoting its political beliefs abroad than with pursuing pragmatic gains at Soviet expense. To some extent democracy may be considered the ultimate stake of the struggle; and if democracy is given short shrift in the present this is, it can be argued, only to ensure that it will thrive in the long term. But cast in these terms, the ideological goal seems to have a roughly comparable function to that which Marxist slogans have for the Soviets: creating a broad sense of legitimacy for foreign policy and assuring both oneself and others that current policy is more than simply a matter of grim and traditional power politics.

The inference so far is that for both superpowers ideological goals are subordinated to the pursuit of short-term Cold-War advantages, which weakens the case for an objective conflict of ideological interest. There is yet another reason for doubting that ideology is a major moving force behind the rivalry (although it may have had something to do with the initiation of the Cold War). If we believe that Y is caused primarily by X, we also would expect shifts in Y to be associated with movements in X. But this has hardly been the case. Have ideological divergences narrowed during the late sixties and seventies (i.e., at the height of détente), or have they intensified at times of increasing confrontation (e.g., the early sixties and late seventies)? It seems more likely that the state of overall US-Soviet relations has marched to the beat of a different drummer.

## DIVERGENT ECONOMIC INTERESTS

Although radical authors especially are prone to account for political phenomena in economic terms, the link between economic differences and social or international conflict has been recognized by authors within the mainstream as well. Economic issues have fueled many international conflicts and, when distilled, fall in two general categories. Historically, nations have felt that one side's economic gain was the other's economic loss when (a) the parties have experienced a rivalry over access to limited export markets or (b) the parties have competed over access to external sources of raw materials. On the whole, neither situation adequately describes relations between the United States and the Soviet Union.

### Competition for Foreign Markets?

Most nations obviously would prefer to expand their presence in foreign markets—both as a means of earning income (especially the foreign exchange required to finance imports), and as a means of generating employment and reducing the costs of goods sold domestically by extending production runs through foreign sales.

Interestingly, competition for export markets did mar relations between America and Russia in the late nineteenth century. At that time the United States was pursuing an open-door policy in Asia with the idea of gaining access to local markets, especially those of Manchuria. The Russians, on the other hand, were bent on acquiring exclusive access to this part of the world, and relations between the two nations suffered the consequences of this rivalry.[27] Yet it is difficult to believe, and not often claimed, that commercial rivalry has had much to do with the tone of US-Soviet relations during the past several decades. Exceptionally, a number of revisionist historians, most notably William Appleman Williams,[28] have suggested that the roots of the Cold War go back to America's attempt to establish an Open Door to commerce with Eastern Europe and to Russia's even firmer determination to permit nothing of the sort. But this certainly is an exceptional interpretation of the origins of the rivalry, and not a particularly convincing one. To begin with, there is no evidence of any significant pressure on either Roosevelt or Truman by influential businessmen with a vested interest in Eastern European markets to ensure their commercial access to these regions. And it is worth remembering that neither president was especially sympathetic to the interests of big business. In fact, as Arthur Schlesinger Jr. reminds us, both presidents had "engaged in bitter struggles with the business community and both were persuaded of the folly and greed of business leaders. . . ."[29] Under the circumstances, it is doubtful that either president would have allowed his foreign policy to be dictated by self-serving businessmen.

Even apart from the Eastern European case, there are several compelling reasons to dismiss export rivalry as a source of US-Soviet enmity. In the first place, the nature of the Soviet system is such that it is not a *demand-driven* economy. In the United States, downswings in the economy's cyclical performance are caused largely by shortfalls in aggregate demand for the goods and services it is capable of producing. Aggregate demand, in turn, is composed of various forms of domestic purchases—by consumers, investors, and government—as well as by foreign demand for American products. Although exports are not as crucial to the US economy as to the economies of many smaller industrialized nations, their role remains significant, and domestic growth and employment levels cannot be separated from the nation's ability to export part of its output.

The USSR economy is in a different position, for it is driven by *supply* rather than demand—by its ability to generate, rather than to absorb, output.[30] The more the Soviet Union produces, the faster its economy grows, while the country's economic plans, by matching demand and supply, ensure that output will find buyers. But there are definite limits to how much can be produced—limitations linked to constraints on production factors (capital and labor) as well as to the economy's inability to generate the modern technology required to offset ultimately declining returns. Exports, therefore, do not play the role they do in market economies. In fact, the Soviet economy would often be unable to meet whatever demand for its goods and services might develop abroad. This does not mean that exports are irrelevant to the Soviet Union, merely that their economic role is not the same, or as important, as in the United States.

For the Russians, the major benefit of foreign sales is to earn the hard currencies needed to purchase the goods and the modern technologies they have not managed to provide for themselves. Accordingly the Soviets would most like to direct their exports to countries with strong and convertible international currencies (e.g., dollars, marks, or yen), in other words toward the nations of the industrialized West. Theoretically then, Russia's export interests could collide with those of other countries (such as the United States) that also service the markets of developed nations. But this theoretical possibility is hardly a practical threat: the Soviet Union is not, and has never been, in a position to compete with the United States in the markets of the industrialized world.

Russia primarily is an exporter of *raw materials* while, apart from grain (which mainly is sold to Russia in any case) and soybeans, America primarily exports *manufactured goods:* a difference that substantially limits the scope of possible commercial rivalry. To the extent Russia does try to sell manufactured goods abroad, their inferior quality and unsophisticated designs make it unlikely that they would seriously challenge the goods of Western producers. For the most part the Soviet Union must be content with Third-World markets for its manufactured goods, its principal clients being nations that simply cannot afford comparable imports from the industrialized West. A Soviet-American contest for export markets is, consequently, a highly implausible source of antagonism.

### Rivalry Over Raw Materials?

Could it be that the two superpowers vie for access to external sources of *raw materials* rather than for export markets? Competition of this sort has, of course, led to many wars in the past; perhaps it also is at the root of US-Soviet rivalry. The idea that the two nations might clash over access to critical natural resources gained some currency in the seventies. By 1980, Secretary of State Alexander Haig announced that "as one assesses the recent step-up of Soviet proxy activity in the Third World . . . one can only conclude that the 'era' of the resource war has arrived."[31] But which resources might be at issue?

The strongest case has been made for the possibility of clashes over access to Persian Gulf oil. Ever since the Arab members of OPEC (Organization of Petroleum Exporting Countries) embargoed oil shipments to the United States in the autumn of 1973 in retaliation for America's support of Israel, the threat of petroleum denial has had a significant impact on US international security policy. A few years after the embargo, the CIA predicted a decline in Soviet oil production and implied that the Kremlin might turn to the Middle East to cover its domestic shortfalls.[32] Under the circumstances some concern was understandable, but the

danger was considerably overstated. The United States reacted to the 1973-74 embargo by taking steps to lessen its
dependence on foreign oil; as a result, the proportion of US
oil consumption met through imports has declined significantly. In addition, estimates of Soviet oil reserves have been
revised upward by the US intelligence community; the Soviet oil future now is reckoned to be reasonably good.[33]

In any case, Russia need not rely too heavily on petroleum for its energy needs. Russia can augment its reliance
on natural gas, with which it is well endowed, and has the
option of increasing the share of nuclear power in its overall
energy consumption. Moreover, despite the accident at
Chernobyl, Soviet commitment to nuclear energy has not
declined appreciably.

But petroleum is not the only natural resource over which
the two sides might quarrel. Although the United States is
a mineral-rich country, it must rely on external sources for
a number of raw materials, including such strategic metals
as chromium, cobalt, platinum-group metals, manganese,
and vanadium. These metals have numerous civilian applications as well as considerable military significance, primarily involving the aerospace industry. Unfortunately, their
primary sources are politically volatile parts of the world—
countries such as Zimbabwe and, especially, South Africa—
which could become the object of direct competition for influence between the United States and the Soviet Union.[34]
Nevertheless, the Soviet Union need not look beyond its
own borders for most of the raw materials that its economy requires.

As Figure 2-2 illustrates, the Soviet Union does import
some cobalt from abroad (mainly from Cuba, Zaire, Zam-
bia) but, apart from this, is basically self-sufficient as to
minerals. Russia is one of the world's largest producers of
chromium and manganese, and a net exporter of platinum-
group metals. Thus unless one is prepared to believe that
superpower relations are determined by, for example, cobalt, it is unlikely that the Soviet Union and the United
States are experiencing a fatal divergence of interest over
access to raw materials.

**FIGURE 2-2**
US-Soviet Reliance on Mineral Imports in 1986*

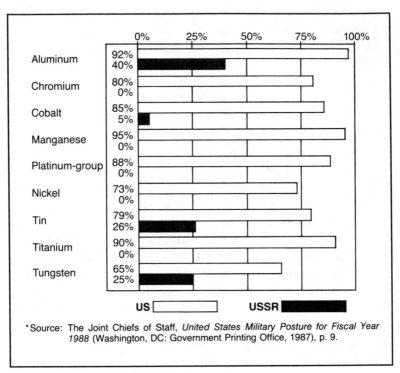

*Source: The Joint Chiefs of Staff, *United States Military Posture for Fiscal Year 1988* (Washington, DC: Government Printing Office, 1987), p. 9.

Even if it has little need to import raw materials, one might argue that Russia may nevertheless try to *deny* crucial raw materials to the United States in an attempt to weaken its principal rival. For example, it might withhold raw materials at their source by gaining control over producing nations or seek to distrupt sea-lanes by which they are shipped to America. Although the point is reasonable and should not be dismissed glibly, it does suggest some *preexisting* conflict of interest, one that could cause either party to desire to hurt or disable the other. In other words, competition over raw materials cannot be said to provide the basis for an *objective conflict of interest,* but at most the basis for one that is derivative.

Economic conflicts of interest do not seem to have

significantly affected US–Soviet rivalry for one other reason: there is no credible coincidence between the various ups and downs exhibited by superpower relations and the economic differences between the two. Economic conflicts (if any) were certainly no more acute in the early sixties (a time of growing tensions) than during the early seventies (the height of détente). And they were not more apparent during Ronald Reagan's first term (a period when relations moved from cool to icy) than during his second term (when the ice again thawed). As pointed out, if two phenomena are linked causally, we expect shifts in the effect to be associated with comparable shifts in the cause—yet no such pattern is discernible regarding economic contention and US–Soviet relations. Although economic competition has often caused hostility, quarrels, and even armed conflict among nations, it does not seem to have shaped relations between the United States and the Soviet Union.

## THE DOMESTIC TRACES OF RIVALRY

There are few, if any, Soviet or American goals—not contingent on the existence of conflict—that either nation can attain solely at the other's expense. Objective conflicts of interest have had a limited impact on the Cold War's beginnings, and have had even less to do with subsequent developments in US–Soviet relations. If accepted, these conclusions damage the demonological perspective most, for of the three perspectives it claims most confidently that inexorable incompatibilities pit the superpowers against each other. Moreover, the demonological approach can draw no strength from the knowledge that derivative conflicts of interest are part of the problem, inasmuch as the contest hardly can be depicted as one between good and evil if the contest amounts to no more than a struggle over the means of pursuing an as yet unexplained rivalry.

These conclusions, however, are less damaging to realpolitik and the game-theoretic approach. Although it is neither credible nor useful to assert that power is sought as an end in itself, the perception of power as a means to an end—and thus as the plausible object of a derivative conflict of interest—is consistent with certain variants of political realism. This perception also is consistent with the prisoner's dilemma, since, though the game assumes some conflict of interest, it does not require that the conflict be of an objective sort. In fact, an assumed incompatibility of interests that flows from perceptual errors would not vitiate its assumptions.

Both approaches might lead to the suggestion that US-Soviet rivalry is, in some fashion, *about itself*—that the rivalry has found the resources to maintain its momentum within its own logic. In a very general way the proposition is true—but cast in these terms it is not particularly enlightening. Additional information is necessary if we are to grasp how a substantial structure of derivative conflicts of interest can repose on so slim a foundation of objectively conflicting needs and goals. And because neither realpolitik nor game theory can guide us toward an answer, the inquiry must take a different direction.

Nations engage in confrontation for a variety of reasons, ranging from objective conflicts of interest to vested domestic interests. Rivalries, however, often perpetuate themselves even when their initial causes have become blurred or had never been entirely apparent. Once animosities are aroused, states may experience a variety of *internal changes*. Expecting external threats, such states adopt appropriate mind-sets, generate additional interests, and devise habits and institutions suited to dealing with hostility. But these changes often encourage further conflictual behavior as hostility and its internal impact perpetuate and reinforce each other—each being the other's cause and effect. An implication is that there often is less merit to searching for the primary sources of confrontation than in identifying conditions that might, with varying degrees of intensity, sustain the hostile relationship.

Two sorts of internal adaptations are particularly important. The first are *psychological;* they affect the ways in which members of the outside world are perceived, and notions of how best to deal with rivals. These perceptions and expectations can be an obstacle to improved relations even when tangible reasons for emnity have disappeared. The second traces involve *political reward structures*—the configurations of interests, beliefs, and power that discourage non-threatening interpretations of the world and conciliatory behavior toward nations defined as rivals. Though the two sorts of traces are logically distinct, they can, and often do, reinforce each other. For example, a perception of hostile intent on the part of an assumed adversary may lead to the creation of institutions designed to confront this adversary but, at the same time, some portion of this institution's resources will be devoted to perpetuating the very perceptions, especially the conviction of external threat, which led to its creation.

In the case of the US-Soviet confrontation, the psychological correlates have been more extensively studied than the political reward structures, and they are better understood. Accordingly, this is where we will first turn our gaze.

## NOTES

1. For a view of territorial contention as a leading source of international conflict, see Patrick O'Sullivan, *Geopolitics* (New York: St. Martins Press, 1986), especially Chapter 1.

2. Richard Pipes, *Survival Is Not Enough* (New York: Simon and Schuster, 1984), p. 37.

3. Richard Nixon, *Real Peace* (Boston: Little, Brown and Company, 1983), p. 5.

4. The following are general overviews of Russian history that provide solid coverage of its territorial growth: A. E. Presniakov, *The Formation of the Great Russian State* (Chicago: University of Chicago Press, 1970); Marc Raeff, *Imperial Russia, 1682–1825* (New York: Alfred A. Knopf, 1971); Melvin C. Wren, *The Course of Russian History* (New York: Macmillan, 1958); J. N. Westwood, *Endurance and Endeavour: Russian History, 1812–1980* (Oxford: Oxford University Press, 1981).

5. Arguments for the continuity of Russian expansionism in pre-revolutionary and post-revolutionary periods are found in Victor S. Mamatey, *Soviet Russian Imperialism* (Princeton, NJ: Van Nostrand, 1964) and Richard Pipes, "Russia's Mission, America's Destiny," *Encounter*, October 1970.

6. Quoted in Philip W. Quigg, *America the Dutiful: An Assessment of US Foreign Policy* (New York: Simon and Schuster, 1971), p. 58.

7. George F. Kennan, *American Diplomacy, 1900–1950* (Chicago: University of Chicago Press, 1951).

8. Nicholas Spykman, *The Geography of the Peace* (New York: Harcourt-Brace, 1944).

9. Same as 8, p. 43.

10. Quoted in Walter Lafeber, *America, Russia, and the Cold War: 1945–1984*, 5th edition (New York: Alfred A. Knopf, 1985), p. 16.

11. Quoted in David Horowitz, *The Free World Colossus: A Critique of American Foreign Policy in the Cold War* (New York: Hill and Wang, 1965), p. 85.

12. See Michael McGwire, *Military Objectives in Soviet Foreign Policy* (Washington DC: Brookings Institution, 1987), especially Chapter 4.

13. See, for example, Allen S. Whiting, *China Crosses the Yalu* (Palo Alto, CA: Stanford University Press, 1960).

14. *International Energy Statistical Review*, (Washington, DC: Central Intelligence Agency, August 30, 1983).

15. *Energy Security: A Report to the President of the United States* (Washington , DC: US Department of Energy, March 1987).

16. On the relative emphasis of maritime versus continental interests, see Keith A. Dunn and William O. Staudenheimer, "Strategy for Survival," *Foreign Policy*, Fall 1952, pp. 22–43; Robert W. Komer, *Maritime Strategy or Coalition Defense?* (Lanham, MD: American University Press, 1984).

17. Quoted in Robert V. Daniels, *Russia: the Roots of Confrontation* (Cambridge: Harvard University Press, 1985), p. 144.

18. This period is described in Robert K. Murray, *Red Scare: A Study in National Hysteria, 1919–1920* (Minneapolis: University of Minnesota Press, 1955).

19. The US intervention is dealt with by George F. Kennan in *Soviet-American Relations, 1917–1920*, II (Princeton, NJ: Princeton University Press, 1958) and by Robert J. Maddox in *The Unknown War with Russia: Wilson's Siberian Intervention* (San Rafael, CA: Presidio Press, 1977).

20. The issues surrounding Poland and Czechoslovakia are described by Lynn E. Davis in *The Cold War Begins: Soviet American Conflict over Eastern Europe* (Princeton, NJ: Princeton University Press, 1974).

21. Same as 10, p. 72.

22. Same as 2, p. 51.

23. The Soviet views of the importance of the Third World and of the outlook for communism in the developing regions are discussed by Roger Kanet in *The Soviet Union and the Developing Nations* (Baltimore: Johns Hopkins University Press, 1974) and by Richard Lowenthal in *Model or Ally? The Communist Powers and the Developing Countries* (New York: Oxford University Press, 1977).

24. One of the early, and most closely argued, statements of this view was provided by Barrington Moore Jr. in *Soviet Politics: The Dilemma of Power* (New York: Harper Torchbooks, 1950), Chapter 17.

25. This mood has been described by many authors. See especially Ruth W. Mouly, "Values and Aspirations of Soviet Youth" in Paul Cocks et al., eds., *The Dynamics of Soviet Politics* (Cambridge: Harvard University Press, 1976). See also Robert Wesson, *The Aging of Communism* (New York: Praeger, 1980), Chapter 2.

26. Seweryn Bialer, *The Soviet Paradox: External Expansion, Internal Decline* (New York: Alfred A. Knopf, 1986), p. 263.

27. This period is described by Thomas A. Bailey in *America Faces Russia: Russian–American Relations from Early Times to Our Day* (Ithaca, NY: Cornell University Press, 1950) and by Barbara Jelavich in *A Century of Russian Foreign Policy, 1814–1914* (Philadelphia: Lippincott, 1964).

28. William Appleman Williams, *The Tragedy of American Diplomacy,* 2nd edition (New York: Dell, 1972) and *American–Russian Relations: 1781–1947* (New York: Rinehart, 1952).

29. Arthur Schlesinger Jr., "The Cold War Revisited," *New York Review of Books,* October 25, 1979.

30. For general surveys of the Soviet economic system, see Paul K. Gregory and Robert C. Stuart, *Soviet Economic Structure and Performance* (New York: Harper and Row, 1981); Franklyn D. Holzman, *The Soviet Economy: Past, Present, and Future* (New York: Foreign Policy Association, 1982); Alec Nove, *The Soviet Economic System,* 2nd edition (London: George Allen & Unwin, 1980).

31. Quoted in Michael Shafer, "Mineral Myths," *Foreign Policy,* Summer 1982, p. 154.

32. *Prospects for Soviet Oil Production* (Washington, DC: Central Intelligence Agency, April 1977).

33. See, for example, *Allocation of Resources in the Soviet Union and China—1981* (Washington, DC: Joint Economic Committee, US Congress, 1981), pp. 81–111. See also J. P. Hardt, "Soviet and East European Energy Supplies," in H. Franssen et al., *World Energy Supply and International Security* (Cambridge, MA: Institute for Foreign Policy Analysis, 1983), pp. 28–64.

34. For the role of natural resources in Soviet foreign trade, see Jochen Beth Kenhaged, "The Soviet Union in World Trade: Energy and Raw materials," in Hans-Joachim Veen, *From Brezhnev to Gorbachev: Domestic Affairs and Soviet Foreign Policy* (Hamburg: Berg Publishers, 1984), pp. 58–69.

# CHAPTER THREE

♦ ♦ ♦ ♦ ♦

# The Psychological Foundations

We rarely respond in a direct and unmediated fashion to the "real" world; rather, we respond to what we think the world is like and, because social cognition is filtered through perceptual lenses, some distortion in our views is virtually unavoidable.

Images, and possibly misperceptions, influence the way nations behave and matter most when we seek to understand why relations sometimes are hostile even though objective conflicts of interest cannot be found; the logic of images is consistent with two of the three approaches to US-Soviet hostility considered in this book. The influence of images is least applicable to the demonological perspective, for there the rivalry is thought to flow from certain incontrovertible facts about the other side—primarily its predatory nature—and adherents would argue that this has nothing to do with perceptions. However, both the game-theoretic approach and realpolitik (particularly if it considers power a means rather than an end) are compatible with psychological reasoning. Both approaches assume that nations feel threatened by one another, but neither approach requires that conflicts of interest be authentic rather than simply products of subjective perceptions. Although game theory makes strong assumptions about rationality, this is not inconsistent with the existence of images and even misperceptions: all that is required is that nations be rational about pursuing their interests, *given* what matters most to them and what they assume (correctly or not) about the other side.

Images are not formed in a vacuum; they take as their point of departure an existing state of affairs, and their subsequent maintenance is encouraged in a variety of ways. Significantly, images often perpetuate the reality of which initially they were but a reflection—thus they may both mirror and sustain a certain state of affairs. For example, hostile images between nations often lead to belligerent behavior that in turn maintains hostile images. Moreover, political structures may be fashioned around existing perceptions and the responses for which they seem to call. For instance, images might produce their own bearers who, in turn, have a stake in their maintenance. A warrior class is unlikely to do anything to dissipate the image of a hostile external world, much as a union of police officers is unlikely to discourage public concern with the prevalence of crime.

To account for the genesis of malevolent images of other nations, the empirical circumstances surrounding their creation must be identified. Usually they are of two types. Initially there is a variety of *situational* conditions—actual experiences—that may provide the parties, through their cumulative effect over a period of time, with indications of each other's unsavory character, predatory intentions, and so forth. Secondly, the birth of images usually is assisted by *dispositional* conditions as well. At the level of individuals, these conditions include such things as personality, motives, and abilities. At the level of nations, the primary sources of dispositional conditions tend to be political ideology and national culture (which are, in any case, intertwined concepts). Both situational and dispositional conditions have molded the images that the United States and the Soviet Union hold of each other, and both types are deeply rooted in the past.

Apart from the light shed on the origins of rivalry, a glance at the history of American and Russian perceptions of each other is enlightening in several ways. For example, it shows a long-term tendency for relations marked by unusual intensity and substantial volatility, even when there are few points of contact between the two countries. Bouts of deep hostility toward Russia alternate with periods of astonishing warmth, neither attitude always reposing on firm logical foundations. Because Americans are often willing to think the worst of Russia, the virulent US response to the Bolshevik Revolution and the transition from World War II alliance to Cold War rivalry do not appear astonishing against the pattern of the more-than-two-centuries-long history of relations between the two countries. Accordingly, the hostile perceptions of the postwar decade should be judged against the longer backdrop of history.

# A HISTORY OF FLUCTUATING PERCEPTIONS

## Before the Revolution

At the time of America's birth, events augured well for future US-Soviet relations—indeed, the nascent republic felt that it had found in Russia one of its truest friends. Not only did the press of Moscow and Saint Petersburg comment sympathetically on America's struggle for independence,[1] but Catherine the Great rejected George III's request to hire some 20,000 Russian troops to help crush the rebellion. Although the Empress had certain pragmatic reasons for rebuffing his request, Americans unanimously interpreted the decision as evidence of her great love for the revolutionaries. The conviction was reinforced when Catherine took the lead in organizing the anti-British League of Neutrals, to which most of nonbelligerent Europe adhered and which was designed to force England to respect the rights of neutral maritime shippers. The League's impact was to weaken Britain and, consequently, to help the American cause—a fact much appreciated by the beneficiaries. Catherine came to be viewed as one of America's major champions, a saint-like Mother of Independence, and the new nation's gratitude seemed boundless.

But admiration for the Russian Empress soon succumbed to the vagaries of international history. In 1793, Catherine and Frederick the Great of Prussia undertook to partition Poland (for the second time in just over 20 years), and Americans commiserated with the Polish underdog. In 1794, sympathy yielded to fervent emotion when the valiant Thaddeus Kosciuszko, revered by Americans for his participation in the War of Independence, led the revolt against Russia and Prussia. Kosciuszko was hailed as the "Washington of Poland," while Catherine—recently the object of a national outpouring of affection—was excoriated as an "abominable tyrant" and a "ravenous she-bear."[2] Feelings certainly had changed but, once again, the intensity of emotion masked the shallowness of their roots: in the next several decades, relations became cordially placid.

Catherine died in 1796, and Alexander I mounted the throne in 1801, the same year that Thomas Jefferson became America's third president. The two men seemed to have a genuine respect for each other. The Czar displayed a polite interest in the civil government of the United States and Jefferson edified the Russian monarch by sending him books on the American Constitution. Alexander provided Russian assistance in freeing an American frigate captured by Tripolitan pirates in 1803 and formal diplomatic ties were established between the two countries in 1809. Relations were warmly amicable, and the US public mood responded accordingly. When the United States found itself at war with England in 1812, the Czar—himself locked in battle with Napoleon—offered to mediate the dispute. The British declined mediation, but Alexander's gesture was interpreted by many as evidence of his solicitude for America.

Nevertheless, relations experienced minor irritants during these years. As Russian forces repelled Napoleon and chased his troops westward into France, reports (in all probability overstated) of rapes, plundering, and pillaging by Cossacks reached the American press. At the same time, some concern was expressed at apparent Russian territorial ambitions in Persia and Turkey, and at encroachments by Russian pioneers in Alaska.

Russia's rulers may also have been nervous about the possible impact of the American experience on their regime. Cordial relations notwithstanding, the two countries' political systems were antithetical. Whereas the United States was successfully establishing the foundations of authentic democracy, Russia never deviated from its tradition of iron-fisted rule by autocratic monarchs. Yet many of the ideals that inspired both reformers and revolutionaries in Russia originated in the Western democracies. For example, the Decembrist Revolt of 1825 was led by liberal military officers attempting to establish a constitutional monarchy on the English model, or a republic along American lines. This was plainly disquieting to the Russian autocracy.

By 1830, feelings once again turned bitter as Poland, chafing under the foreign yoke, revolted against its Russian overlords. As in 1793, Americans enthusiastically supported the Poles and voiced their outrage against the Russians. Horror stories (again probably exaggerated) circulated about Nicholas I's repression of the insurrection, and the Czar was aggrieved by the US stance and offended by the anti-Russian outbursts in the American press. Nevertheless, Washington's attitude was more restrained than that of the American public and, though relations cooled, official diplomacy was still courteous and correct.

Toward the second half of the nineteenth century, the pendulum of American feelings once again swung from hostility to affection. Attitudes toward Russia have been warmest during some of the most trying moments in US history, and the Civil War was no exception. Although the European powers were officially neutral, most had evident sympathies for one side or the other; Saint Petersburg, however, stood fully behind the North. Britain had been pretty much at loggerheads with the United States since the War of Independence, and many Englishmen felt that a divided America was less threatening to their interests. Professing neutrality, France nevertheless flagrantly supported secession by the South. Because Russia wholeheartedly favored the Union cause, the American public extended considerable respect and affection to Alexander II, who ascended the throne in 1855. Unlike Nicholas I, Czar Alexander displayed genuine reformist inclinations, and his emancipation of the serfs in 1861 was compared with Lincoln's decision, a few years later, to free the slaves. Even though Russia was struggling once again to put down a revolt by the Poles, this action was now compared to the North's attempt to deal with insurrection by the South. The parallels between the two leaders were deemed striking, and the perception of similar destinies between the two nations appealed to many Northerners.

Moreover, but not altogether accurately, Americans viewed the Czar as the major force deterring French and perhaps even British intervention on behalf of the Confederacy. Gratitude peaked when two Russian fleets sailed into New York and San Francisco in the fall of 1863. Although it has since been established that the vessels were merely seeking safe anchorage in friendly ports, Americans were convinced that they had come to protect the Union against European intervention.[3] The ships' crews were treated to endless rounds of banquets and passionate oratory, and the image of a Russia intent on protecting the new republic excited US enthusiasm and gratitude. "God bless the Russians," exclaimed Secretary of the Navy Wells, and much of the country echoed his feelings. Sentiment ran so deep that when Russia sold Alaska to the United States for just over $7 million, the modest price was interpreted as further proof of its deep sentiment for America.

But as before, effusive expressions of mutual affection soon yielded to hostile recriminations. Two types of circumstances conspired to alter Americans' perceptions of their erstwhile protectors and benefactors. To begin with, and for the first time, the two nations experienced the stirrings of commercial rivalry. Russia's belated industrialization brought with it protectionist pressures, and this, despite America's own trade barriers, rankled many US businessmen. As historian Thomas Bailey perceptively observed, "Our people will stand for a great deal, but not for prohibitively high tariffs imposed by other nations."[4] The commercial rivalry extended to the Far East as the United States, in pursuit of its open-door policy, sought commercial access to Manchuria, which Russia was bent on transforming into its exclusive economic preserve.

Although partly determined by economic interest, perceptions of Russia were colored even more profoundly by images of autocratic injustice and repression. Alexander II died at the hands of an assassin in 1881, and was succeeded by a far more ruthless monarch. Indeed, many of the most unsavory traits of Russian politics became starkly evident during the reign of Alexander III, qualities soon brought to the indignant notice of the American public. Persecution of Russian Jews accelerated toward the end of the century with a rash of pogroms. Many of the terrorized and destitute victims debarked on America's eastern shores, providing visual evidence of the inhumanity of their treatment back home.

Petitions poured into Congress demanding action on behalf of Russia's Jews. America's moral position, however, was weakened by the extermination of certain Indian tribes and the increased incidence of lynchings of blacks in the 1890s. Consequently, Washington did little to protest another country's treatment of a minority.

At approximately this time Americans became generally aware of the extent of political repression in Czarist Russia. This was largely the achievement of George Kennan, a journalist (and distant relative of the historian-diplomat) who reported widely on the horrible conditions of Siberian prison camps, the arbitrary exercise of political power, press censorship, and the like. Accompanied by the artist George Frost, Kennan dispatched illustrated articles to US magazines detailing the sordid character of Russian autocracy. American passions were inflamed, and many shared the feelings of Mark Twain when he declared that if the regime could be ended only with dynamite, "then thank God for dynamite."[5] And when Russia found herself at war with Japan in 1905, American public opinion overwhelmingly supported the Japanese—while a deep chill engulfed relations between America and Russia.

Thus by the beginning of the twentieth century, the image of Russia as a nation of poverty and injustice, ruled by repressive despots with unwelcome external designs, was imprinted on the American consciousness. This set of images, occasionally exaggerated but on the whole accurate, provided the foundation upon which many subsequent US attitudes toward the Soviet Union have developed. Nevertheless, such images cannot have been indelibly graven. Because periods of intense wrath had not precluded phases of surprising affection in the past, it is not inconceivable that the pendulum could once again have swung in the other direction. This possibility was all the more real since, though Americans objected to much that Russia represented, generally they did not feel they had much to fear from her. After all, Saint Petersburg had not expressed any hostile feelings toward the United States or American democracy, and Russia was hardly a military power of intercontinental caliber. Perhaps the old friendship could have been rekindled, but the Bolshevik Revolution altered the terms in which Americans viewed Russia.

## The Bolshevik Revolution and Its Aftermath

As we saw earlier, the United States joyfully welcomed the overthrow of the Russian monarchy. Democracy, it was thought, finally had come to a deserving people and, as two like-minded and powerful nations, America and Russia surely would mold a better world together.

Under the circumstances, it is understandable that the Bolshevik victory was greeted with shock and horror in the United States. It knocked out the last prop from under relations established over nearly a century and a half, for the basis of animosity now seemed infinitely profound. Whereas the Czarist regimes had been merely offensive, the Bolshevik regime was perceived as a direct threat to US values and institutions: a force striving to subvert that for which the United States stood and claiming, with haughty confidence, to have history on its side. Not just political dislike, but clashing conceptions of Manifest Destiny were now at issue. In addition, by signing a separate peace with Germany the Bolsheviks had violated a commitment to fight the Kaiser, a covenant America considered sacred. Thus the Bolsheviks had, in US eyes, provided additional telling proof of their perfidious character.

A natural reaction to unbearable news is to deny that it can be true. According to a study conducted by Walter Lippman and Charles Merz, between November 1917 and November 1919 the *New York Times* predicted the fall of the Bolsheviks 91 times—nearly once every week.[6] Nevertheless, reality set in as the new rulers nationalized the land and factories, repudiated the national debt, confiscated church property, and dealt harshly with their political opponents. For the moment at least, the Communists were here to stay, and lurid tales were told about their actions and policies.

Woodrow Wilson dispatched two battalions of US troops in support of anti-Bolshevik forces. Accounts circulated of an electrically driven guillotine capable of decapitating 500 persons an hour,[7] and Lenin and Trotsky, it was stated confidently, were actually German agents. Part of the anti-Bolshevik mythology was a report, repeated many times between 1918 and 1922, that the Soviets actually had ordered the nationalization of Russian women. In certain Russian provinces, so the story ran, every eighteen-year-old girl was required to register with a government "bureau of free love," whereupon she was assigned a husband without her consent or, alternatively, could select a man without his consent.[8] Japanese intervention in Siberia met with considerable public approval and, when President Wilson decided to send US troops into the Russian fray, the only criticism in the popular press was that he was sending too few soldiers.[9] One observer captured the national perception when he proclaimed that "Bolshevism means chaos, wholesale murder, the complete destruction of civilization."[10] The paranoia produced by the Russian revolution ramified throughout American society as several thousand suspected Communists were seized in 33 American cities during the Red Scares of 1919, and the New York state legislature went so far as to seek the expulsion of six elected socialist members.

Nevertheless, by the late twenties the hysteria had subsided. Lenin's death in 1924 removed from the scene the man to whom the US press had referred as "another scourge of God," "one of the great wreckers of history," and as one who had attained "the very eminence of infamy." By the same token, Stalin's rise to power, and his rupture with Trotsky, was regarded as a portent of moderation. In any case, the American public's capacity for hostility was not inexhaustible and, by the late twenties, cool distrust had replaced the frenzied antagonism of the years immediately following the Revolution. There was also, at this time, a pragmatic basis for improved relations between the two countries.

During the early thirties the United States was weathering the Great Depression, which had produced a collapse of the stock market, a substantial drop in industrial activity, and unprecedented levels of unemployment. The Soviets were

not displeased with these developments, and America's economic predicament was contrasted with the success of the
Soviet Union's first Five-Year Plan (1928–1932). Yet there
were ways in which economic cooperation could be good
for both nations, and this was as apparent to Russia as it
was to the United States. Whereas the United States could
benefit from access to Soviet markets, the Russian economy
could use both US imports and capital (Russia produced an
extremely narrow range of goods, and its growth was constrained by severe capital shortage). Thus a basis for renewed cooperation emerged, and political relations benefited.
Moscow dangled the prospect of billion-dollar orders from
abroad, and opinion polls in the United States showed
growing support for diplomatic recognition of the Soviet
regime. A recognition which—almost alone among the
Western democracies—Washington had so far refused to
grant. In 1933 the two nations finally reestablished diplomatic relations, the irrationally diabolic perception of the
Soviet Union having ceded to a cold antagonism combined
with a modicum of pragmatic tolerance.

Although some of the more bizarre images of the Bolshevik regime had faded by the early 1930s, the basis for
US-Soviet relations nevertheless had changed since the Revolution. Not only was there nothing resembling the affection expressed during the War of Independence and the Civil
War, but feelings went beyond the ire aroused by Catherine
the Great's repression of Poland, or by the pogroms and
Siberian prison camps described by George Kennan. On such
occasions, Americans merely expressed revulsion for political practices of which they disapproved, but which did not
concern them directly. After the Bolshevik Revolution,
however, the American way of life was thought to be
threatened directly. Plainly the Soviet Union was no military threat, yet an insidious form of political infection was
nonetheless feared. The fact that the dimensions of Soviet
subversion were always modest—never even remotely successful—did not remove the concern, the threat being seen
as rooted in permanent features of Russian Communism.
The likelihood that the pendulum would swing again toward

amity was accordingly remote, but the possibility was not excluded totally. Some level of civility and modest cooperation had been restored and, as no two nations are ever so far apart they cannot be drawn together by a sufficiently dire common threat, the specter of Hitler's Germany, in principle, could have offset their other differences. But the actual effects of the Hitlerian danger were more ambivalent, and the expectation never materialized fully.

## The Common Threat and the Onset of the Cold War

By the mid-1930s the attention of the Soviet Union, and to a lesser extent of the United States, had shifted toward Central Europe. In January 1933, the Nazis rose to power on the economic frustrations of the German Depression and through a great deal of successful political infighting, intrigue, and propaganda. Moscow was particularly disturbed by Nazi rumblings. Much of Hitler's ethnic hatred was directed against the Slavs, and his proclaimed intention, as outlined in *Mein Kampf* and in a constant stream of fiery oratory, was to provide Germans with vast new living space in Eastern Europe. The fact that German communists and socialists were perishing in gestapo torture cells probably meant less to Stalin than Germany's direct menace to Russia, and the Soviet dictator emerged from his cocoon of anti-Western isolation to seek a common front against Hitler. But his attempts to galvanize a joint effort to stop the Nazis met with a lukewarm response from the Western democracies.

Partly because the West felt less-directly concerned by the German threat and partly because Stalin's purges of the late thirties had made him a particularly unsavory bedfellow, there was little enthusiasm for cooperation with Moscow. Appeasement was seen as more acceptable than resistance, and neither France nor Britain acted when Hitler boldly reoccupied the Rhineland in 1936—an example of flaccid Western will that was not lost on Stalin.[11] As Hitler began encroaching on neighboring states, the Kremlin again sought a common effort to stop him, but the West demurred. When Germany moved to absorb Austria into the Reich in 1938, both London and Paris agreed not to thwart him. And when Czechoslovakia was dismembered and then occupied by the Nazis, the West again acquiesced in the vain hope that Hitler's appetites finally would be satiated.

The thought occurred to Moscow that the West would not be displeased if Germany and the Soviet Union bled each other dry in battle, and that the fate of Czechoslovakia was connected to a desire to open Hitler's gateway to Russia. Moreover, Stalin understood that Russia was in no position at that time to confront the Germans singlehandedly—having recently liquidated many of his own most capable generals in the purges. The immediate solution to this predicament was to buy time by deflecting, temporarily at least, the German threat. In August 1939, to the shock of most Western democracies, the Soviet Union and Nazi Germany signed a Nonaggression Pact. By the terms of the accord, each side foreswore aggression against the other and, in a secret protocol, agreed to divide Poland between them, while reserving Finland, Estonia, and Latvia for the Soviet Union. Western opinion of the Soviet Union dropped to a new low.

Hitler eventually overstepped the bounds of Western forbearance, and German invasion of Poland marked the beginning of World War II. Predictably, the Führer soon tired of the agreement with Stalin and, in June 1941, launched a major offensive—Operation Barbarossa—against his former associate. Although the United States welcomed Moscow's change of camp, the perceived reasons were not always reassuring to Stalin. As Senator Harry Truman of Missouri explained, "If we see that Germany is winning we should help Russia and if Russia is winning we should help Germany and that way let them kill as many as possible, although I don't want to see Hitler victorious under any circumstances."[12]

Nevertheless, a strained collaboration got underway as, faced with the Nazi threat, each side understood the other was an unsavory but vital partner. Even before Pearl Harbor officially brought the United States into the war,

Washington extended loans to the Soviets and provided large amounts of equipment under the lend-lease program. The Russians, for their part, fought with the ferocious determination of a people defending its homeland against an enemy bent on its total destruction and subjugation. Progressively, the cement of common cause—and Russia's stoic bravery—produced a mellowing of American attitudes. At approximately the same time as the attack on Pearl Harbor, Joseph E. Davis, a former US ambassador to Russia, published a best-selling volume entitled *Mission to Moscow,* which provided a generally sympathetic assessment of the Soviet Union. Steadily, images of stouthearted patriots replaced images of godless libertines and subversives. By 1942, a majority of Americans considered communism a less offensive form of government than fascism.[13] By the eve of the San Francisco Conference in 1945, the majority of Americans surveyed trusted Stalin—to whom Roosevelt referred familiarly as "Uncle Joe"—to cooperate with the United States after the war.[14] The warming perceptions of America's new associate were understandable; in retrospect, however, any optimism concerning future relations seems overblown.

The basis of Roosevelt's thinking was that Russian suspicion of the West was rooted in the latter's tendency to treat the Bolshevik regime as an international pariah and in Russia's fears of capitalist encirclement—fears that were founded in the foreign intervention of the immediate post-revolutionary years. The obvious solution was to undo the hard feelings by treating the Soviet Union precisely as most nations would wish to be treated. If the United States simply granted the Soviets all they needed for their war effort, and treated them with trust, respect, and generosity, surely they would abandon all ideas of world revolution and cooperate with the Western democracies in building a better postwar world.[15] But Roosevelt underestimated Soviet suspicion of the capitalist world: nothing did as much to fuel this distrust during the war as the issue of the *second front.*

German troops had driven deeply into the Soviet Union—wreaking enormous human and material devastation—and Stalin pleaded with both Britain and the United States for an invasion of France. The idea was to spearhead a second front in Central Europe, relieving some of the disproportionate military pressure shouldered by the Russians by drawing off some of the German forces from the USSR. Indeed, by Churchill's own account, by early 1943 the Russians were engaged with 185 German divisions, the West with a mere 12.[16] On two occasions the British and US leaders promised an invasion of Western Europe, but on both occasions were forced to renege. They chose instead to invade North Africa and Italy, thus gradually to encircle and squeeze Germany from these positions. This may have made military sense, but Stalin was not convinced. Russians were being made to bear most of the struggle against the Nazis, convincing Stalin that the real purpose was to let Germany and Russia reduce each other to a state of prostration—making it easier for Western democracies to deal with both on their own terms. The accusation was unfair; nevertheless, the conviction became firmly embedded in the Kremlin's mind, and Stalin's perceptions of the West were shaped accordingly.

Paradoxically therefore, mutual cooperation and Soviet distrust developed hand-in-hand during the war years. What could have provided the basis for dissipating the intolerance and suspicions of the interwar years actually heightened the existing distrust. Under the circumstances, it is not surprising that postwar differences should have assumed, in both Washington's and Moscow's eyes, their ultimate magnitude. As the Soviet Union installed prefabricated communist regimes in the nations it liberated from the Nazis, Western misgiving about the Kremlin once again rose to the surface. The Nonaggression Pact and the 1939 invasion of Finland loomed larger in Western consciousness in 1945 than they had in the middle of the war, and fears of Russian expansionism were exacerbated further by its pressure on Iran and Turkey in 1946. At the same time, the Soviet Union's conviction that the capitalists desired its demise was strengthened further by the West's unhappiness with Russia's presence in Eastern Europe, a presence to which Russia felt entitled by her role in the war. Moreover, America's detonation of an atomic bomb in the summer of 1945 was not, understandably enough, interpreted by Stalin and his lieutenants as a means of expediting Japan's surrender, but as an asset designed to force Russia into an unfair postwar settlement and, quite conceivably, as an instrument of future Western aggression against its Communist rivals.[17]

Thus, as World War II drew to a close, Soviet-American relations degenerated to the level of vituperation and suspicion characteristic of much of the interwar period. By 1945 virtually all ambiguity was reduced to zero by the black and white prism of Cold War perceptions. And it may be that neither country could have done anything, given the political constraints under which both operated, to convince the other that its intentions were benign. As the chill deepened, each superpower became, in the other's eyes, not just an odious rival but an absolute enemy.

## IDEOLOGICAL CONFIRMATION OF HISTORICAL IMAGES

These then were the major events surrounding the history of relations between the two superpowers, events that provided the raw material from which their images of each other were formed. Although history had given both nations reasons for fearing and distrusting each other, an objective observer probably would have interpreted their behavior less ominously than the superpowers were inclined to do—a predisposition to assume the worst that requires further explanation. We have allowed that images are determined by both situational and dispositional influences, and that, while historical circumstances define the situation, national culture and ideology provide the stuff of which perceptual dispositions in international affairs are made. In many respects the two societies were separated by a wide cultural gap, yet their conceptions of each other crystallized following the Bolshevik Revolution, as antithetical political ideologies made it easier to interpret the other's nature and behavior in a threatening light.

In international relations, and certainly in US–Soviet relations, political beliefs have played an important part in these filtering mechanisms. Even in the absence of objective conflicts, the rival ideologies have shaped superpower relations by establishing rules and cues with which to make sense of the other's, often cryptically disquieting, behavior. In the early years of the Bolshevik Revolution, Soviet leadership appeared to take quite seriously the implications of its own ideological tenets. As Lenin observed:

> As long as capitalism and socialism remain, we cannot live in peace. In the end, one or the other will triumph—a funeral requiem will be sung either over the Soviet Republic or over world capitalism.[18]

The United States, as demonstrated by its initial reactions to the Bolsheviks' political victory, viewed the revolution as "a direct challenge to American values."[19] But ideology can mold perceptions in a circuitous, as well as direct, fashion. In addition to images that nations have of themselves and of other nations, they also have images of themselves through the eyes of *other* nations, and they assume that such images are determined by the other nations' ideological predilections. Thus, superpower policies have been determined not only by the guidelines provided by each side's beliefs but by how each side thinks its rival's beliefs impelled it to behave.

In US eyes, Moscow's ideological claims meshed well with historical facts to produce an especially menacing vision of the Soviet Union. For example, the proclaimed Soviet belief in an inevitable and general class struggle seemed to threaten the concept of natural social harmony, an assumption at the very core of American political beliefs. Moscow's claim to being at the helm of this struggle, and its insistence that the Soviets would emerge victorious, gave Russia the status of a total enemy simply on the basis of its own assertions. All this might have been taken with amused indulgence had not Russia's history, its postrevolutionary experience in particular, given the rhetorical challenge substance. After all, each of America's prior conflicts were limited by the stakes of the conflict (e.g., rival designs on Cuba during the Spanish-American War) and by the duration of the confrontation. Now Soviet ideology seemed to proclaim that the issue was infinitely large (the victory of one social system over the other) and that the duration of the rivalry was virtually unlimited—an assertion not taken with equanimity.

The images conjured up by this apparently total ideological challenge were strengthened by the impression of Russia that prior history already had imprinted on the American mind. Visions of repression, prison camps, and of a passive, robot-like society were carried over from the nineteenth century, from the memories of Nicholas I and Alexander III, and from Kennan's reports on conditions in Russia. In any case, it may not have been difficult to incorporate the specifics of the new political threat into the unpleasant images that Russia might have evoked for many Americans. Thus the disposition to view Soviet activities in their most ominous light—following the Revolution of 1917 and World War II—is not astonishing.

At the same time, at both these junctures the Soviet Union showed numerous signs of believing that the United States, fearing the influence of Soviet Marxism, would do everything, in Lenin's words, to prevent "the sparks from our fire from falling on their roofs."[20] Similarly, as one Soviet student of the United States observed of US strategy at the height of the Cold War: "[It] proceeded from the notion that the presence of the socialist camp, to say nothing of its expansion, was a direct threat to the very existence of the United States."[21] Consequently, the Kremlin probably believed that its main task was to defend its political order and sphere of influence from US attacks that, given the nature of American values and beliefs, must constantly be expected.

US-Soviet relations in the postwar decades cannot be explained exclusively, or even principally, by the images that had evolved by 1945. But history suggests that the basic elements of mutual perceptions had been sufficiently formed by this point to no longer require explicit justification. And, no longer requiring rational articulation, images could resist numerous changes in objective political conditions. Subsequent stability in superpower responses to ambiguous or contrary information about each other has been an abiding fact of the rivalry.

## THE NATURE AND IMPACT OF COLD WAR IMAGERY

Social psychology, which deals principally with relations between individuals, also has been helpful in understanding international relations—especially the matter of how countries perceive one another. Because individuals and nations are social entities of a very different order, one should not project uncritically the former's psychological attributes on to the latter. Although individuals ultimately make a nation's foreign policy decisions, institutional roles and ideological and political constraints that must be respected mold their motivations and perceptions in ways that have no parallel within the normal realm of social psychology. Nevertheless, at a certain level of abstraction the insights of psychology help illuminate some extremely important facets of the relations among nations, one of these being the stability of the images nations have of each other.

### The Stability of Images

Images are composed of several related components, and the stability of Cold-War images derives largely from the ability of their various parts to sustain one another. An indication of how perceptions of hostility can be perpetuated is given by the psychological principle of *cognitive consistency,* according to which people tend to seek a balance, or structured consistency, among the various beliefs they hold.[22] Clashes and inconsistencies among the various elements of their belief systems are not tolerated easily, and discrepant convictions and perceptions usually are modified to bring them into balance with their other beliefs. For example, we usually expect a person whom we like and admire to have ideas we agree with. And if such a person were to adopt a belief we disliked, we could resolve the inconsistency in two ways: deciding the person was not particularly likable after all or concluding the belief is not as objectionable as we had thought initially.

Similarly, political leaders, as well as their publics, dislike dissonance in their perceptions of other nations. As a major contributor to the psychological understanding of international relations has pointed out:

> We tend to believe that countries we like do things we like, support goals we favor, and oppose countries we oppose. We tend to think that countries that are our enemies make proposals that would harm us, work against the interests of our friends, and aid our opponent.[23]

The belief that bad things go together with regard to our rivals also explains why negative images often are more stable than actual circumstances might justify. In order to maintain the integrity of the overall image we have of the Soviet Union, we tend to interpret and reinterpret each of its components so that there is a psychologically coherent relationship among them: making the whole more stable than any of its parts might otherwise be. The implications for specific elements of the overall image are obvious are well. Because Americans generally disapprove of the Soviet political system, they may assume that Russia's external objectives must also be generally unpalatable. For example, Americans may find it hard to believe that a nation which has allowed its citizens scant political freedom could have nonthreatening intentions vis-à-vis a nation which, like the United States, has made liberty the cornerstone of its political life. Similarly, it is difficult to believe that a nation which appears to harbor unfriendly designs toward us would increase its military capacity for any reason other than to do us harm. Thus, increased defense outlays usually are not attributed to the Kremlin's concerns with China, to the expense of policing Soviet Bloc nations, or simply to a need to placate its defense establishment.

A related mechanism is the tendency for perceptions to be shaped by *expectations*. Psychologists have revealed—and most people understand from personal experience—that incoming information is very often interpreted in a manner consistent with what we have come to anticipate. This is "the assimilation of information to pre-existing beliefs"[24] that few statesmen manage to escape. This implies that once hostility comes to dominate relations between nations, each side comes to expect the worst of the other and, expecting unfriendliness, tends to see unfriendliness and to act with corresponding hostility, thus managing to remove all doubt about its hostile inclinations from the other side's perspective. An engine of self-reinforcing negative perceptions is thus created, and its momentum is hard to reverse.

This is why historical experience has so tenacious an impact. Ralph White, who has combined the insights of political science and psychology to analyze US-Soviet relations, compared this process to "a great flywheel, too heavy to be set in rapid motion all at once by an ordinary amount of force but having much momentum once it is started."[25]

Such mechanisms were illustrated in the thinking and perceptions of John Foster Dulles, whose name is associated closely with what has been called the "inherent bad faith" model of the Soviet Union. A pioneering study of foreign policy perceptions by political scientist Ole Holsti sought to identify the various components of the Soviet Union's negative image and to examine how that image correlated to actual evidence concerning Moscow's behavior.[26]

Through a careful quantitative analysis of Dulles' speeches and writings, Holsti managed to map out the structure of a belief system that, as far as the Soviet Union was concerned, consisted of one core element and three related perceptions. The core element was Dulles' intense dislike for the Soviet political system; the three related perceptions were, his view of the degree of Kremlin *hostility* toward the United States, the extent of Soviet foreign policy *success,* and an assessment of Russian *capabilities* for pursuing its external objectives. Shifts in each of these component perceptions were monitored for the period 1953–1958 to evaluate their stability and the extent to which they covaried (Was the Soviet Union viewed as more or less hostile or successful in its external ventures? Was Russian capability thought to be increasing or decreasing? Was the Soviet system becoming more or less objectionable? And so forth.).

The study revealed that Dulles' appraisal of the Soviet Union was remarkably resistant to change: no matter what turn events might take, no matter how the Soviets behaved, he would not alter his fundamentally negative evaluation. When Soviet hostility toward the United States seemed to decrease, Dulles would conclude that Moscow's foreign policy had been less successful—temporarily causing the Russians to change the course of their behavior. Alternatively Dulles would perceive that Soviet capability had declined: the reason the Soviets were behaving in a less confrontational manner was because they had no choice, not because they had changed in any significant way. As Holsti pointed out, "So long as good behavior is attributed to necessity, there is no need to attribute it to virtue."[27] The resistance of Dulles' central beliefs to any evidence of acceptable Soviet behavior was reflected in numerous specific ways. For example, in 1956 when the Russians reduced their military spending, Dulles did not interpret this as evidence of a less-threatening Soviet posture. Rather, he attributed the reduction to economic problems and to the fact that the reduction would release men from military service so they could be employed building more weapons!

The implication drawn by Dulles was that there was never any reason to behave in a conciliatory fashion toward the Kremlin. If Soviet hostility was declining, this was precisely when the enemy should be permitted no "relief from harassment," inasmuch as lack of success or declining capabilities accounted for this change of tune—not a change in Soviet objectives. If anything, at such times it made more sense to "sit on the lid" and turn up the heat. However, this surely is not a recipe for effective tension-reduction: the Soviet Union would have no incentive to improve its attitude if, whenever it did so, the United States became more confrontational.

Similar interpretational mechanisms have operated in the Soviet Union, the Kremlin as well seeking to make its various perceptions of the United States mutually congruous and consistent with its overall expectations of US behavior. For example, an ideologically determined image has long maintained that the American government is at the service of, or operating in close association with, "monopoly capital." Although perceptions are considerably more sophisticated now than in the days when Lenin explained that "the stock exchange is everything, while parliament and elections are marionettes,"[28] the belief that American business ultimately calls the tune continues to be a central element of the Soviet belief system. And as business interests benefit from expanded military production, the belief is that such interests are driven to demand foreign adventurism of their government. Nevertheless, Russians have had to deal with such dissonant information as the fact that American business often has reacted positively to portents of peace. For example, it did not escape the notice of some Soviet observers that, during the Vietnam war, Wall Street tended to react positively to signs that a peace settlement was at hand.[29] Their explanation: any money the US military saved on conventional forces would simply be channeled to the potentially more lucrative nuclear weapons industry.[30] Thus the dissonance was interpreted away to maintain the integrity of the basic image of militaristic capitalists.

### The Moral Self-Image

Although a variety of perceptual mechanisms continue to confirm that the other side is no good—even in the presence of ambiguous or contrary evidence—it is important to note that political leaders' images are *reversed* when it comes to perceiving their own activities. What White refers to as the *diabolical enemy image* is thus complemented by the *moral self-image:* a tendency not only to perceive one's own actions as nonthreatening but to assume that others, including adversaries, view them as such. As historian Herbert Butterfield has described it:

> It is the peculiar characteristic of the . . . Hobbesian fear . . .
> that you yourself may vividly feel the terrible fear you have
> of the other party, but you cannot enter into the other man's
> counter-fear, or even understand why he should be particularly nervous. For you know that you yourself mean him no
> harm, and that you want nothing from him save guarantees
> for your own safety; and it is never possible for you to realize
> or remember properly that he cannot see the inside of your
> mind, he can never have the same assurance of your intentions
> that you have. As this operates on both sides, the Chinese
> puzzle is complete in all its interlockings and neither party can
> see the nature of the predicament he is in, for each only imagines that the other party is being hostile and unreasonable.[31]

The result is an inflexible self-righteousness and lack of empathy for the threat that the other side might reasonably perceive from one's behavior. For example, Dulles once claimed that "Khrushchev does not need to be convinced of our good intentions. He knows we are not aggressors and do not threaten the security of the Soviet Union."[32] Dulles may have believed this, but he was almost certainly wrong, since American military power along with Dulles' own anti-Soviet rhetoric caused considerable trepidation in Russia. Similarly, the Soviet Union seems to have felt that the United States understood that the 1979 invasion of Afghanistan was not directed against US interests. Consequently, Washington's indignation was interpreted to stem from America's own designs on Southwest Asia, and from its desire to undermine the Soviet Union's regional security. Although surveys of Americans in leadership positions conducted in 1976 and 1980 revealed a general consensus to the effect that Soviet foreign policy is expansionist rather than defensive,[33] the leading study of the perceptions of Soviet leaders concluded that they perceived their own actions as being fundamentally defensive.[34] Thus moral self-image implies an inability to see oneself from an opponent's perspective, making one insensitive to the kind of information that could encourage such conciliatory behavior.

The effect of images is complemented by yet another, though related, mechanism: one through which specific causes are attributed to behavior. To some extent this mechanism overlaps the psychology of cognitive consistency, but the emphasis is different.

## The Logic of Attribution

Attribution theory is the subfield of social psychology that studies patterns of people's causal attributions.[35] The theory seeks to understand how individuals perceive the causes behind the behavior of others, and many of its conclusions can apply to perceptions among nations.

A basic principle of attribution theory is that typically we account for our undesirable conduct in terms of external pressure, whereas the misbehavior of others—especially those to whom we feel ill disposed—tends to be explained by their inherent negative traits. If we act violently, for example, we are likely to feel that we have been "driven" to it by outside circumstances (e.g., a gratuitous provocation); when others (particularly those we dislike) engage in violent behavior, it is probably explained in terms of their unattractive or flawed character. The application to relations among hostile nations is straightforward. For instance, if the Soviet Union expands its military outlays, US political leadership would probably interpret this in terms of aggressive designs, Communist militarism, and so forth. America's own military growth, on the other hand, would likely be attributed to the pressure of external circumstances, most notably the Soviet threat. Presumably, the Kremlin would simply reverse the terms of the explanation.

An important attributional extension observes that when the other superpower behaves in a manner contrary to one's own interests, such behavior usually is attributed to the rival's very essence (as revealed in its ideology, political system, and so forth). Yet when the other superpower behaves in a cooperative or nonthreatening fashion, such behavior is usually attributed to one's own toughness and resoluteness. The tendency already has been revealed in the case of John Foster Dulles, who explained unwelcome Soviet behavior in terms of inherent bad faith, whereas he maintained that cooperative Soviet behavior stemmed from frustration caused by foreign policy failures or from a declining ability to pursue expansionary objectives. More recent instances of this sort of attributional bias can be found as well.

The Soviet Union welcomed détente both because of the implied decreased risk of conflict and because of the potentially improved access to Western goods and technology but also because it interpreted *America's* desire for improved relations in terms of necessity rather than goodwill. Moscow's explanation for the new US "realism" stressed, as a central fact, that the international "correlation of forces" was no longer as obviously in America's favor as it had been previously, and that parity between the two superpowers called for accommodation with the Soviet Union.[36] Washington's realization (brought home by US failure in Vietnam) that it could not always get its way through military means, the Soviet Union's improved capacity for force projection, and, especially, the attainment of strategic parity between the two sides ushered in a new type of relationship between the superpowers. The United States, according to Moscow, had no choice but to treat the Soviet Union as an equal; it was this circumstance, Moscow claimed, that ultimately led to détente. Sophisticated Russian observers appear to have understood that détente was facilitated by the shift of political power within the United States from Cold-War elites to groups more willing to cooperate with the Kremlin,[37] a shift also explained in terms of the new balance of power. In fact, it was the declining utility of military instruments of foreign policy under conditions of strategic parity that would weaken the grip of the military-industrial complex on US politics and would permit the emergence of new political forces.

But pro-détente feeling in the United States had less to do with Soviet power than the Kremlin supposed. Although the desire to reduce the risk of nuclear war and to control strategic weaponry were important, the greatest pressure for East–West détente came from generational change within the US polity and from growing concern, during the sixties and early seventies, with domestic economic and social problems, at the expense of international issues.[38] In retrospect, domestic considerations appear to have been more important than strategic circumstances in explaining détente's appeal to many Americans.

The Soviet explanation for the new American attitude was not only biased and simplistic, but was counterproductive as well. The implication drawn by the Kremlin from its analysis was that only improved Soviet strength would ensure continued US accommodation—a boost for Russia's own advocates of military growth and of assertiveness toward the United States. As later became apparent, however, the Soviet Union's expanding military outlays in the seventies, and its interventions in Angola and the Horn of Africa, turned away many Americans from support for superpower conciliation and ushered in the growing anti-Soviet mood of the late seventies. In other words, the policy conclusions drawn by the Soviets about the sources of the US movement toward détente ultimately undermined American support for improved relations.

Similar attributional reasoning has operated in the United States—and has been comparably misguided. No recent president has placed so much emphasis on military strength and on firmness toward the Soviets as Ronald Reagan, an attitude particularly pronounced during his first years in office. From the Reagan Administration's perspective, toughness soon produced results. In 1982, for example, Israel invaded Lebanon with the objective of weakening the Palestinian Liberation Organization's position in the southern part of the country. During the invasion, the Israelis destroyed the MIGs and SAMs provided Syria by Moscow—with no Russian retaliation. The Soviet Union's apparent meekness, and the contrast with its blustering stance in 1973, convinced Reagan and his advisers that the change in Soviet behavior was due to their hardline policies.

But Moscow's restraint probably was linked to a different set of causes.[39] Russia was bogged down in the costly quagmire of Afghanistan and was appropriately concerned over developments in Poland (a country of enormous security significance to the Soviets) where Communist rule was being challenged effectively by the newly emerged Solidarity movement. Moreover, domestic imperatives were rising to the forefront of Kremlin concerns, as it faced the issues of leadership succession and slackening economic growth rates. In many ways this was a period when priorities were being reassessed, and when risky and costly action in the Middle East was not an appealing proposition. As Strobe Talbot has since pointed out:

> Whatever restraint, uncertainty, and even passivity the USSR may have displayed during that period did not mean leaders had concluded that the correlation of forces had permanently shifted against them or that the most prudent course in the long run was to cut their losses in a new set of arrangements with the United States on American terms.[40]

In the event—and despite a certain amount of self-congratulation by the Reagan Administration—the Soviet Union actually may have come out ahead in this situation. The lost MIGs and SAMs were replaced quickly with improved versions, Israel became entangled in its own morass in Lebanon, and the US image in the Middle East suffered the result of its perceived association with the Israeli invasion.

Thus the tricks of attributional psycho-logic can point to misleading conclusions about the roots of the other superpower's activities and encourage ill-advised and counterproductive responses. This does not mean that the superpowers have *systematically* distorted images or that they are incapable of learning to view each other more accurately. But a fair amount of astigmatism does characterize their mutual perceptions, often nudging Soviet-American relations toward more hostility and intolerance than the extent of their true differences should reflect. This incongruity is amplified further in two ways.

Other nations, especially those considered adversaries, are perceived to be more *monolithic* than they actually are.[41] Thus a rival's actions are seen as emanating from a single decisional center—a powerful leader, a government acting in unison, a conspiratorial group firmly in control of governmental decisions—and the more monolithic the decisional center, the more purposeful its behavior appears. Accordingly the threat seems even greater than if the perception simply were that the other country was driven by bureaucratic inertia, political compromises, or a tendency to muddle through.

For example, it is interesting to note how Soviet views on what drives US foreign policy evolved during the years of détente. Previously the perception was that the American power structure could be described as "state-monopoly capitalism." Under this system the US government operated under direct instructions from monopoly capital that, because it viewed Soviet socialism as the principal threat to its interests, encouraged a hostile foreign policy.[42] As Anatoly Gromyko (related to the long-time Soviet foreign minister) explained in 1968, "Monopoly capital is the main and decisive force which controls American foreign policy."[43] No room was recognized for noneconomic influences or for interests beyond those of the "bourgeois ruling class." However, with the onset of détente the US leadership structure came to be viewed in more differentiated terms. Businessmen were no longer regarded as the political leaders' puppeteers; rather, the government was recognized as an autonomous political force whose interests did not invariably overlap with that of "monopoly capital."[44] For the first time too, public opinion and elections also came to be recognized as independent influences on US policy.

In addition, the notion of a monolithic adversary, and the other psychological mechanisms thus far surveyed, are sustained by the pressures toward conformity that, to a greater or lesser extent, are present in all societies. Once a majority comes to accept an image or endorse an attitude, the pressure for all members to conform becomes powerful, a phenomenon that has come to be known as "groupthink".[45]

Such pressures usually are subtle—the case with most socialization—but occasionally they become more obvious and heavy-handed. The net effect is that independence of thought often requires considerable courage and a capacity to bear ostracism and ridicule. As few people can manage this, most accept the prevailing wisdom or remain prudently discreet about their own beliefs.

## THE STRUCTURE OF POPULAR IMAGES

Although the focus so far has been on the images held by political leadership, these images usually are reflected in the perceptions of the general public as well. That America's Soviet policy frequently mirrors public moods stems from the nature of democratic politics and, especially, from electoral considerations. But public attitudes have impacted America's Soviet policies even outside the context of electoral politics, simply in the normal play of influence between people and government. For example, it appears that Truman's initial decision to move away from cooperation with the Soviet Union had much to do with public irritation over Moscow's postwar behavior. Arthur Schlesinger Jr. points out that "[it was] the mass of ordinary people who first became angry over Soviet actions and then turned the Truman administration around."[46] Similarly, near the end of his incumbency, Jimmy Carter's increasing assertiveness vis-à-vis the Kremlin reflected the average American's growing anger with Russia in the late seventies. Adam Ulam, a Harvard political scientist, observed that regarding the nation's Soviet policy "powerful gusts of popular emotion rather than factual data about the international situation determined the main lines of American foreign policy."[47]

The government, however, does not merely respond to public feelings regarding the Soviet Union; it seeks independently to build domestic support for whatever line of policies the government considers most advisable by molding public preferences accordingly. But whatever the dominant direction of influence (people to government or the other way around), US political leaders must take into account national moods, and these are determined by how the public views the USSR.

The average American's image of the Soviet Union has been overwhelmingly negative and, with the possible exception of the brief interlude of wartime collaboration, has been so since the Bolshevik Revolution. In 1982 respondents were asked to express how warmly they felt about 24 countries by rating them on a "feeling thermometer." The Soviets finished last with a chilly 26-degree average temperature—as opposed to a warm 74 degrees for Canada and a balmy 68 degrees for Great Britain. Admittedly, 1982 was a bad year for US-Soviet relations; but a glimpse at the comparable figures for 1986, a year when relations had taken a turn for the better, reveals much the same picture (Table 3.1). Public attitudes do shift as the tone of relations changes. Still, fluctuations occur within a band ranging from cool to frigid, and the proportion of the American public willing to express even the mildest level of approval of the Soviet Union has always amounted to less than half the total.

Tethered to this disapproval is a good deal of distrust: most Americans simply do not believe the Soviets can be relied upon to keep their promises and live up to their commitments. Most Americans favor the pursuit of arms control agreements with the USSR but, at the same time, some two-thirds of all those surveyed typically doubt the Soviets would comply with the terms of an arms-control agreement, or of an agreement to reduce tensions between the two countries (Table 3.2).

That Americans fear the Soviet Union and disapprove of its politics is scarcely surprising—both Russia's behavior and the deluge of negative information attending that behavior virtually preclude any other feelings. Less understandably, Americans know little about Soviet *society*, and the opinions they express are often quite at variance with reality. Although most Americans routinely would claim that the problem is with the Soviet government and not its people, feelings toward the former have been instrumental in

**TABLE 3-1**

Approval Ratings of Twenty-Three Countries
by US Public: 1982 and 1986*

| Country | 1982 | 1986 |
|---|---|---|
| Canada | 74 | 77 |
| Great Britain | 68 | 73 |
| West Germany | 59 | 62 |
| Japan | 53 | 61 |
| Mexico | 60 | 59 |
| Israel | 55 | 59 |
| Philippines | — | 59 |
| France | 63 | 58 |
| Italy | 55 | 58 |
| Brazil | 54 | 54 |
| Poland | 52 | 53 |
| China | 47 | 53 |
| Taiwan | 49 | 52 |
| South Korea | 44 | 50 |
| Saudi Arabia | 52 | 50 |
| Egypt | 52 | 49 |
| India | 48 | 48 |
| South Africa | 45 | 47 |
| Nigeria | 44 | 46 |
| Nicaragua | — | 46 |
| Syria | 42 | 34 |
| Soviet Union | 26 | 31 |
| Iran | 28 | 22 |

*Sources: John E. Reilly, ed., *American Public Opinion and U.S. Foreign Policy* (Chicago: Chicago Council on Foreign Relations, 1983), p. 19 and John E. Reilly, "America's State of Mind," *Foreign Policy* (Spring 1987), p. 47.

**Table 3-2**

US Public's Faith in Soviet Compliance with Agreements

| To Build No More Nuclear Weapons* | | To Relax US-Soviet Tensions** | | To Abide by a US-Soviet Agreement*** | |
|---|---|---|---|---|---|
| Very likely | 6% | Cannot be trusted | 66% | Cannot be trusted | 66% |
| Fairly likely | 27% | Can be trusted | 24% | Can be trusted | 23% |
| Not at all likely | 60% | Not sure | 10% | Not sure | 12% |
| No opinion | 7% | | | | |

Sources: *The Gallup Report,* April 1981, p. 8. **/***NBC News/Associated Press surveys, October 16–17, 1978. Reported in Everett Carl Ladd, "The Freeze Framework," *Public Opinion,* August/September 1982, p. 36.

shaping opinions of the latter. Twice, in 1942 and again in 1966, a Gallup poll presented a sampling of Americans with a list of adjectives, asking them to select those that best applied to the people of Russia, Japan, and Germany. On the first occasion, during wartime collaboration between the two countries, such adjectives as "warlike" and "treacherous" were applied most often to the Japanese, whereas generally favorable adjectives were attached to the Russians. Fourteen years later, when relations between the superpowers had deteriorated, the Russians became "warlike," "treacherous," and "sly," whereas the Japanese were now described in positive terms.[48]

In September 1985, not long before the first summit meeting between Reagan and Gorbachev, the *New York Times* conducted a survey designed to assess US understanding of Soviet society.[49] The dominant conclusion was that Americans perceive Russians as very dissimilar to themselves—considerably more so than the British, the Germans, and, despite ethnic differences, the Japanese. This is almost certainly the product of postwar relations between the two countries. In 1966, the first things the American public thought of regarding the Soviet Union were military threat and political differences; just one half of one percent of respondents (i.e., one in two hundred) mentioned the experience of fighting together against Nazi Germany during World War II. A mere six percent of those polled had such positive thoughts about the Russians as "people like us" or "World-War II allies."

Feelings toward a nation's government and its policies are probably never entirely independent of the way its people and society are viewed. On grounds of cognitive consistency, disdain for the people or dislike of the society may make it easier to think ill of the political system. It therefore comes as no surprise that Americans do not think highly of Soviet society; nevertheless, their views are powerfully distorted.

A significant plurality of those surveyed believed that Americans were more patriotic than Soviet citizens and that Americans cared more about their children. As virtually

everyone who has had any direct experience with Soviet society would confirm, Russians are extremely warm and car-
ing parents, and it is a virtual cliché with knowledgeable
observers that Russians are fiercely patriotic. By contrast,
most Americans believe that Soviet citizens are harder
working than themselves—a belief that is, by all accounts,
just about 100 percent wrong. Whereas few people are as
industrious as Americans, the average Soviet citizen's deftness at shirking work has made the Soviet Union, in the
words of an experienced journalist, "one of the world's
greatest goof-off societies."[50]

Other stereotypes, while pretty much off target, are more
understandable. The average American is convinced that his
or her Soviet counterpart detests the regime and would gladly
choose US-style democracy if given the chance. Yet this is
not obviously so. Russians do grumble about shortages, are
fond of jeans and Western music, produce visible dissidents,
and indulge in copious political joke-making. Nevertheless,
there seems to be a reasonably firm consensus between government and governed; Glasnost notwithstanding, there is
as yet no widespread public feeling that a radically different
political arrangement would be preferable.[51] Russians appear
to believe their current form of government is well-equipped
to defend them against the sort of foreign threats that have
ravaged their society in the past. And although living standards do not approach those of developed capitalist societies, Russians enjoy the economic security and cradle-to-grave
welfare with which they are provided.

Russians appear convinced that much chaos and uncertainty attends life in the West; everything in Russian historical experience has persuaded them that social existence must
be orderly and that the purpose of government is to be
obeyed. Challenges to established authority do not easily fit
in with the Russian conception of the natural order of things.
For example, it has been reported that when the US em-
bassy in Moscow invited a number of Soviet officials to watch
videotapes of the televised debates between Jimmy Carter
and Gerald Ford during the 1976 electoral campaign, many
Russians were repelled by the spectacle, feeling that the sharp

questioning to which the men had been submitted was "humiliating" to a national leader.[52] Authority is authority, and chaos as well as economic insecurity are undesirable. Thus, American expectations that Russians detest their regime and yearn for democracy are perfectly understandable, but by and large mistaken.

Still, the compelling fact of American opinion is its disdain for Soviet society and its antipathy toward the Communist regime—making it easier to cast specific intentions and policies in an ominous light. And because US foreign policy is formed against a background of public moods as well as international events, the actual structure of national opinion does little to facilitate improved US-Soviet relations.

## IMAGES IN US-SOVIET RELATIONS: THE ISSUE IN PERSPECTIVE

The images and attributional mechanisms with which US-Soviet relations are impregnated produce consequences of two sorts. First, these perceptions establish a level of conciliatory behavior beyond which even the most reasonable and farsighted leaders can go only at significant political cost. Cooperative gestures typically are viewed as "appeasement," and statesmen seen as lacking in sufficient toughness may suffer the sanctions wielded by the political system. For example, Gerald Ford's decision to abandon all reference to détente during the primary election season of 1976 reflected the domestic risks of appearing too conciliatory toward the nation's principal rival. Second, these perceptions increase the amount of *contrary evidence* needed to think well of the other side—far beyond what is required to establish good intentions between nations whose mutual images are less marred by negative bias. Indeed, initial cooperative gestures on the rival's part may well be taken as signs of weakness rather than goodwill. Consequently, any improvement in relations requires an exceptionally large number of explicitly conciliatory gestures by one or both countries. At the same time, even modest indications of the other side's predatory nature could quickly undo the effect of numerous indications of friendliness.

Although psychological mechanisms have tipped the conflict–cooperation scale toward continued hostility, the bias need not *inevitably* drive the superpowers away from conciliation, and reasonable starts toward improved relations have at times been made. These starts, in turn, were rooted in two types of circumstances. To begin with, the dominant image of the adversary occasionally has shifted away from a Manichaean dichotomy in response to contrary evidence about the rival. In other words, images have at times been moderated by learning. Secondly, there have been instances where one side or the other has felt that the perils of continued rivalry outweighed the claims of antagonism, and decided to take steps toward conciliation *despite* continued negative perceptions of the adversary. Images need not have changed, but the two countries occasionally have risen above them. And when relations eventually tipped back toward hostility, this was not because images reasserted themselves in any *automatic* manner, but because more tangible pressures blocked the path toward expanded cooperation. Thus, two arguments militate against according excessive weight to psychological mechanisms. First, images sometimes do change in response to changing international conditions. Second, relations also have been shaped by nonpsychological forces that have motivated leaders to act in apparent defiance of their own images.

### Rivalry and the Capacity to Learn

Because some minds are less closed than others, people have unequal abilities to learn from experience. As we have seen, John Foster Dulles held an immutable view of the Soviet Union, and he resisted any information inconsistent with his opinions of it. Others have demonstrated a greater ability to adapt personal images to experience and changing information.

For example, during the early years of his political

career, John F. Kennedy's image of the USSR mirrored that of the nation's more virulent cold warriors. In 1946, Kennedy called on Americans to "recognize the fact that internally Soviet Russia is a ruthless dictatorship and externally is on the march."[53] He castigated Roosevelt for insufficient toughness toward Moscow and enthusiastically endorsed Truman's containment policy. As a young congressman, Kennedy's views were not significantly different from Dulles'. But Kennedy's mind was not impermeable to experience and, as he moved from the House to the Senate, his views of the Soviet Union became more nuanced and complex. By the time he stepped into the presidency, Kennedy's perceptions had evolved considerably. In 1960, according to Arthur Schlesinger Jr.:

> The John Foster Dulles contrast between the God-anointed apostles of free enterprise and the regimented hordes of atheistic communism bored him. Seeing the world as a historian rather than a moralist, he could not utter without embarrassment the self-serving platitudes about the total virtue of one side and the total evil of the other. . . . The stereotypes of the fifties, he thought, were not only self-serving, but, worse, they simply did not provide a useful way of thinking about international affairs.[54]

Thus, leaders' perceptions can become more sophisticated and flexible, the result of experience and expanded insight, and when this happens relations are more likely to take a turn for the better. Occasionally too, people whose thinking was never really afflicted with the usual biases enter office bringing new and more productive ways of thinking to national policy. Henry Kissinger is a case in point.

Unlike Dulles, Kissinger considered the opposition of communism and democracy less significant to international relations than the more basic dichotomy between order and upheaval.[55] For Kissinger it was more meaningful to distinguish legitimate states seeking to preserve the general outlines of the status quo from illegitimate, revolutionary states wishing to disrupt the established order. In Kissinger's opinion, the Soviet Union had become pretty much a status-quo nation, and thus less a threat to US interests than his predecessors had believed. Most importantly, Kissinger kept a rather open mind about Russia, allowing his images to be shaped by the flow of circumstances rather than by the iron clasp of ethical convictions.

A worthy piece of research—using a methodology similar to Holsti's—compared Dulles' images of Russia with those of Kennedy and Kissinger.[56] As in Holsti's study, the authors distinguished four components of US policymakers' images of the Soviet Union: their overall evaluation of Russia, their perception of Russian hostility toward the United States, their estimates of Russian capability, and their views on the success of Russian foreign policy. The study's central conclusion was that Kennedy, and especially Kissinger, saw Moscow in a less-hostile light than did Dulles. Moreover, their perceptions of hostility tended to diminish progressively while their general evaluation of Russia tended to become more favorable with time. Most importantly, whereas Dulles' overall opinion never changed—even when he perceived Soviet hostility declining—the other statesmen were more willing to let their opinion of the Soviet Union be influenced by its perceived hostility toward the United States.

The key is that Kennedy, and particularly Kissinger, managed to escape the constraints of certain psychological mechanisms—especially the tendency to have perceptions determined by unchanging expectations—and to attribute cooperative Soviet behavior to duress rather than to goodwill. Dulles, as we have seen, explained decreases in Soviet hostility in terms of necessity (lowered capacity or diminished success) rather than Moscow's genuine desire for improved relations. Thus there was never any reason to think better of the Russians. Kissinger was less willing to account for improved Soviet behavior in such cynical terms. And Kennedy, although never eager to give Moscow the benefit of the doubt, nevertheless did not explain away ebbs in Soviet hostility in the Dulles tradition.

The implications of these findings are encouraging. Although negative images tend to perpetuate themselves through a variety of psychological stratagems, they are never totally inflexible and some leaders are able to free themselves from their grip. Of course, learning can operate in the opposite direction as well. President Carter's views of the Soviet Union deteriorated during his term in office. A few days after the invasion of Afghanistan, Carter admitted that his "opinion of the Russians has changed more drastically in the last week than ever in the previous two and a half years before that."[57] Yet this does not alter the conclusion that even though superpower relations are affected by perceptual *bias,* they are not the victim of psychological *determinism.* Furthermore, public images can be modified in the course of experience as well. We saw that traditionally the US public has taken a dim view of the Soviet Union, but its perceptions have not been immutable. The long-term, postwar trend has been in the direction of decreasing disapproval (Figure 3-1). Although opinion has fluctuated around the trend, it usually has done so in reasonable response to Soviet behavior and the overall tone of East–West relations.

Nevertheless, learning does occur and images can change, even between nations who consider each other mortal rivals. As a major American statesman observed:

**FIGURE 3-1**
US Public Approval of the Soviet Union*

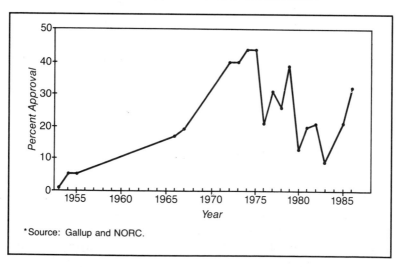

*Source: Gallup and NORC.

> We concur in considering the government . . . as totally
> without morality, insolent beyond bearing, inflated with van-
> ity and ambition, aiming at the exclusive domination of the
> [world]—of deep-rooted hatred towards us, hostile to liberty
> wherever it endeavors to show its head, and eternal disturber
> of the peace of the world.[58]

This is not John Foster Dulles or Ronald Reagan castigating
the Soviet Union, but Thomas Jefferson describing England
in the early nineteenth century. At roughly the same time,
England's Lord Palmerston explained:

> [In] dealing with Vulgar minded Bullies, and such unfortu-
> nately the people of the United States are, nothing is gained
> by submission to Insult & wrong; on the contrary the sub-
> mission to an Outrage only encourages the commission of
> another and a greater one.[59]

Nevertheless, by the latter part of the century, the English
and American perceptions of each other had changed dramatically and a friendship now entering its second century
took root.

Countries then can learn to change their images. And
while not much is understood yet about the mechanisms of
governmental or societal learning,[60] the important issues are
that no one is totally impermeable to experience and that
cycles of misperception are never totally closed or wholly
binding. Even views of a diametrically opposite society can
be altered in the face of new and reliable information—as
the example of US perceptions of the Japanese has demonstrated. Under the circumstances, one should ask under what
conditions learning might be promoted or impeded in US-
Soviet relations.

### Circumventing Images

Not only can images be modified by experience, but decision makers' behavior is sometimes at variance with what
their stereotypes would lead one to expect; consequently,
policies may change even when images remain inflexible.
One such influence is the *fear* of consistently allowing

hostile images to guide foreign policy, especially when doing so increases the likelihood of nuclear war. When such fear intensifies, one or both sides might seek to establish relations on a friendlier footing—even in the face of unchanging adversarial images. The Cuban Missile Crisis in 1962 provided an example of this very situation.

The discovery, in October 1962, of Soviet missile emplacements on Cuban soil, and the threat of US military action to remove them, led the world closer to the nuclear precipice than ever before. According to Khrushchev, "The smell of burning pervaded the air." And Kennedy reckoned the odds of a confrontation claiming some 100 million lives on each side as "between one out of three and even."[61] Although it did in fact lead both sides to the brink of destruction, this brief glimpse into the nuclear abyss also jolted the superpowers from their lethargic approach to mutual accommodation and military restraint. It was not that the superpowers suddenly thought better of each other—they were simply, and appropriately, terribly frightened of the consequences of uncontrolled rivalry.

Both nations had been unsuccessfully discussing the issue of nuclear test bans for several years, a major stumbling block being Soviet unwillingness to permit on-site inspections of its compliance. But by December 1962, Khrushchev made a significant concession by agreeing to permit two or three yearly inspections on Soviet soil. In June of 1963, Kennedy delivered a major speech at American University in which he recognized the USSR's abhorrence of war, as well as its past sufferings and current achievements. In July 1963, the Limited Test Ban Treaty—which prohibited nuclear testing under water, in the atmosphere, and in outer space—was signed. Other developments followed. Six months after the missile scare, the Hot Line was established between the White House and the Kremlin in an important step at improving crisis management. Within the next few years, movement occurred toward limiting the spread of nuclear weapons to other nations (the Treaty on the Non-Proliferation of Nuclear Weapons was signed in 1968), and the first serious talks on limiting strategic missiles were undertaken in 1967. By the end of the decade, the momentum created by the Cuban missile crisis had spent itself; nevertheless, the institutions for arms limitation had been created and, even after the memory of the near-holocaust had dimmed, some halting progress was registered along the course it had charted.

The Cuban Missile Crisis was, admittedly, a startling example of an external shock with salutary effects for superpower cooperation; other, less obvious, examples could also be mentioned. The point is that there have been, and will continue to be, occasions where the fear of acting on negative images comes to outweigh the impulse to do so; under such conditions, images can be set aside and their consequences occasionally circumvented. Nevertheless, the risk of nuclear disaster cannot be manipulated for policy purposes, and (as discussed further in Chapter 6) few practical lessons can be drawn from our understanding of its occasional benefits.

Pressures for improved cooperation, even in the face of mutual negative perceptions, can be rooted in domestic sources as well. Mikhail Gorbachev's push for improved East–West relations—despite what must have been a dire image of the United States created by President Reagan—had much to do with Soviet domestic needs. The declining rates of Soviet economic growth and the growing drag that huge military budgets exerted on the economy increased the appeal of arms control for the Kremlin. Moreover, Gorbachev's desire to unleash more of Russia's creative potential in further pursuit of accelerated scientific, technological, and productive growth required a loosening of internal controls on Soviet life. But internal relaxation is difficult to justify to Soviet hardliners, especially in the presence of continuing East–West tension—hence another reason to seek accommodation with the United States. Although it is unlikely that Gorbachev's initiatives were founded on significantly altered perceptions of the United States—in fact, the evidence indicates otherwise—domestic needs required that such images be partially ignored.[62]

President Nixon's pursuit of détente was, to some

extent, also linked to anticipated domestic benefits. Public weariness with confrontation in the aftermath of the Vietnam involvement made the pursuit of improved relations with the Soviet Union good electoral strategy for both his first and second terms. Though Nixon was a reasonably pragmatic man, and though he did benefit from Henry Kissinger's counsel, he retained, as his later published work revealed,[63] an abiding distrust of Russia and a continuing belief in her expansionist nature. Nevertheless, Nixon managed to navigate around his images in anticipation of domestic political rewards.

Without doubt, psychology is important; yet, psychology can never fully create its own reality. And governments, like people, can learn, and negative perceptions can be circumvented when there appears to be a sound reason to do so. Accordingly, one may ask why learning is permitted to occur at certain times but not at others? Why do leaders occasionally act in defiance of their apparent perceptions but at other times do not? Why hasn't the movement toward improved relations created sufficient momentum to become self-sustaining and to progressively erode the foundations of illwill and confrontation that have permeated Soviet-American relations? The answers to these questions may provide the keys to understanding superpower rivalry—answers which lie within the political structures and practices that, for both superpowers, have evolved around their mutual rivalry.

## NOTES

1. Nikolai N. Bolkhivitinov, *The Beginnings of Russian-American Relations: 1775–1815* (Cambridge: Harvard University Press, 1975), Chapter 2.

2. Thomas A. Bailey, *America Faces Russia: Russian-American Relations from Early Times to Our Day* (Ithaca, NY: Cornell University Press, 1950), p. 10.

3. Frank A. Golder, "The Russian Fleet and the Civil War," *American Historical Review* (July 1915), pp. 801–812.

4. Same as 2, p. 174.

5. Quoted in William Appleman Williams, *American-Russian Relations: 1781–1947* (New York: Rinehart, 1952), p. 25.

6. Walter Lippman, "More News from the Times," *The New Republic* (August 11, 1920), p. 299.

7. Same as 2, p. 246.

8. Peter G. Filene, *Americans and the Soviet Experiment: 1917–1933* (Cambridge: Harvard University Press, 1967), p. 46.

9. Same as 8, p. 45.

10. Gertrude Atherton, "Time as a Cure for Bolshevism," *New York Times* (March 16, 1919), p. 3.

11. Stalin's feelings during this period are described by George F. Kennan in *Russia and the West Under Lenin and Stalin* (Boston: Atlantic Monthly Press, 1960), pp. 304–306.

12. Quoted in Robert V. Daniels, *Russia: The Roots of Confrontation* (Cambridge: Harvard University Press, 1985), p. 205.

13. *Public Opinion Quarterly* (Winter 1944–1945), p. 522.

14. *Public Opinion Quarterly* (Spring 1945), p. 103.

15. See, for example, Forrest Davis, "Roosevelt's World Blueprint," *Saturday Evening Post* (April 10, 1943), pp. 20–21.

16. Winston Churchill, *The Hinges of Fate* (New York: Bantam), pp. 663 and 679.

17. For the views of two Soviet historians on this period, see Nikolai V. Sivachev and Nikolai N. Yakovlev, *Russia and the United States* (Chicago: University of Chicago Press, 1979), Chapter 6.

18. Quoted in David Shub, *Lenin: A Biography* (London: Penguin Books, 1977), p. 445.

19. Michael H. Hunt, *Ideology and U.S. Foreign Policy* (New Haven, CT: Yale University Press, 1987), p. 115.

20. Quoted in Morton Schwartz, *Soviet Perceptions of the United States* (Berkeley: University of California Press, 1978), p. 118.

21. Yuri P. Davidov, " 'Doktrina Niksona'—Krizis Globalizma," in Yuri P. Davidov, V. Zhurkin, and V. S. Rudnev, *Doktrina Niksona* (Moscow: Nauka, 1972), p. 12.

22. Examples of relevant literature include Leon Festinger, *A Theory of Cognitive Dissonance* (Palo Alto, CA: Stanford University Press, 1957) and Robert Zajonc, "Cognitive Theories in Social Psychology," in Gardner Lindzey and Elliot Aronson, eds., *The Handbook of Social Psychology,* I, 2d ed. (Reading, MA: Addison-Wesley, 1968), pp. 345–353. For applications to international relations, see Robert Jervis, *Perception and Misperception in International Politics* (Princeton: Princeton University Press, 1976).

23. Same as 22, Jervis, p. 118.

24. Same as 22, Jervis, p. 76.

25. Ralph K. White, *Fearful Warriors: A Psychological Profile of US-Soviet Relations* (New York: The Free Press, 1984), p. 169.

26. Ole R. Holsti, *The Belief System and National Images: John Foster Dulles and the Soviet Union* (doctoral dissertation: Stanford University, 1962).

27. Same as 26, 140.

28. Vladimir I. Lenin, *Lenin on the United States* (New York: International Publishers, 1970), p. 401.

29. For the relationship between stock-index movements and portents of peace in Vietnam, see Bruce M. Russett and Elizabeth C. Hanson, *The Foreign Policy Beliefs of American Businessmen* (San Francisco: W. H. Freeman, 1975), Chapter 4.

30. See John Lenczowski, *Soviet Perceptions of U.S. Foreign Policy* (Ithaca, NY: Cornell University Press, 1982), p. 63.

31. Herbert Butterfield, *History and Human Relations* (London: Collier, 1951), p. 19.

32. Same as 22, Jervis, p. 68.

33. Ole Holsti and James N. Rosenau, *American Leadership in World Affairs: Vietnam and the Breakdown of Consensus* (London: George Allen & Unwin, 1984), pp. 188, 229, 231, 233, 271, 282.

34. Richard K. Herrmann, *Perceptions and Behavior in Soviet Foreign Policy* (Pittsburgh: University of Pittsburgh Press, 1985), especially Chapter 6.

35. See, for example: Harold Kelley, *Attribution in Social Interaction* (Morristown, NJ: General Learning Press, 1967); Edward Jones and Richard Nisbet, *The Actor and the Observer: Divergent Perceptions of the Causes of Behavior* (Morristown, NJ: General Learning Press, 1971); Richard Nisbet and L. Ross, *Human Inference: Strategies and Shortcomings of Social Judgment* (Englewood Cliffs, NJ: Prentice-Hall, 1980); Harold Kelley and J. L. Michela, "Attribution Theory and Research," *Annual Review of Psychology*, XXXI, 1980, pp. 457–501.

36. Same as 20, p. 141; same as 17, p. 253.

37. Same as 20, p. 142.

38. This was a period when concern with crime and inflation rose to the forefront, and when, in the wake of Vietnam, the nation underwent an unprecedented period of introspection and self-reappraisal.

39. Strobe Talbott, *The Russians and Reagan* (New York: Vintage Books, 1983).

40. Same as 39, p. 35.

41. Same as 22, Jervis, Chapter 8.

42. Same as 20, p. 35.

43. Same as 20, p. 36.

44. See, for example, V. Petrovsky, "Anatomy of Presidential Power," *International Affairs* (June 1976), pp. 128–130.

45. Irving L. Janis, *Victims of Groupthink* (Boston: Houghton Mifflin, 1973).

46. Arthur Schlesinger Jr., "The Cold War Revisited," *New York Review of Books* (October 25, 1979), p. 17.

47. Adam B. Ulam, *Dangerous Relations* (Oxford: Oxford University Press, 1983), p. 7.

48. Robert Holt, "Stereotyped Images of the Enemy: A Preliminary Study" (unpublished manuscript: New York University, 1987).

49. Adam Clymer, "Polling Americans," *New York Times Magazine* (November 10, 1985), p. 32.

50. David K. Shipler, "The View from America," *New York Times Magazine* (November 10, 1985), p. 76.

51. See, for example, Seweryn Bialer, *The Soviet Paradox: External Expansion, Internal Decline* (New York: Alfred A. Knopf, 1986), pp. 36–38.

52. David K. Shipler, *Broken Idols, Solemn Dreams* (New York: Times Books, 1983), p. 368.

53. Robert Nurse, *America Must Not Sleep* (unpublished doctoral dissertation: Michigan State University, 1971), p. 26.

54. Arthur Schlesinger Jr., *A Thousand Days* (Boston: Houghton Mifflin, 1965), p. 298.

55. The best available study of Kissinger's political thinking is provided in Harvey Starr, *Henry Kissinger: Perceptions of International Politics* (Lexington, KY: University Press of Kentucky, 1984).

56. Douglas Stuart and Harvey Starr, "The 'Inherent Bad Faith Model' Reconsidered: Dulles, Kennedy, and Kissinger," *Political Psychology* (Fall/Winter 1981–82), pp. 1–33.

57. Quoted in Jerel A. Rosati, "The Impact of Beliefs on Behavior: The Foreign Policy of the Carter Administration," in Donald A. Sylvan and Steve A. Chan, *Foreign Policy Decision Making: Perception, Cognition, and Artificial Intelligence* (New York: Praeger, 1984), p. 172.

58. Same as 48, p. 1.

59. Quoted in Kenneth Bourne, *Britain and the Balance of Power in North America* (Berkeley: University of California Press, 1967), p. 182.

60. See, however, John R. Raser, "Learning and Affect in International Politics" in James N. Rosenau, ed., *International Politics and Foreign Policy* (New York: The Free Press, 1969), pp. 432–441; Lloyd Etheredge, "Government Learning: An Overview" in S. Long, ed., *Handbook of Political Behavior*, II (New York: Plenum Press, 1981), pp. 73–161; Lloyd Etheredge, *Can Governments Learn?* (New York: Pergamon Press, 1985).

61. Quoted in Graham T. Allison, *The Essence of Decision* (Boston: Little, Brown, and Co.), p. 1.

62. See, for instance, "How Gorbachev Sees America: A Gloomy Land," *New York Times*, November 15, 1985, p. 1.

63. For example, *Real Peace* (Boston: Little, Brown and Company, 1983), p. 5.

# CHAPTER FOUR

◆  ◆  ◆  ◆  ◆

# America's Soviet Policy and the US Political System

According to George Kennan, one of the most per-
ceptive observers of US foreign policy:

> The motivations for American policy toward the Soviet Union
> from the start have been primarily subjective not objective in
> origin. They have presented for the most part not reactions to
> the nature of an external phenomenon (the Soviet regime) but
> rather the reflections of emotional and political impulses mak-
> ing themselves felt on the American scene[1].

Most of what we have seen so far leads us to share Kennan's
view. There is reason to suspect that each superpower's behavior toward the other is deeply rooted in its domestic politics, an assertion that springs not from some abstract theory
of the link between national politics and foreign policy (a
theory we lack) but from the record of actual policy shifts
during the past several decades. We know that relations took
a decisively hostile turn toward the end of World War II,
and the circumstances that initially led to animosity were
traced in Chapter 3. However, it is considerably more difficult to account for the subsequent course of superpower
relations. Psychological explanations are helpful but, as we
have seen, their light illuminates but part of the question.
And objective conflicts of interest have not provided a clear
justification for the development of the rivalry. However,
the role of domestic influences cannot be judged properly if
the impact of the Soviet Union's conduct is not also established. As a point of departure, then, it is useful to trace the
major postwar shifts in America's Soviet policy with a view
to determining to what extent they can be attributed to the
USSR's international behavior.

## COLD WARS AND SOVIET CONDUCT

Over the past four decades the trend has been towards progressively declining tension, but it has traced a sinuous
course—periods of increasing hostility have been followed
by occasional plateaus and movements toward improved
cooperation, efforts which, in turn, have regularly ceded to

new periods of rising belligerence. Broadly speaking, there have been three periods of surging hostility. The first, which may be thought of as the First Cold War, extended from the mid-forties to the early fifties. Another, which shall be termed the Second Cold War, spanned the late seventies and the early eighties. Between the two, a somewhat lesser crest of pugnacity appeared in the late fifties and very early sixties. Relations also witnessed two major thaws (the late sixties through the mid-seventies and the phase of decreasing tension underway since the mid-eighties) as well as plateaus during which hostility neither rose nor fell (the mid-to-late fifties and the mid-sixties). What all these shifts in US policy share is the fact that they cannot be explained fully by international events or by the Soviet Union's external behavior.

## The First Cold War

Several events, in addition to Russia's presence in Eastern Europe, confirmed US visions of a Soviet menace to the West. Moscow's apparent designs in Iran, Turkey, and Greece, and tension surrounding Berlin, all have been viewed as major causes for deteriorating US-Soviet relations. But Cold War history is more complex than traditional thinking suggests, and the extent of the threats could have been viewed in several equally plausible ways. In each case, however, the most ominous interpretation was selected and the corresponding hardening of America's attitude was expressed in two documents that have become landmarks of Cold War history.

The first document was President Truman's speech of March 12, 1947, in which he observed that "at the present moment in world history nearly every nation must choose between alternative ways of life." America's own survival required the defense of democracy at the international level and this, in turn, could not be achieved

> unless we were willing to help free peoples to maintain their institutions and their national integrity against aggressive movements that seek to impose upon them totalitarian regimes.[2]

The speech was followed by a request to Congress for $400 million in aid to Greece and Turkey, heralding America's decision to assume Britain's responsibilities in that region, as part of its global struggle against communism. Truman's actions indicated a readiness to confront Russia where necessary and, in the words of a White House advisor, represented "the opening gun in a campaign to bring people up to [the] realization that the war isn't over by any means."[3] And in 1948 when the Soviet Union imposed a blockade on Berlin, Truman's warnings seemed entirely prescient.

The second major reflection of America's escalating Cold-War attitudes was a 1950 position paper drafted for use within the National Security Council and entitled NSC-68. Its principal author was Paul Nitze, head of the State Department's Policy Planning Staff and, for several subsequent decades, a leading advocate of the demonological approach to the Soviet Union. The most significant features of NSC-68 were its apocalyptic description of the Soviet threat and its emphasis on military responses. As expressed by the report:[4]

> The Kremlin's policy toward areas not under its control is the elimination of resistance to its will and the extension of its influence and control. It is driven to follow this policy because it cannot . . . tolerate the existence of free societies; to the Kremlin, the most mild and inoffensive free society is an affront, a challenge, and a subversive influence.

The position paper described chances for a diplomatic settlement of differences as "poor, given the immutability of Soviet objectives and its advantage in military power." The paper further asserted:

> An indefinite period of tension and danger is foreseen for the United States and for the West—a period that should be deemed less as a short-term crisis than as a permanent and fundamental alteration in the shape of international relations.

According to the authors:

> This means virtual abandonment by the United States of trying to distinguish between national and global security. It also

means the end of subordinating security needs to the traditional budgeting restrictions, of asking "How much security can we afford?" . . . Security must henceforth become the dominant element in the national budget, and other elements must be accommodated to it.

The Soviet Union was thus described as an incurable evil, a threat comparable to that which Nazi Germany had presented several years earlier. As in dealing with Nazis, not much faith should be placed in diplomacy; rather, an all-out effort should be made to confront the Soviets with superior US military might. A diplomatic settlement would not be possible until the nature of the Soviet Union's political system changed. "NSC-68 proved to be the blueprint for waging the Cold War during the next twenty years."[5]

The question, of course, is whether the conclusions embodied in the Truman Doctrine and NSC-68 were a logical response to Soviet behavior. Historians may debate the matter at length, but it seems that although the Truman Administration's interpretation of the Soviet threat was not entirely fanciful, other, less ominous, readings of Soviet intentions were just as plausible.

Consider, for example, the Turkish crisis. At the Teheran Conference in 1943, Churchill had expressed the opinion that Russia should be granted warm-water ports after the war. This was interpreted by Stalin as a promise of a base in the Dardanelles, a promise which, in the Russian dictator's mind, was amply justified by Turkey's wartime collaboration with Germany. Nevertheless, confronted with the strength of US feelings on the matter and the decisiveness of its response, the Soviets did back down. Might this episode not have been viewed as a self-serving interpretation of a wartime pledge and an expression of limited geopolitical ambition on Stalin's part? Was it so obviously an example of single-minded and aggressive Soviet expansionism? Similarly with regard to Iran—a country that for many decades it had regarded as part of its security perimeter, as a center for foreign intrigues, and as a base for possible military operations against Russia. Moreover, inasmuch as the West had obtained postwar oil concessions, Moscow felt that, as Iran's third occupying force, it was entitled to as much. Nevertheless, the Kremlin did withdraw in the face of Western opposition.

The image created on both occasions was of a nation bent on global domination. But could it not have been argued just as credibly that these events reflected local Soviet ambitions (both Turkey and Iran border on the Soviet Union), and that their outcomes demonstrated that the Kremlin could be flexible? Although several explanations were possible, in both instances the interpretation that most strongly emphasized Soviet aggressiveness and expansionism was selected.

The situation in Greece was even less ambiguous. The communist side in the Greek civil war was not supported directly by the Soviet Union but by Yugoslavia. Moreover, there is every reason to believe that Belgrade was acting in pursuit of its own, rather than Moscow's, interest: Marshal Tito was, at that time, intent on forging a Balkan federation of communist nations. Instead of welcoming Tito's ambition, Stalin objected to what he viewed as a challenge to Soviet authority in the region.[6] Why then was this event viewed not as a struggle for power within the Balkans, but as further evidence of the Kremlin's global designs? While there is considerable room for honest disagreement, the former interpretation appears approximately as compelling as the latter.

And what of the 1948 Berlin Blockade? This event certainly represented a major Soviet challenge to Western interests, one to which the US airlift was a measured and appropriate response. Nevertheless, the common assessment that Moscow was trying to force the United States and its allies out of Berlin was, in all likelihood, inaccurate. Still fearful of German intentions, the Soviets were adamant about preventing the emergence of an economically and militarily reinvigorated, and unified, West Germany. As Adam Ulam, among others, has explained:

> It should have been abundantly clear from everything the Russians said and did that their real objective in the first as

well as in every subsequent Berlin crisis was a resolution of the German problem as a whole, more specifically in this case prevention of a rearmed West German state.[7]

In retrospect, it is not apparent that the hardening of America's attitude was a direct, proportionate, and necessary response to the Soviet Union's activities. At the very least, a variety of interpretations could have been placed on Moscow's intentions and capabilities; yet in each case the most threatening interpretation was selected. Is it not reasonable then to ask whether this inclination may not, to some extent at least, have had domestic roots? The same question applies to other phases of the Cold War.

## A New Crest in Hostility: The Late Fifties and Early Sixties

Although hostility never rose to the levels of the First Cold War, both the tone and the reality of the rivalry intensified during the late fifties and early sixties. The new wave of belligerence formed around two issues: competition for positions within the Third World and an accelerating strategic arms race. In both cases it was claimed that new Soviet initiatives, pregnant with aggressive intent, called for bold US responses and that, if relations had deteriorated in a spiral of action and reaction, the fault was entirely on the Russian side.

With the exception of areas contiguous to the Soviet Union, Stalin did not consider the developing world either powerful enough or of sufficient political importance to merit Moscow's attention. But this view changed with Stalin's death in 1953 and with the emergence of the Third World as an independent political force of nonaligned nations born at the Bandung Conference of 1955. Khrushchev—recognizing the political significance of non-Marxist liberation movements—embraced the nonaligned countries as part of an emerging "zone of peace." Increased Soviet military aid and economic assistance was directed toward the Middle East (initially Egypt) and Asia. By the end of 1956, fourteen economic and military assistance agreements had been signed—the major recipients being North Vietnam, Indonesia, Iran, Afghanistan, Turkey, and Egypt. The scope for clashing superpower interests thus expanded beyond its original European confines.

In 1960 the United States viewed with concern Russia's attempts to insert itself into sub-Saharan Africa, a concern that peaked during the civil war that wracked the Congo following its independence from Belgium. While United Nations forces strove to restore order and while Belgian troops attempted to consolidate their country's interests in secessionist Katanga, the Kremlin joined the fray on the side of Congo's official government led by Patrice Lumumba. Aircraft and trucks for transporting troops were shipped to the Congo, and apparently hundreds of Soviet agents, in the guise of diplomats, technicians, and instructors, swarmed the country. The United States threw its support behind the UN forces, declaring it would do whatever was needed to prevent the intrusion of Soviet military forces into this part of the world. The matter was finally settled when Lumumba was ousted from power and the Soviets expelled from the country.

By the time Kennedy assumed office, the Third World had become a central focus of American foreign policy attention. Faced with Castro's successful revolution and its increasingly apparent Marxist character, as well as with the deepening US involvement in Laos and South Vietnam (in each of which a right-wing government faced armed Communist opposition), the new Administration convinced itself that a global struggle was being waged in the developing regions. As President Kennedy declared in a special message to Congress on May 21, 1961: "The great battleground for the defense and expansion of freedom today is . . . Asia, Latin America, Africa, and the Middle East, the lands of the rising peoples."[8]

Military means of confronting the threat were emphasized: arms sales, security assistance, and preparations for guerrilla warfare. The response also focused on economic means, as US assistance programs increased and as the

Alliance for Progress—one of the most ambitious foreign-aid projects in the developing world—was launched. Thus, a competition previously centered on the European rimland now acquired a global scope. Every political development within the Third World was viewed through East–West lenses, and any sign of political change was scrutinized for signs of Communist subversion. The opportunity for clashes increased dramatically.

A second aspect of intensified Cold-War activity was linked to the superpowers' strategic programs. NSC-68's prophecy that Soviet military power could surpass America's by 1954 was not borne out. On the contrary, the US strategic edge was so overwhelming that John Foster Dulles could threaten massive nuclear retaliation in the event of Soviet intervention into any region deemed important to US security. But the next several years brought a shattering blow to Washington's complacency.

Although the development of certain light missiles began soon after World War II, serious work on intercontinental missilery (ICBMs) was not undertaken before the early days of the Eisenhower Administration and, by the summer of 1957, the United States had yet to launch its first ICBM. One reason for the missing sense of urgency was the Soviet Union's perceived technological inferiority. The notion of USSR backwardness was so widely accepted that the first Soviet flight test of a long-range missile in August 1957 came as an extremely jarring revelation—surpassed in impact only by the launching of Sputnik, the first artificial earth satellite, just two months later. The adversary's ICBM capability was unambiguously and unexpectedly demonstrated.

At approximately this time, a presidentially commissioned study of the US-Soviet strategic situation was produced. Entitled *Deterrence and Survival in the Nuclear Age,* it came to be known as the Gaither Report, after the review committee's chairman. The report claimed, in the same general vein as NSC-68, that the Soviets had just about overtaken the United States in strategic power and that soon they would have a sufficiently large arsenal of ballistic missiles to overwhelm US defenses. The Report urged increased military budgets, as well as the creation of the crisis mentality essential to generating national support for an intensified military effort.

At first these recommendations were not taken very seriously. Eisenhower knew more than did the report's authors about the true state of US-Soviet military balance, and he dismissed many of its conclusions. In addition, the President's fiscal restraint militated against major new defense programs. By 1959, however, a presidential election loomed on the horizon, and again the threat of a "missile gap" was pushed to the forefront of public debate. The issue, seized upon by many of the Democratic contenders for the presidency, played a prominent role in John F. Kennedy's campaign. Upon entering the White House, JFK set out to rectify the problem through a substantial buildup of US strategic forces. In 1962 the first Minuteman squadron became operational; by 1964 the United States had over 400 ICBMs (as opposed to 90 for the Soviet Union).[9] However, the military buildup was not limited to strategic missiles: in 1961 the Administration increased the defense budget by 15 percent, doubling the number of combat-ready divisions in the Army's strategic reserve, expanding the Marine Corps, adding 70 vessels to the active fleet, and augmenting the tactical air forces.

Obviously, the new investment in military force could not be justified without a strong hypothesis of foreign threat, and this was reflected in the vigor of the Administration's Cold-War rhetoric. Accordingly, at both the level of pronouncements and of military activity, the quality of US-Soviet relations deteriorated from the stability attained during the mid-fifties. The relevant question is whether this deterioration could have been explained by Soviet actions themselves. As before, the answer is not clearly affirmative.

It is unlikely that the Kremlin's sudden concern with the developing regions represented a credible threat to fundamental US interests. Soviet ability to lure Third-World governments with economic or military aid was limited to the bait it could toss, bait that was always dwarfed by what a much wealthier United States could offer. Nonetheless, subversion was feared more than bribery. From the Kennedy Administration's point of view, the real menace came from revolutionary ("national liberation") movements in developing nations that, it was feared, were actively sponsored by Moscow or, at the very least, might come to discover shared interests with the Soviet Union.

Although the early sixties certainly were marked by considerable instability in the developing world, the Kennedy Administration's view of the problem was not compelling. Almost invariably the roots of social turmoil are internal; the flames may be fanned, but rarely ignited, from outside. It would have been at least as logical to blame such turmoil on the economic inequity, squalor, and despair that characterized life in many developing societies as to blame it on Soviet subversion. And even though the Alliance for Progress demonstrated the President's awareness of the economic roots of revolutionary fervor, the dominant Administrative reflex was to invoke the Soviet threat and to stress military solutions.

In any case, it takes two to compete, and the Soviets appeared rather unconcerned about America's own moves in the developing regions. In 1958, for example, 14,000 US troops landed in Lebanon to quell a civil war that, it was feared, might be exploited by Iraq and Egypt (both of whom the Administration deemed too sympathetic to Russian interests). Although Lebanon was far closer to Soviet than American shores, the Kremlin's reaction was mild, and Egypt's President Nasser was rebuffed by Khrushchev when Nasser flew to Moscow to request a Soviet response.

While there certainly was increased Soviet activism in the Third World at this time, it appears simply to have been an opportunistic pursuit of limited advantages. In this respect Soviet activism presented a legitimate challenge to the United States; nevertheless, the apocalyptic implications drawn by many US political leaders were, it seems, overdrawn.

And what of the "missile gap" that had caused such concern and had prompted the increased defense effort as well as the rhetoric essential to justify it? The bulk of the evidence indicates that the threats highlighted by the Gaither Report and invoked by several Democrats (as well as some Republicans) during the 1960 election campaign were exaggerated. President Eisenhower appeared unconvinced that a Soviet lead in strategic delivery vehicles really existed: American U-2 spy planes had been overflying Soviet missile test ranges since 1956 and, by the late fifties, the absence of a crash ICBM program on the Russian side must also have been apparent to the White House. In any event, the Kennedy Administration soon discovered the true state of affairs. At his first off-the-record session with journalists on February 6, 1961, Secretary of Defense Robert McNamara informed reporters that he could find no signs of major Soviet missile construction or development,[10] indicating thereby that the controversy—though it may have suited various political purposes—had lacked a solid factual foundation.

Although none of these facts and events suggests that Soviet activities should not have been viewed with responsible concern, US responses during this brief surge of Cold-War activism were not unambiguously connected to an external threat. Accordingly, the Communist challenge to US interests in the developing world does not appear to fit the description given it at the time, and the acceleration of the arms race cannot be linked objectively to trends in Russia's military might. However, the picture is incomplete, and more must be provided by way of explanation.

### The Second Cold War

It is not easy to determine exactly when détente yielded to the bitterness, stridency, and surging militarism of the Second Cold War; it is, however, certain that the seeds of derailment were planted several years before either the invasion of Afghanistan or Ronald Reagan's election to the Presidency.

The first indication that détente might be in trouble occurred in 1973 at the time of the Six-Day War in the Middle East. Washington suspected that Soviet leadership had prior knowledge of Egypt's plan to launch, together with Syria, a surprise attack on Israeli positions in occupied territories—and there was a feeling that Russia should have alerted the United States. Although the damage to détente was not felt immediately, the foundations of cooperation were weakened, and soon additional problems arose.

In 1975, Cuban forces intervened in the Angolan civil war in support of the Marxist MPLA faction; the United States supported (but without benefit of direct military assistance) the MPLA's opponents. Two years later, thousands of Cuban troops and several hundred Soviet military advisers intervened in Ethiopia to assist in its struggle against neighboring (and equally Marxist) Somalia. Moreover, in 1978, Zairan opponents of President Mobutu marched from their camps in Angola against Zaire's wealthy Shaba province. There was evidence of Cuban support for the invaders, and it was inferred by some that the Kremlin was involved. To many Americans it seemed that the Soviets, assisted by Cuban proxies, were on the prowl in Africa and that the United States, lulled by the delusions of détente, was being outmaneuvered at every turn. Furthermore, and despite the signing of the SALT I agreements limiting offensive missiles and missile defenses, there was new concern over an emerging strategic gap to America's disadvantage.

Dissatisfied with the Central Intelligence Agency's estimates of the Soviet military effort—which portrayed the effort in a less-than-menacing light—the Foreign Intelligence Advisory Board pressured President Gerald Ford to appoint a non-CIA team (Team B) to provide an outside estimate of Soviet military strength (reminiscent of earlier blue-ribbon commission reports). Virtually all the Team B members were vocal hawks and critics of détente; not surprisingly, their report painted a picture of a successful Soviet thrust for "military superiority" and called for a vastly upgraded program to counter it.

In addition to the apparent imbalance of military force, proponents of greater US military growth pointed to a specific danger as well—the so-called *window of vulnerability*. The size and accuracy of Russia's warheads, it was claimed, made it possible for the Kremlin to launch a preemptive first strike against US land-based missiles. The United States would then be left only with its submarine-launched missiles, which—because they were less accurate—could be used against civilian, but not strategic, targets. Unwilling to undertake the carnage of innocent Soviet civilians, America would be at Russia's mercy. The Kremlin, having no such compunctions, could then use its remaining missiles to threaten American cities and economic centers. US decision makers could do little to counter the Soviet threat since, having lost our accurate land-based missiles, there would remain no means with which to destroy the balance of the Soviet warheads. The United States would then have no choice but to yield to various (usually unspecified) forms of Soviet blackmail.[11]

The growth of Soviet strategic capabilities was coupled, in the view of opponents of détente, with disturbing news regarding USSR defense spending. According to CIA figures there was indeed cause for concern. Using a technique known as dollar–cost comparison, the extent of Soviet military capacity was estimated, after which the cost of replicating the same capacity in the United States was computed. The latter, dollar-denominated figure, was taken as a measure of Soviet defense spending.

In his 1981 inaugural address, President Ronald Reagan invoked the CIA's dollar–cost estimate of Soviet military outlays to claim that Russia had outspent America on defense by $300 billion during the previous decade. In the eyes of US critics of détente, the Soviets were demonstrating not only that they would exploit Third-World conflicts for their expansive goals, but that they were aiming for military, and especially strategic, superiority.

Indications of a new Soviet threat thus seemed to be mounting. Although the Soviet invasion of Afghanistan in late December 1979 erased all American doubts, movement toward anti-Soviet sentiment was in evidence years earlier. By the late seventies, most American sympathy with détente had waned, and few aspirants to national political office could afford to deny the need for increased assertiveness on East–West matters. A major new military buildup—which was to last until the mid-eighties—was initiated toward the end of the Carter Administration. Moreover, the pugnacity of President Reagan's first term in office seemed the natural outcome of the US-Soviet climate that had been developing since 1973. But was the evidence of a Soviet threat as plain as all that? Was the hardening of the US stance a natural and direct reaction to Soviet activities?

No doubt the Kremlin was aware of Egypt's plans to attack Israeli positions in 1973, but did not explicitly alert the White House. This omission was interpreted by Washington as a Soviet attempt to gain a unilateral advantage at America's expense, and thus as a violation of the 1972 Basic Principles Agreement by which both sides promised not to seek Third-World gains at the other's expense. However, because Egypt was a Soviet ally at the time, it may have been unreasonable, even under conditions of détente, to expect that Moscow would jeopardize its standing in the Arab world by alerting Washington to Cairo's plans—especially since the United States certainly would have felt bound to warn Israel. One wonders, had the roles been reversed, whether Washington would have alerted Moscow? In any case, the Nixon Administration was itself intent on undermining the Soviet Union's position in the Middle East;[12] by Kissinger's own admission, this goal had been central to his efforts at diplomatic peacemaking in the area at that time. But this is not at all surprising. By most standards the United States was behaving pretty much as was logical for one superpower, in a state of continuing competition with the other superpower, to behave. Still, under the circumstances, protestations of Soviet misbehavior may have been disingenuous.

Other examples of unilateral Russian attempts at gaining a geostrategic advantage at US expense are amenable to a variety of plausible interpretations as well. Moscow may or may not have been behind the 1978 invasion of Zaire's Shaba province, but the Carter Administration supplied the transport aircraft that enabled Belgian and French paratroopers to recapture the copper mines of Kolwezi from the invaders.[13] Was this anything other than routine US-Soviet sparring for position in the developing world? And although there is little doubt that Russia was associated closely with Havana's involvement in the Horn of Africa or that Washington's concern over this matter was legitimate, the Kremlin probably played a minor role in the Cuban presence in Angola in 1975. Fidel Castro seems to have had his independent ideological agenda[14] and, as Kissinger told a *New York Times* reporter: "It was not, as commonly alleged, a proxy war fought by the Soviet Union with Cuban troops."[15]

Nor was talk of a military gap to Russia's advantage entirely convincing. Although the Soviets had been developing new strategic missiles in the seventies, the United States had been involved vigorously in *modernizing* its existing missiles. Actually, the implications of both programs for the balance of strategic capacity may have been similar.[16] Even the President's Commission on Strategic Forces (the Scowcroft Commission) concluded in 1983 that the "window of vulnerability" had, in fact, been a myth all along. While the report recognized that US land-based missiles had become more vulnerable, it also concluded that no assailant could be confident of the ability to destroy sufficient enemy ICBMs to avoid unacceptable levels of retaliatory damage. In any event, the Report concluded—as should have been obvious all along—that the US force of submarine-based strategic missiles (SLBMs) provided an assured retaliatory capability no matter what happened to the land-based missiles.[17]

Finally, in 1982 the CIA released new figures on Soviet military spending that suggested the level of military outlays previously imputed to the USSR had been overstated. It transpired that instead of spending some $300 billion more than the United States over the previous decade, Russia had actually spent nearly $300 billion *less*.[18] Moreover, in 1983 the CIA concluded that during the preceding seven years the rate of Soviet military spending growth had been a mere 2 percent a year—about half the figure previously brandished to demonstrate that the Russians were outspending the United States on defense[19].

What are we to conclude? Plainly, some Soviet activities did call for a US response—there was nothing ambiguous about the invasion of Afghanistan. However, other behavior (regarding the Middle East and Shaba, for example) amounted to no more than routine superpower jockeying for international position—the sort of activity the United States considered acceptable from the point of view of its own activities. Lastly, certain allegations held self-evident by opponents of détente—such as those concerning the window of vulnerability and Soviet defense spending—have been flatly contradicted.

It is increasingly evident that shifts in superpower relations cannot have been accounted for exclusively (perhaps not even principally) by international events or by Soviet conduct. Because neither instances of growing tension nor halting attempts at cooperation are fully understandable when viewed in such terms, we must cast a wider explanatory net. We know that the logic of perception and the dynamics of negative images create (at least in the short run) a ceiling beyond which relations cannot improve, and we understand that such forces cause ambiguous information to be interpreted in an especially ominous light. Were it not for the demonstrated capacity of statesmen to learn coupled with the fact that occasionally they manage to ignore their own images, we might simply say that, at each juncture in the history of US–Soviet relations, psychological forces have ensured that the path of improved cooperation would be eschewed.

But this is not convincing. We have examined the two periods of improved cooperation (détente and the period following the Second Cold War), that cannot be associated easily with the logic of misperceptions. And even when superpower relations suffered a setback, it has not been easy to identify a specific psychological cause. Soviet behavior often has been ambiguous—a combination of assertive and prudent activities—and at times the United States has seemed more prone to draw grim conclusions from such behavior than at other times. Why has this been so? We cannot progress much further unless we go beyond both international events and psychological images to focus our attention on domestic conditions—on certain abiding features of the interests, values, and power distributions that comprise the US political system. Because this focus has several layers of implication for East–West relations, we begin with the basics.

The search begins by locating the nexus between America's Soviet policy and the structure of American domestic politics. If the two interests are somehow connected, we then must identify their primary points of contact—for it is there that clues to the explanation may lie. A useful first step is to recognize that, in the final analysis, policy is the product of policymakers—of individuals—who are driven by a variety of interests and are buffeted by various pressures, but whose ultimate objective is personal political benefit. Accordingly, the following two basic questions must then be asked: What are the principal rewards toward which policymakers, including those most responsible for foreign policy, are driven? and, How are these rewards affected by US policy toward the Soviet Union? The aim is to determine whether the pursuit of political rewards tends to bias an individual's Soviet policy in a particular regard. And whether the political reward structure exerts pressures more powerfully at certain times than at others.

## THE POLITICAL REWARD STRUCTURE, ELECTORAL POLITICS, AND AMERICA'S SOVIET POLICY

Effective explanation, especially in its initial phases, requires that reality be simplified in order to more easily gain a handle on that which interests us most. Accordingly, we begin by relying on a working assumption frequently made by political scientists—that the central and overriding concern of political leaders is to acquire or retain office.[20] In other words, the principal reward offered by the American political system is incumbency—which, in a democracy, requires the elected to maintain the favor of the electorate, with an eye toward the upcoming election. Clearly there are several other influences on a politician's behavior, and soon they will complicate the story somewhat; but, for the moment at least, we shall limit our focus to the most evident truths. The salient question then is whether American Soviet policy is linked to the political aspirations of our nationally elected leaders.

Electoral politics have more frequently led to greater foreign policy combativeness than to improved superpower relations. It is not inevitable that intensifications of US-Soviet hostility should coincide with our national elections, yet a correlation between the two has nevertheless become apparent. As presidential elections involve the level of leadership with the greatest impact on US-Soviet relations, it is there that we should expect to find the clearest association— and indeed this was the case in 1952, 1960, and 1980, when relations plainly deteriorated. This was largely true of 1976 as well. And while some presidential elections have had no obvious bearing on the tone of the rivalry (e.g., 1964, 1968, 1984), it is hard to think of any that actually has led to a more *conciliatory* stance toward the Soviet Union. Thus, although there is nothing deterministic about the link, there is at least evidence of a structural bias.

It is not difficult to see why this should be so. In principle, an actual or aspiring political leader can be punished by the electorate for two major types of errors regarding the Soviet Union. The first is to mistakenly *understate* the extent of the threat and the magnitude of the necessary response—thus jeopardizing traditionally accepted security and diplomatic interests. The second is to incorrectly *overestimate* the extent of the peril—thus increasing the level of bilateral hostility and spurring the nation's military buildup beyond the actual requirements of security. So the political leader is faced with the potential for making two types of major errors, and the decision to chance one or the other will depend on the relative severity of the electoral punishment expected for each. And herein lies the structural bias. Punishment for understating is almost always more severe than for overestimating (whereas rewards for correct assessments are not vastly different), leading to a preference for confrontation over conciliation whenever (as is usually the case) there is any ambiguity concerning Soviet behavior or intent. As Joseph Nye has pointed out: "So central is the Soviet Union to American security that mishandling of the relationship is a handy stick with which to beat incumbents."[21] The same can apply to the policy platforms of contenders for office.

The bias flows from the nature of the values at stake and from the interests and political power involved. To begin with, a leader who fails to take adequate action in the face of an authentic, or imagined, Russian threat will be found guilty of imperiling national interests that rank near the very top of the hierarchy of US values—those that bear on the security of the nation and its normative order. Such a failure would not be considered an easily forgivable offense. Conversely, a leader who increases the tone of US-Soviet hostility will not have endangered values that are especially meaningful to many people (unless such action brings the nation close to the brink of war). Treating the Soviets cordially is not a highly prized national goal. And increasing the level of US-Soviet tension matters only at the margins, when there is a perceptible increase in the likelihood of nuclear war (not something easily measurable or readily apparent to many people). Also, as we shall see presently, there are many organized interests devoted to ensuring that the United States is never overly forthcoming toward the Russians, but very few interests with the resources to lobby effectively against excessively belligerent postures. Thus the asymmetry is apparent and the consequences predictable—since no rational politician will knowingly expose himself or herself to greater political risk than absolutely necessary.

Although the *political reward structure* may be a potent obstacle to improved East–West cooperation, the accuracy of the hypothesis is an empirical matter that requires an examination of the major national elections with an eye to their impact on the tone and content of the nation's Soviet policy.

Foreign policy, never the principal issue upon which national elections have been decided, has not been irrelevant either; in fact, on several occasions actual or aspiring political leaders have sought to gain an edge at election time by demonstrating that they, unlike their political opponents, were most willing to stand up to the Russians. This tactic has resulted in an increased level of Cold-War rhetoric and calls for greater military outlays. The tone of discourse, then, has set expectations for future policy and increased Moscow's perceptions of threat. The logical consequence has been heightened East–West tension and accelerated military competition. Accordingly, US-Soviet relations may be hostage to a biased structure of political rewards that favors confrontation over conciliation and that comes into full play at election time.

### The Election of 1952

1952 was a time when Cold-War passions had peaked; it also was a time when one might have considered resolving several East–West differences. From the US point of view, there was no doubt about America's strategic lead or its economic superiority. The course of the Korean war suggested victory for neither side, and the European situation had stalemated, with scant likelihood of meaningful Soviet encroachments on the West's European interests. Although both sides had acquired nuclear weapons, far better *delivery* systems—provided by aircraft carriers bearing nuclear-capable aircraft—and military bases in Europe ensured that the United States would not be dealing from a position of weakness. Nevertheless, the election campaign was conducted, particularly on the Republican side, on the basis of implacable Cold-War positions.

Indeed, denunciations of Truman's foreign policy were a principal focus of Eisenhower's campaign, although it is not immediately apparent why this should have been so. It is hard to believe that anyone could credibly have charged Truman, the US president most closely associated with the doctrine of containment, with "softness" toward Russia. In fact, there is little evidence that Eisenhower had any profound sense of dissatisfaction with the Truman Administration's approach to containment.[22] Still:

> Presidents are rarely made by endorsing their predecessors . . .
> and Eisenhower quickly came under pressure to put distance

between himself and the incumbent administration in the area of foreign affairs.[23]

Theoretically, this distance could have been achieved either by adopting a softer or a harsher line than Truman's with respect to the Soviet Union; nevertheless, the choice was, in light of our hypothesis, predictable. John Foster Dulles—a vocal advocate of a hard line on Soviet matters— was appointed the campaign's foreign policy spokesman, and he rapidly took the political offensive. In this, Dulles was supported by other conservative Republicans, such as Senator Robert Taft, who castigated the "pro-communist group in the State Department who surrendered to every demand of Russia at Yalta and Potsdam, and promoted at every opportunity the communist cause in China."[24]

Some of the most virulent rhetoric came from within the Eisenhower campaign itself. Guided by Dulles, Eisenhower made the improbable but electorally rewarding claim that he, unlike the Democrats, would not only *contain* the Soviet Union but actually would *roll back* Communism. As one plank in the 1952 Republican platform announced: "Containment is defensive, negative, futile, and immoral [in abandoning] countless people to a despotism and Godless terrorism." The Republicans, unlike their predecessors, would employ all means to secure the liberation of Eastern Europe. A worthy-sounding enterprise, but one inspired at least as much by domestic politics as by international missionary zeal. And as John Lewis Gaddis has pointed out, this Republican claim was "motivated in fact far more by determination to lure East European voting blocs away from the Democrats than from any realistic expectation of 'rolling back' Moscow's sphere of influence."[25]

Though its primary motivation may have been linked to electoral ambitions, we may assume that such talk stirred the Soviet Union's darkest fears. No region was of greater geopolitical concern to the Kremlin than Central Europe; talk of rollback must have confirmed Kremlin suspicion that Washington was bent on depriving the Soviet Union of a secure buffer on its western borders.

Eisenhower won the election and, campaign rhetoric

notwithstanding, rollback was never attempted. Rather, during much of the decade US-Soviet relations reached a plateau that reflected neither significant deterioration nor notable improvement. Nevertheless, the early fifties had presented opportunities for an initial thaw,[26] opportunities never acted upon. It is at least a matter of reasonable speculation that had electoral politics not intruded, meaningful steps at resolving several differences may have been undertaken.

### The Election of 1960

John F. Kennedy's campaign often is remembered for his frequent hammering away at the issue of a "missile gap" to America's disadvantage that Republicans had allowed to develop and that he, with more generous funding for the military and greater determination, would be sure to close. But charges of excessive complacency on the part of the Eisenhower Administration went beyond that.

Kennedy's rhetoric contrasted with the somewhat placid tone that had characterized US-Soviet relations during the latter part of the fifties. Kennedy insisted that "the enemy is the Communist system itself—implacable, insatiable, unceasing in its drive for world domination."[27] It should therefore be a matter of the highest national priority to check its advance and, eventually, to roll back the challenge. Having defined the issue, Kennedy attacked Vice President Nixon's foreign policy leadership as "weakness, retreat, and defeat," declaring that "never before" had the American nation "experienced such arrogant treatment at the hands of our enemy."[28] Nixon, preferring to emphasize his background in foreign affairs and, in particular, his experience at dealing with Khrushchev, nevertheless was quite prepared to sharpen the tone of his own Cold-War oration as well. Nixon worried aloud over Soviet-sponsored subversive wars in the Third World that, he explained, were "aimed at conquering them just as surely as they would be conquered if they were to roll over them with the Red Army."[29] And Nixon too promised to increase defense spending to ensure the United States would have a military force second-to-none—even if this meant increasing taxes.

Although Kennedy won by a slim margin, it is unlikely that foreign policy was of paramount concern to those who voted for him. Yet campaign rhetoric had created expectations of toughness, and the immediate consequence was increased US investment in both strategic and conventional forces, as well as increased American activism in the Third World. Moreover, the pace of this strategic buildup was unaffected by the discovery, soon after Kennedy assumed office, that the missile gap had been a myth and that any such gap as might have existed favored the United States.

Domestic politics aside, Kennedy assumed the presidency without the Manichaean mind-set of a John Foster Dulles, and firmly believed in the need for improved superpower cooperation. In particular, the Cuban missile crisis convinced both Kennedy and Khrushchev that serious steps were required to set relations between the two countries on a less dangerous footing—and the President's 1963 speech at American University represented a sincere call for productive negotiations.

It is apparent that, freed from the political dictates of an election, constructive initiatives were possible; however, the bias of the political reward structure could never be ignored completely. For example, the US intervention in Vietnam was justified principally by the need to counter the spread of Soviet influence via the "domino" effect. The first steps toward direct American involvement in Vietnam were taken by the Kennedy Administration and, as US involvement escalated, additional obstacles to meaningful gestures, by either superpower, were created. Yet again, domestic politics played an important role in perpetuating this involvement—even in its initial phases. Kennedy's White House Chief of Staff, Kenneth O'Donnell, reported that the President soon concluded that the costs and risks of further involvement in Vietnam were great, and that a complete US pullout was desirable. But, as Kennedy admitted to Senator Mike Mansfield, "I can't do it until 1965." Kennedy apparently felt "that if he announced a total withdrawal of American military personnel from Vietnam before the 1964 election, there would be a wild conservative outcry against returning him to the presidency for a second term."[30]

On the subject of Vietnam, it is worth noting that Lyndon Johnson's decisions to escalate US military involvement reflected a similar appreciation of domestic political realities. Although Johnson did not face immediate electoral concerns at the time, he too feared the political consequences of perceived softness in Vietnam.

> If I don't go now and they later show I should have gone, then they'll be all over me in Congress. They won't be talking about my civil rights bill, or education, or beautification. No sir, they'll shove Vietnam up my ass every time. Vietnam, Vietnam, Vietnam.[31]

Thus the sixties in general, and the Kennedy election in particular, suggest that confrontational pressures may originate within political systems—a suggestion confirmed by subsequent developments.

## The Elections of 1976 and 1980

We have surveyed certain of the circumstances attending the collapse of détente in the late seventies. And we have seen that although instances of Soviet misbehavior existed, the interpretations placed on them—even before the Soviet invasion of Afghanistan—were often more threatening than they need have been. Again, domestic politics almost certainly contributed to the hardening of America's attitudes toward the USSR during the Second Cold War.

By the mid-seventies, dissatisfaction with détente—always simmering just below the political surface—became increasingly vocal. This dissatisfaction included organized opposition within both political parties and involved the emergence of powerful lobbies, backed by an increasingly restive public opinion, that attacked US self-restraint and urged a new drive for military superiority. In 1976 the assault was led by Ronald Reagan in his bid to wrest the Republican presidential nomination from Gerald Ford. Reagan denounced relaxed relations with Moscow and the pending arms control talks, declaring that "there is little doubt in my mind that the Soviet Union will not stop taking advantage of détente until it sees that American people have elected a new president and appointed a new secretary of state."[32] As an act of political prudence, Ford decided to place some distance between himself and the conciliatory policies of previous years. Although Ford had signed the Vladivostok Accord with Leonid Brezhnev in 1974, as a temporary measure restricting strategic missile deployment pending a final SALT II agreement, the latter and more ambitious treaty fell victim to the electoral climate. According to his own admission, by January 1976, Ford reckoned that any chance of signing a SALT II treaty was eroding rapidly as, with an approaching election, "it would be impossible to discuss complex issues like SALT II in a rational way."[33] And in a further break with previous policy, Ford declared that détente would no longer be part of his vocabulary, echoing Henry Kissinger's comment that détente "is a word I would like to forget."[34]

Although Soviet activities must assume their share of responsibility, the shift in US policy cannot be understood fully if its domestic context is ignored. This fact became especially evident as the 1980 election approached. Carter's initially ambivalent Soviet policy—which combined a quest for arms control with criticism of Moscow's human rights practices—soon yielded to an accelerated military buildup, an inclination to replace talk with muscle, and a declining willingness to give the Kremlin the benefit of the doubt. Angola and the Horn of Africa plainly had much to do with this, but so did the rapidly approaching 1980 election.

Again the attack was spearheaded by Ronald Reagan who had, without much trouble, secured the Republican party's nomination. Reagan declared that Carter's policy, by "bordering" on agreement, actually had encouraged Soviet invasion of Afghanistan and could, indeed, be inviting another world war.[35] "They were right," Reagan declared. "The Soviet Union has bet that Mr. Carter is too weak to respond to the invasion of Afghanistan. And they were right."[36]

Moreover, the Republican party platform charged that the Soviet threat was greater than ever before and, in a departure from Nixon's and Kissinger's stress on "essential equivalence," called for the pursuit of US military *superiority* over the Russians. While it can safely be assumed that such superiority has always been the aim of military planners,[37] making superiority a matter of official policy symbolized, with particular clarity, a complete lack of faith in détente or arms control.

In any case, Reagan won the election. While it is hard to disentangle the effects of the economy (especially the high inflation rates) on the average voter's choice or the impact of the spectacle of American hostages in Iran, the impression again was left that insufficient toughness vis-à-vis the Soviets carried very real electoral costs.

It appears obvious that a politician who errs on the side of underestimating the Soviet threat will incur far greater punishment than one judged guilty of overestimating it. Faced even with slightly ambiguous Soviet behavior, a rational American leader will tilt toward a confrontational rather than a conciliatory response—a tendency especially pronounced at election time, when the principal rewards and punishments are meted out.

Even so, there have been notable exceptions. Although the elections of 1952, 1960, 1976, and 1980 were associated with an increasingly strident foreign policy, not so the elections of 1946, 1964, 1968, 1972 or 1984 (1956 is a somewhat ambiguous case). Thus the reward structure is not *inevitably* tipped toward confrontation. At times, it seems, the bias is strong and at other times less strong; the challenge is to identify the circumstances that cause this to be so.

## THE SHIFTING IMPACT

Several explanations for the uneven movement of political pressure come to mind. According to one interpretation, forcefully advanced by Alan Wolfe, the most striking feature of surges in anti-Soviet hostility is that the surges tend to occur when Democrats hold the presidency.[38] The idea is that because Democrats, unlike Republicans, have an abiding fear of appearing insufficiently anti–Communist, they feel politically vulnerable to charges of excessive softness on East–West matters. Moreover, since the United States has never spawned a significant working-class movement—one that could provide the Democratic party with needed support when under attack from the hard-line right wing—Democrats rarely hazard a truly conciliatory policy. Republicans, to the contrary, are not subject to such pressures, and thus are better equipped to deal with the Soviet Union on a realistic basis, unfettered by fears of a right-wing backlash.

This view has some merit, but is not unassailable. Most obviously, the hypothesis runs into trouble with the Second Cold War, which coincided with the first term of Ronald Reagan (a man who had little to fear from the right). Of course, it can be argued that Reagan picked up where his predecessor had left off, and that the collapse of détente originated with the Carter Administration. Yet even this view leaves unexplained the fact that President Carter stepped into office fully prepared to get along with Moscow and eager to rid the country of its "inordinate fear of communism." One could reply that this scenario simply proves the point: the right wing (military pressure groups, conservative citizens lobbies, and so forth) eventually will drive Democratic presidents toward a hard-line position. However, this view runs counter to the record of the Kennedy Administration, which came into office concerned about missile gaps and promising war against left-wing subversion, yet moved toward the sort of conciliatory statesmanship displayed by the President in his 1963 American University speech and in his arms control initiatives. Wolfe's hypothesis has some validity, but does not sufficiently reflect the historical record.

Inasmuch as the political reward structure increases the *probability* of confrontational behavior—but does not do so under all circumstances nor with uniform force—we must examine certain additional explanations for its shifting effect.

### The Pull of the Middle of the Road

An interpretation perhaps nearer the mark would emphasize the American public's impatience with sustained departures from what it views as the proper balance between peace and strength. Although the point of equilibrium in public preference generally is closer to the hard-line than to the conciliatory pole, the average American is apprehensive about extended departures from the notion of responsible moderation. Accordingly, when weariness with either the Cold War or with détente sets in, and as the political reward structure modifies its idea of where excesses lie, the American public is more likely to lend a sympathetic ear to arguments in favor of opposite policies.

Thus the circumstances of the time partially explain why the 1968 and 1972 Republican and Democratic presidential nominees did not bring major Cold-War themes to their campaigns. For the most part, the nation was weary of East–West strife, a condition amplified by the Vietnam involvement (justified almost exclusively in terms of Cold-War imperatives). Similarly, the elections of 1956 and 1984 occurred soon after the two Cold Wars peaked, and against a background of national fatigue with tension and military buildups. Consequently, these elections did not cause a resurgence of anti-Soviet feelings and policy. However, the same logic operated in reverse concerning the elections of 1960, 1976, and 1980. The election of 1960 followed on the heels of a plateau in superpower relations, whereas the elections of 1976 and 1980 followed in the wake of a failing bout of détente. Correspondingly the elections of 1968 and 1972 were associated with expanding détente, the elections of 1976 and 1980 linked to the Second Cold War, whereas the election of 1960 produced a slight upsurge of confrontation.

Just as the public generally is wary of departures from middle-of-the-road policy, it is suspicious of aspiring political leaders whose rhetoric deviates too far from the mainstream of national thinking. A frequent development, as we have seen, is that a political aspirant attempts to exploit to political advantage an opponent's "softness" on East–West issues, whereas the opponent, in order to overcome this vulnerability, becomes more unyieldingly anti-Soviet than would otherwise have been the case. Although the usual consequence is a deterioration in US-Soviet relations, the mechanism does not always play itself out. While motivated by electoral opportunism, such exploitive charges and countercharges, claims and counterclaims, must lie within accepted parameters of political sentiment if they are to serve their purpose. This mainstream generally flows in an anti-Soviet direction, but is limited on both its hawkish and dovish sides. Attitudes that spill over these limits fail to sway a significant segment of political society, and generally may be ignored by those whose positions continue within the limits of broad public acceptability.

If a candidate drifts too far toward the confrontational pole, his or her claims are easily dismissed as too extreme to be politically threatening; by contrast, the opponent's claims will appear reasonable and responsible. By the same token, a candidate positioned too far toward the conciliatory pole will be considered unacceptably "soft," whereas the opponent will be seen as having a statesmanlike respect for US strength and thus will not be required to raise the level of Cold-War rhetoric. And although the definition of mainstream changes with time (more liberal in the sixties and seventies, more conservative in the fifties and eighties), it nevertheless defines the limits of acceptable discourse, and increases in Cold-War fervor usually are linked to political pressures originating *within* its boundaries. On two major occasions, American political candidates strayed beyond these limits; accordingly, America's Soviet policy was basically unaffected by the elections.

Barry Goldwater's 1964 challenge to President Johnson ended in an electoral fiasco rooted in his ultra-conservative positions in virtually every politically sensitive area. Although New-Deal issues, as well as the matter of general competence, appear to have sealed Goldwater's fate, the fear that peace would suffer the consequences of a Goldwater presidency mattered as well.[39] Moreover, there was never any serious reason to think that Johnson might lose. In December 1963, 75 percent of those surveyed expressed a preference for Johnson, whereas only 20 percent backed Goldwater[40]—and these figures experienced no major shift until election day. Goldwater's distance from the center was so great, at least on US-Soviet issues, that Johnson never felt compelled to preempt Goldwater support. George McGovern's problem was a mirror-image of Barry Goldwater's: his positions on both domestic and foreign affairs placed him too far left of center to draw away major sources of Richard Nixon's support. In any case, Nixon's generally conciliatory Soviet policy left McGovern little maneuvering room within the boundaries of acceptable policy positions.

Thus, a prolonged period of Cold War tension will generate pressures for greater conciliation, and vice versa—a phenomenon elsewhere termed the *politics of opposites*.[41] Similarly, elections will not generate significant pressures for increased hostility if either presidential candidate strays too far outside the political mainstream (or if, as in 1948, the candidates have quite similar foreign policy positions, both within the mainstream). Both effects are the natural consequence of the simultaneous existence of a political reward structure biased toward confrontation and of public impatience with political behavior considered extreme.

By focusing on elections we have probed the inner core of the US political reward structure, but there are layers and facets as well. Electoral interests are not all that drive national leaders, nor is theirs the only will that shapes the conduct of external affairs. Consequently, we must expand our view of the concerns to which politicians respond and our cast of participants in the foreign policy-making process. It is useful to view such participants as comprising a system with two layers: one composed of elected national leaders (and of officials, such as cabinet members, whose fortunes are linked directly to those of elected officials), the other consisting of participants (e.g., bureaucrats, lobbyists) who care a great deal about actual policies but only incidentally about their electoral context. Each layer has its dominant pattern of interests and beliefs, and each plays a role in determining the course of America's Soviet policy.

Although elected leaders, always concerned with the ballot, also act on an agenda that reflects their personal beliefs, they do not all have identical views of Russia: some regard it as more wicked, powerful, and predatory than others; some are more pessimistic about the outlook for cooperation than others. Consequently, US attitudes toward the Soviet Union partially depend on *who* is in power—a matter often decided on grounds that have little to do with foreign policy. For example, Reagan's 1980 election was determined primarily by domestic issues—such as the economy[42]—his foreign policy beliefs, however, shaped the course of East–West relations for the eighties.

The policy preferences of elected leaders are also affected by Russia's international behavior and by the state of its military capacity. Yet the case should not be overstated, for the impact of Soviet international behavior depends as much on a shifting US willingness to perceive it as menacing as on the reality of the threat. This willingness is conditioned partly by pressure originating from the *second* layer of the policy-making process, whose various members are numerous and often committed to a more complex set of policy objectives than are nationally elected officials. Recognizing the impact of electoral calculus and political beliefs on the major bearers of foreign-policy power, the remaining interest to which they must be responsive also should be examined.

### The Push from the Second Layer

It is useful to distinguish three sources of foreign-policy motivation at the second layer: bureaucratic interests, economic interests, and normative values and beliefs—what might be termed "pure" policy objectives. Each source provides grist for the foreign-policy mill, and each has a bearing on the course of US–Soviet relations.

BUREAUCRATIC DRIVES   It is recognized generally that national policy is not simply the product of calculated decisions by national leaders, but that it is also the result of governmental institutions acting on their routines and perceptions, and pursuing their organizational interests with parochial zeal. Over time, these institutions acquire a specific character and established needs. Whatever priorities and perceptions an organization's official might bring to the job, the nature of the position itself will largely determine his or her conduct in that role.[43] And as a bureaucracy's functions are limited to the missions with which it is charged, the national interest will come to be viewed in terms of such missions. (Officials of the Pentagon and of the Department of Commerce are not likely to view the sale of advanced technology to the Soviet Union in identical terms). Thus, American foreign policy cannot be understood fully unless bureaucratic *views* of external needs and challenges are adequately considered.

Foreign policy also is shaped by the institutional *objectives* of bureaucracies. Each organization seeks to expand its turf—the funds it is allocated and the range of issues within its jurisdiction—both absolutely and relative to competing bureaucracies. The State Department and the Pentagon, for example, both feel they should be allocated a larger slice of the foreign-policy pie. Definitions of external problems and proposed solutions are structured to buttress each organization's claim to a larger share of authority and budgetary resources. As Bertram Gross pointed out several decades ago: "The average unit of the bureaucracy is far more deeply committed to its own particular program than to the program of the Administration as a whole."[44]

There is nothing unusual about this—all bureaucracies pursue their corporate weal, convinced that this is where the true national interest lies. But the fact remains that foreign policy cannot be understood fully if bureaucratic politics are ignored. Most importantly, power is as much a component of the political reward structure as are interests and beliefs—and it is significant that some of the most powerful federal bureaucracies owe their existence to the assumption of an active Soviet threat.

The three largest and most influential foreign-policy bureaucracies are the Defense Department, the Central Intelligence Agency, and the State Department. Because the first
two entities define their primary function as countering a
USSR threat, it would be surprising if they did not define
the national interest accordingly or if their organizational goals
could prosper in a world stripped of East–West hostility.
However, the State Department's interests cannot be defined as crisply. At the extremes of confrontation, where
diplomacy is replaced entirely by a contest in coercion, its
role would certainly shrink. Short of that, the State Department would do well under conditions of either Cold War
or détente. In a Cold War, the State Department would
muster international support for US positions; in a period
of détente, it would attempt to promote cordial superpower
relations. Finally, such institutions as the Department of
Commerce or the Department of Agriculture usually place
greater emphasis on the benefits of closer economic ties with
the Russians; indeed, they occasionally seek the support of
the Department of State in overcoming Pentagon objections
to improved commercial ties between the two countries.[45]

If foreign policy partly results from the interests and
power of various government bureaucracies, one would
suspect an inclination against a conciliatory policy since, by
most standards, organizations whose interests are linked to
confrontation are significantly more powerful than those that
benefit from cooperation. As with initial threat perceptions,
this situation is a consequence of both World War II and of
the early phases of the Cold War. Nevertheless, the dispar-
ity in bureaucratic clout has a significant bearing on Soviet-
American relations.

The Defense Department (by just about every measure
the most powerful federal bureaucracy) is especially effective in influencing the course of America's Soviet policy. Its
power does not come only from its size, funding, or the
nature of the values under its protection, but also from its
deftness at playing the political game. As Samuel Huntington has pointed out, the Founding Fathers were not as interested in limiting the power of the military (which had not

emerged as a major professional organization at the time) as with creating checks to prevent any single governmental institution from controlling the professional soldier.[46] Although consistent with the Madisonian tenet of equilibrated power, this intention ultimately benefited the influence of the military since "a government of splintered functions allowing for myriad points of access to the decision process was created."[47] Indeed, a sophisticated ability to create alliances within the executive branch and a considerable skill at pursuing its interests through the legislature are probably more characteristic of the Defense Department than of most other federal bureaucracies.[48]

ECONOMIC INTERESTS    It is argued in Chapter 2 that economic conflicts of interest are not a major cause of the rift between the United States and the Soviet Union, but this does not exhaust the role of economic considerations. Radical critics often preach that US foreign policy is shaped by domestic economic interests, mainly those associated with big business. Conservative observers tend either to dismiss or to minimize the extent to which policy is determined economically. Either way there is considerable room for exaggeration; the challenge is to keep matters in sensible perspective.

With regard to dealing with the Soviet Union, the economic interests at issue generally are connected to defense production. The military sector represents a substantial presence in the national economy, and those benefits are garnered by large and influential corporate entities. These entities—together with the segments of the military establishment that consume their goods, the labor unions whose members owe their employment to the military effort, and the political representatives of regions within which the production takes place—represent a powerful alliance of interests devoted to promoting a buoyant demand for military products. Because this demand, in turn, requires a plausible foreign challenge to crucial interests, it is natural for the alliance to promote the notion of an impending and nefarious Soviet threat. Although this conception of the military-industrial complex—a phenomenon first described by C. Wright Mills[49] and cautioned against by Dwight D. Eisenhower—can be overdrawn, it is futile to pretend that defense spending is not an essential component of American economic activity.

In 1985 the military sector accounted for approximately seven percent of gross national product and nearly one-third of total federal spending,[50] and many jobs, directly or indirectly, are linked to defense activity. Some four and one-half million people are employed by defense-related federal agencies, and the private sector employs huge numbers of workers in military production. For example, in 1985 more than 700,000 workers were employed by the aircraft industry—a major portion of which involves military aircraft—and more than 100,000 were employed by producers of guided missiles and space vehicles. Several hundred thousand were engaged in producing military communications equipment, and so forth. In addition, there is substantial evidence that profits in military-related production tend to be substantially higher than profits in industries producing goods with a civilian application.[51] All this notwithstanding, because excessive defense spending can create considerable economic problems, short-term gains must be balanced against inevitable economic costs. For example, economists report that the defense dollar creates fewer jobs than do many other forms of economic activity and that it is more inflationary than most other forms of public or private spending.[52] At the same time, military contractors are major contributors to the election campaigns of Congressional candidates, especially to the campaigns of members of committees with jurisdiction over defense-related matters.[53] Obviously, one must not slip into exaggerated statements about the economic significance or political consequences of defense spending; however, neither can its implications be ignored, nor the fact that the defense establishment cannot prosper in a state of placid US-Soviet relations.

"PURE" POLICY OBJECTIVES    Organizational parochialism and economic interests are not the only, nor necessarily the primary, motivating force within the second layer. Like elected officials, second-layer participants in the policy process often are driven by priorities rooted more in their beliefs than in their self-interest. For example, many have a deep distrust of the USSR. Private groups and citizen lobbies pressing for tougher and more defiant policies toward the Soviet Union have established a permanent presence on the postwar US political scene. However, because even the most committed groups do not display a constant level of anti-Soviet activism, we must ask what accounts for their occasional surges of energy? Why, for instance, were such groups more active in the early fifties and late seventies than at other times?

Similar questions also must be asked regarding the vigor of bureaucratic and economic drives. For it is quite probable that such interests establish levels beyond which US-Soviet relations cannot improve in anything but the long run. But, in the meantime, the state of relations does shift from cool to frigid, from phases of rapid deterioration to periods of uneventful stability, to occasional thaws. Vested interests and deeply held beliefs can explain secular trends in relations, but nothing yet discussed sheds much light on shorter-term movements in America's Soviet policy. What we lack is a plausible link between interests and policy shifts, and it is to this that our attention must be directed.

### Ends, Means, and Policy

That various groups have characteristic needs and beliefs does not suffice to explain their activities. Occasionally it is not shifting needs or goals but changing *means* that determine policy commitments. In other words, what we want to do and how we want to do it often depends on the means at our disposal—and, at times, the acquisition of the means for pursuing policy is viewed as a significant political reward in and of itself. That is, the interests that are part of the political reward structure may clamor for gratification with particular vigor when new means of pursuing preferred foreign policy appear available. Here two points are especially significant with regard to America's Soviet policy.

To begin with, the major foreign policy instruments available to the United States for dealing with Moscow are diplomacy and military coercion. Diplomatic resources are relatively stable, but military resources fluctuate significantly the result of budgetary constraints and technological possibilities. Thus, to the extent that shifts in capacity mold policy toward the Soviet Union, it is most likely to involve national *military* capacity. Secondly, military capacity and actual policy are closely linked: just as capacity frequently determines the substance of policy, so do real or apparent policy needs establish the justification for capacity. The problem is that the acquisition of capacity often is a protracted and expensive business, one that calls for a willingness to accept the inevitable fiscal costs and psychological mind-set. The greater the burden involved, the more pressing the need must seem if the acquisition of the desired instrument of policy is to be justified.

Inasmuch as military capacity is considered vital to dealing with Russia, and since its procurement requires a powerfully justified need, we can assume that pressures for national mobilization around a presumed Soviet threat surge when the possibility for acquiring major new military systems arises. In other words, those mainly concerned with the strategic and diplomatic implications of such systems (i.e., with pure policy goals) may see a chance to advance America's position relative to Russia's—if only the nation can be brought to accept the need for the new acquisitions. Similarly, national security bureaucracies and those whose economic fortunes are linked to defense production may see a chance to advance their own parochial interests—if only the nation can be brought to see things their way.

When the possibility of acquiring a substantial but costly military system presents itself, we can expect that groups whose interests or beliefs are gratified by confrontational policy will press most vigorously for an expanded conception of security needs. In turn, this may require an upgraded estimate of the Soviet threat. The initial pressures may originate inside or outside government, but thereafter certain common features emerge. New light is focused on the more pessimistic intelligence estimates of Russia's military capacity, the image of an enemy plotting America's destruction is revived, and new military vulnerabilities remediable only by acquiring the new military system are discovered. Coalitions between the concerned interests are created, a blue-ribbon commission is created to report on the vulnerabilities, and a hardening of America's Soviet policy ensues.

The record indicates that the activation of Cold-War drives tends to coincide with the emergence of major new categories of weapons. Although the association is not perfect and although there is an inevitable chicken-and-egg problem, the three major upswings in anti-Soviet hostility have overlapped with three surges in the possibilities for new strategic developments and procurement. The First Cold War was associated closely with the development and initial deployments of a strategic bomber force. The upsurge in hostility in the late fifties and early sixties coincided with the transition to ballistic missiles. And the Second Cold War emerged in tandem with the expansion of multiple-warhead missile forces and quantum improvements in missile accuracy.

During the late forties, two major strategic bombers were under development. The first was the B-36, a piston-engine bomber capable of flying a 10,000-mile round trip, that carried a single atomic weapon and became operational in 1951. The second was the B-47, the first American jet-powered bomber. Although it lacked the range to reach the Soviet Union from bases in the United States, the B-47 was the most advanced bomber available at the time and an important element of America's nuclear delivery capability. The B-47 also joined Strategic Air Command squadrons in 1951, its final numbers totaling more than 2,000.[54]

At approximately the same time, initial steps were taken toward acquiring an aircraft carrier capable of accommodating nuclear weapons. In the late forties the Navy experimented with various aircraft for this purpose, and by 1951, nuclear-equipped *Savage* tactical bombers were being deployed on *Midway*-class carriers in the Mediterranean. Subsequently, additional aircraft carriers, including the smaller *Essex*-class ships, were fitted to accommodate nuclear weapons.

These were ambitious and expensive projects backed by substantial bureaucratic, economic, and political interests, which probably would not have found their way into US nuclear arsenals without a powerful assumption of foreign threat. Similar conclusions apply to the long-range *missilery* that characterized the second wave of strategic deployments.

As the late forties and early fifties were the years of the bomber, so the late fifties and early sixties were dominated by the ballistic missile. Battlefield nuclear weapons, including short-range rockets, were introduced into Europe in the mid-fifties, and intermediate-range Jupiter and Thor missiles were deployed toward the end of the decade. But the centerpiece of US strategic planning was the intercontinental ballistic missile (ICBM). Two ICBM systems reached advanced development at this time. The first was the 5,500-mile range Atlas, first deployed in 1959; the second was the 6,300-mile range Titan I, delivered in 1960. No sooner had the Atlas and Titan I missiles been deployed than they were followed by two second-generation missiles: the Minuteman, introduced in 1961, and the Titan II, deployed in 1962. In the early sixties, initial planning provided for 1,200 Minutemen and 120 Titan IIs—the largest strategic project to date.[55] Nor were submarine-launched missiles (SLBMs) ignored. The first Polaris SLBM was flight-tested in 1958, and the Navy built 41 Polaris missile submarines between 1959 and 1967. Thus the final leg was added to the strategic triad consisting of bombers, ICBMs, and SLBMs.

The development of new strategic systems has interacted significantly with transformations in US nuclear doctrine to influence the course of superpower relations. In the 1960s, the primary function of strategic missiles was retaliatory. To be used for offensive purposes—in the form of a preemptive first strike or for waging a protracted nuclear war—the missiles would have to have been considerably more accurate than they were. In the sixties, the most appropriate targets for strategic weapons were population centers or large industrial targets whose destruction did not require that they be hit with great precision. As neither side's nuclear arsenal was vulnerable to a preemptive first strike, each could use its weapons to retaliate against major civilian targets—thus endowing nuclear missiles with a purely deterrent function. But technology does not stand still. And by the seventies, a third wave of strategic weapons was ushered in, one which carried the threat of *offensive* applications.

A major development in this regard was the MIRV, a missile equipped with multiple warheads. Since several warheads could now be directed at each target, the likelihood that even small and hardened military targets could be preemptively destroyed increased. Just as importantly, missile accuracy was making major gains during the late seventies. Advances in inertial-guidance technology allowed ICBMs to be fitted with increasingly precise warheads, a major example of which was the Mark-12 warhead retrofitted onto Minuteman III missiles. The D-5 SLBM warhead brought the promise of increased accuracy to submarine launched missiles as well. Toward the end of the decade a large, multiple-warhead, highly accurate missile named the MX entered the development stage. Cruise missiles also were being introduced into strategic arsenals and, by using a guidance technique known as terrain-contour-matching (TERCOM), were extremely accurate as well.

The aggregate effect of MIRVs, together with the new generation of highly accurate warheads, was to make feasible a substantial overhaul of the US strategic arsenal, implying the possibility of strategic missions involving *military* targets. But this meant that actual nuclear combat must be recognized as a credible contingency, which in turn required an extremely dire view of the Soviet Union and of the superpower rivalry. It may or may not be a coincidence that the new wave of strategic technology, like the first two, was associated with deteriorating East–West relations.

A pattern is discernible. Major waves of strategic weapons development have coincided with periods of hardening US attitudes toward the Soviet Union and, while correlation need not imply causation, the possibility of a causal nexus cannot be dismissed. This is not to say that strategic growth stood still *between* periods of deteriorating relations. For example, the plateau of the mid-fifties coincided with the introduction of the B-52 long-range bomber, and the plateau of the mid-sixties was associated with a significant expansion of the US ballistic missile arsenal. Even the period of détente witnessed the first deployments of MIRVs. For the most part, however, these developments either involved the introduction of a single major weapon or a quantitative expansion of an existing system. On the other hand, the three major waves surveyed coincided with the introduction of entire *classes* of strategic weapons, implying significant strategic discontinuities and involving major costs. Neither probably could have been justified under halcyon international conditions. The evidence admittedly is circumstantial, but even circumstantial evidence can be telling.

### National Mobilization and the Logic of Overreaction

Anti-Soviet hostility proceeds both from domestic influences and Moscow's own conduct, and, whatever its sources, the marginal value of heightened assertiveness is stronger at certain times than at others. Yet governments that push for a harder line may perceive a gap between their own level of determination and that of other relevant segments of American society. Because of the relative decentralization and fragmentation of power within the US political system, the process of developing or altering a consensus can be sluggish. Democracy, especially in a large and diversified society, does not lend itself to nimble responses to real or perceived changes in international conditions. Although this is at once a source of strength and a source of weakness, it nevertheless means that it often is difficult to galvanize society for quick and dramatic action.

In addition to bureaucratic inertia, the public usually will have adjusted to the previous measure of Cold-War commitment and not to the new level policymakers have in mind.

Certain groups may be pushing for more assertive policies or increased US military power—and this may be justified by international events—but a gap often exists between what the public has been led to consider appropriate and that which leading political figures deem necessary. Driven by impatience to have their new programs implemented, supporters of a tougher line may feel that the extent of the Soviet threat must be dramatized powerfully and, if need be, overstated considerably.[56] The result is a vastly upgraded estimate of the Soviet threat, dire warnings of an actual or impending military gap (measured in terms of missiles, spending, or strategic vulnerability), and a call for national mobilization to confront the peril.

But rhetorical and other symbolism creates its own substance. If overblown statements and an overheated tone are deemed necessary to jar the nation into a higher state of Cold-War anxiety, it is difficult to escape the consequences of the climate thus created. In particular, a successfully aroused public and Congress may not only overtake the leadership in the extent of its confrontational zeal, but may also impose strictures on successors who prefer a more conciliatory East–West policy. Because certain expectations have been created, the government's freedom of action is limited.[57]

At this point the logical converse of the initial policy might be to *understate* the extent of the foreign threat—but the structure of political rewards and punishments makes this a risky enterprise. Thus a bias. In other words, inflated assessments of threat rarely are matched by deflated estimates; yet, given the frequent difficulty of changing a policy consensus (another structural feature of the political system), overstatements of Soviet hostility and military capacity occur somewhat regularly. This catch-22 is akin to a vehicle that must accelerate swiftly to master each incline, yet cannot decelerate swiftly once it reaches level ground.

MOBILIZATIONAL OVERREACTION AND THE FIRST COLD WAR  The pattern of express mobilizational overreaction was, in all likelihood, associated with the Truman Doctrine and its aftermath. We saw just after World War II that Turkey was subjected to Soviet pressure and that Greece was torn by a vicious civil war opposing communists and monarchists. In addition, US domestic pressures for increased assertiveness toward Russia were increasingly apparent. In February 1947, Britain declared it was no longer in a position to bear the economic costs of aiding Greece and Turkey, and asked the United States to assume the task. The problem, from Washington's point of view, was the absence of a firm domestic consensus favoring extension of America's postwar commitments. Congress was leery of ventures that placed additional demands on the budget. Republicans were intent on reducing taxes by 20 percent and cutting $6 billion from Truman's budget. If the United States was to expand its role in the East–West contest, residues of domestic resistance had to be overcome, the first task being to mobilize congressional support for increased activism and new security commitments.

On February 27, 1947, a meeting was held with congressional leaders that, from the Administration's standpoint, began poorly. Secretary of State George Marshall presented a restrained argument for assistance to the two Balkan countries based on abstract humanitarian grounds, and the audience appeared unimpressed. At that point Undersecretary of State Dean Acheson spoke up, recasting the argument in what were to become conventional Cold-War terms. As Acheson described it: "No time was left for measured appraisal." Instead, he launched into apocalyptic warnings:

> Soviet pressure on the Straits, on Iran, and on Northern Greece has brought the Balkans to the point where a highly possible Soviet breakthrough might open three continents to Soviet penetration. . . . It would also carry infection to Africa through Asia Minor and Egypt, and to Europe through Italy and France. . . . The Soviet Union [is] playing one of the greatest gambles in history at minimal cost.[58]

The congressional leaders were suddenly impressed. According to Acheson:

A long silence followed. Then Arthur Vandenberg said solemnly, "Mr. President, if you will say that to the Congress and the country, I will support you and I believe that most of its members will do the same." Without much further talk the meeting broke up to convene again, enlarged, in a week to consider a more detailed program of action.[59]

A few weeks later President Truman appeared before Congress to request $400 million in aid to Greece and Turkey, warning that the world must now "choose between alternative ways of life." What was needed was a US commitment to help "free peoples" and oppose "totalitarian regimes." The approach was successful. The Truman Doctrine, responding to congressional suggestions to "scare hell" out of the country, had the effect of mobilizing domestic support for America's new international role.

The Marshall Plan and the North Atlantic Treaty Organization (NATO) were the Truman Doctrine's logical sequel. In retrospect it seems clear that Congressional support for both was dependent largely on there being a sufficiently urgent sense of Soviet threat and that the Administration felt that it must generate just that.

Less obvious instances of cultivated threat perception, designed to strengthen the Administration's hand when dealing with more reticent segments of the political system, can be found as well. For example, in 1948 before the Senate was to act on the Marshall Plan, General Lucius Clay, commander of United States forces in West Germany, dispatched a telegram warning that war, resulting from a Soviet attack, "may come with dramatic suddenness." Although the peril appeared imminent, the most President Truman would do was provide grim assurances that war was not likely within the next 60 days! Clay later admitted that he had sent the cable for domestic political purposes, the idea being, according to his biographer, "to assist the military chiefs in their Congressional testimony; it was not, in Clay's opinion, related to any change in Soviet strategy."[60]

NSC-68's purpose was to whip the American public and Congress into a state of heightened concern over the

Russian threat, and especially to impress both with the need
for expanded military outlays. However, Truman's guidelines for the 1951 budget, prepared in mid-1949, set a ceiling
of $13 billion on the defense budget. Thus, as in 1947, in-
creased Cold-War activism encountered budgetary barriers.
Moreover, there was resistance within the Administration
itself to whipping up excessive anti-USSR feeling, especially
among such veterans of Soviet policy as George Kennan and
Charles Bohlen. Accordingly, NSC-68's apocalyptic warnings were intended largely, as Dean Acheson later explained, "to so bludgeon the mass mind of 'top government'
that not only could the President make a decision but that
the decision could be carried out."[61] It was an instrument
of consensus-building rather than a reasoned estimate of the
threat but, as before, the perceptions and expectations it created colored the tone of future relations.

Consequently, a congealing of anti-Soviet feeling within
America, and probably heightened Russian anxiety regarding the United States, resulted from a drive to ensure pas-
sage of the Administration's national security program. The
need to overcome a residue of domestic reluctance induced
a greater level of US-Soviet tension than international events
by themselves might have warranted.

The fear of national lethargy on security issues—the desire for greater anti-Soviet awareness—has been a recurring
theme in American political life. The fear was felt during
the early years of the Kennedy Administration, and it no
doubt had something to do with the desired ICBM buildup
and the extension of *containment* to national leftist movements within the Third World. The fear was even more apparent in the late seventies and early eighties.

MOBILIZATIONAL OVERREACTION AND THE SECOND COLD
WAR   For the first time successful pressure to reactivate the
Cold War did not originate from an incumbent administration, but originated from those who felt that the United States
had been hoodwinked by détente. As in the late 1950s, the
idea of a military gap to Russia's advantage gained considerable credence, critics lamented the apparent loss of

national will, and some went so far as to regret that the Sino-Soviet rift had removed the anxious urgency characteristic of earlier Cold-War sentiment.[62] The feeling crystallized in the demands of conservative citizen lobbies, retired national security officials, and others for far greater assertiveness and an accelerated strategic buildup.

The new drive originated within both of the major political parties. For example, the Democratic neoconservative movement found a voice in the Coalition for a Democratic Majority; such groups as the American Conservative Union and the Emergency Coalition Against Unilateral Disarmament drew membership mainly from Republican ranks. However, two organizations provided especially effective anti-détente lobbies. The Committee on the Present Danger, a bipartisan group led by such previous administration stalwarts as Paul Nitze and Eugene Rostow, launched a vigorous public information campaign arguing the existence of a dangerous Russian military lead. Similar efforts were made by the American Security Council, whose leadership was comprised largely of retired military and intelligence officers, and which boasted a national membership of 230,000.[63]

Although the anti-détente drive originated outside the government, it nevertheless closely reflected the Administration view after 1980. Paul Nitze, one of President Reagan's principal arms control counselors, previously had warned Henry Kissinger:

> It is not only wrong but dangerous to lull the Western public by proclaiming an end to the Cold War, a substitution of negotiation for confrontation and a generation of peace.[64]

The idea of a nation that had let down its guard, whose naive trust was exploited routinely by the Kremlin, was a theme repeatedly stressed by Reagan and his associates. As Richard Perle, Assistant Secretary of Defense and one of the Administration's most influential players on matters of Soviet policy, explained in 1983:

> Democracies will not sacrifice to protect their security in the absence of a sense of danger. And every time we create the impression that we and the Soviets are cooperating and

moderating the competition, we diminish that sense of apprehension.[65]

If one assumes that for sufficiently powerful segments of American society a "sense of danger" had become a value in its own right, then one must also assume that a quasi-automatic domestic mechanism designed to counter conciliation has managed to take root. In any case, surges in anti-Sovietism and East–West tension often may be a partial product of the sort of mobilizational overreaction displayed during the two cold wars.

## POLITICAL STRUCTURE IN CONTEXT

The principal conclusion thus far is that America's Soviet policy is at least as much a product of domestic political circumstances as it is a product of Russia's behavior. Instances of Soviet aggressiveness, or of threatening increases in military capabilities, may always provide a *sufficient* condition for a rise in US hostility, but neither circumstance represents a *necessary* condition—a more confrontational posture can also stem from internal forces. A political reward structure that tilts toward hostility—and at least four mechanisms that further affect the bias—account for shifts in US attitudes toward the USSR even in the absence of meaningful changes in the Soviet Union's behavior.

The sources of United States policy toward the Soviet Union must be considered against the backdrop of issues raised in Chapters 2 and 3. To begin with, domestic actors are affected by perceptual distortions associated with enmity and distrust. These distortions partially account for the nature of political rewards and for the unequal punishments meted out for the two kinds of misestimates (erroneous understatements and erroneous overstatements) of Soviet threat. Perceptions thus provide another layer of causality. Moreover, the fact that domestic drives behind hostility are usually effective suggests a public receptivity to threatening views of Russia, a receptivity grounded in the public image discussed in Chapter 3.

Just as clearly, the nature of the incompatibilities that separate the two sides, and that are assumed rather than explained in most conventional approaches to superpower rivalry, cannot be understood without reference to their domestic political setting. We have managed to identify a set of derivative conflicts of interest in US-Soviet relations, but have discovered very few of an objective nature. If derivative incompatibilities do not repose on a solid foundation of objective clashes, we may wonder how they are in fact sustained. Yet if the pursuits associated with these incompatibilities (e.g., rival military growth) are connected to powerful *domestic* interests, their maintenance, even in the absence of objective conflicts, is much easier to understand.

All such pressures are part of the structure of US politics. And although that fact is neither especially sinister nor particularly mysterious, it makes a resolution of the superpower rivalry quite difficult. For even though history provides many clues on how to deal with objective conflicts, history has less to suggest when it comes to addressing antagonism nourished by derivative conflicts, perceptual distortions, and domestic politics. Of course things are complicated further when the impact of Soviet political structure is also taken into account.

## NOTES

1. George F. Kennan, *The Nuclear Delusion: Soviet-American Relations in the Atomic Age* (New York: Pantheon Books, 1983), p. 229.
2. The speech is reported in "Truman Acts to Save Nations from Red Rule," *New York Times*, March 13, 1947.
3. Quoted in Walter Lafeber, *America, Russia, and the Cold War*, 5th Edition (New York: Alfred A. Knopf, 1985), p. 53.
4. The text of NSC-68 (declassified in 1975) is reprinted in Thomas H. Etzold and John Lewis Gaddis, *Documents on American Policy and Strategy: 1945–1950* (New York: Columbia University Press, 1978), pp. 385–442.
5. Same as 3, p. 96.
6. Adam B. Ulam, *Expansion and Coexistence: Soviet Foreign Policy, 1917–1973*, 2d Edition (New York: Praeger, 1974), p. 462.

7. Adam B. Ulam, *The Rivals: America and Russia Since World War II* (New York: The Viking Press, 1971), p. 148.

8. U.S. Government Printing Office, *Public Papers of the Presidents, J. F. Kennedy, 1961* (Washington, DC: 1962), p. 397.

9. For data on trends in comparative numbers of missiles during this period, see Bruce M. Russett and Bruce G. Blair, eds., *Progress in Arms Control* (San Francisco: W. H. Freeman, 1979), p. 6.

10. Robert McNamara, *Blundering Into Disaster* (New York: Pantheon Books, 1986), p. 44. Also John Prados, *The Soviet Estimate* (New York: The Dial Press, 1982), pp. 114–115.

11. Major discussions of the "window of vulnerability" are found in Paul Nitze, "Assuring Strategic Stability in an Era of Détente," *Foreign Affairs,* June 1976. See also, Fred M. Kaplan, *Dubious Specter: A Second Look at the Soviet Threat* (Washington, DC: The Transnational Institute, 1977).

12. See Alexander L. George, "The Arab-Israeli War of October 1973: Origins and Impact" in Alexander L. George, ed., *Managing US-Soviet Rivalry: Problems of Crisis Prevention* (Boulder, CO: Westview Press, 1983), pp. 139–155.

13. Richard J. Barnet, *Real Security: Restoring American Power in a Dangerous World* (New York: Touchstone, 1981), p. 76.

14. William M. Legrande, *Cuba's Policy in Africa: 1959–1980* (Berkeley, CA: Institute of International Studies, 1980).

15. "Kissinger Believes Cuba 'Exports' Revolution Again," *New York Times,* February 5, 1976.

16. Les Aspin, "Judge Not By Numbers Alone," *Bulletin of the Atomic Scientists,* June 1980, pp. 5–32.

17. "Report of the President's Commission on Strategic Forces" (Washington, DC: U.S. Government Printing Office, 1983).

18. Joint Economic Committee, Congress of the United States, *USSR: Measures of Economic Growth and Development, 1950–1980,* December 8, 1982, p. 123.

19. "CIA Analysts Now Said to Find US Overstated Soviet Arms Rise," *New York Times,* March 3, 1983.

20. For the analytical power this basic assumption can yield, see Anthony Downs, *An Economic Theory of Democracy* (New York: Harper and Row, 1957).

21. Joseph S. Nye Jr., "The Domestic Environment of US Policy Making," in Arnold Horelick, ed., *US-Soviet Relations: The Next Phase* (Ithaca, NY: Cornell University Press, 1986), p. 113.

22. John Lewis Gaddis, *Strategies of Containment: A Critical Appraisal of Postwar American National Security Policy* (New York: Oxford University Press, 1982), p. 127.

23. Same as 22, p. 128.

24. Richard Stebbins, *The United States in World Affairs, 1950* (New York: Harper and Row, 1951), p. 57.

25. Same as 22, p. 128.

26. Same as 7, pp. 19, 156, 162.

27. Quoted in Benjamin Page, *Choices and Echoes in Presidential Elections* (Chicago: University of Chicago Press, 1978), p. 86.

28. "Kennedy Attacks Nixon 'Weakness,' " *New York Times*, August 25, 1960.

29. "Nixon Gives Arms Budget Priority," *New York Times*, August 25, 1960.

30. Kenneth O'Donnell, "LBJ and the Kennedys," *Life*, August 7, 1970.

31. Quoted in David Halberstam, *The Best and the Brightest* (Greenwich, CT: Fawcett, 1972), p. 643.

32. Ronald W. Reagan quoted by Gerald R. Ford in, *A Time to Heal: The Autobiography of Gerald R. Ford* (New York: Harper and Row, 1979), p. 337.

33. Same as 32, p. 353.

34. "Department of State Bulletin," December 1, 1975, p. 767.

35. "Reagan is Stressing a Tough US Stance in Foreign Affairs in Bid to Gain Ground," *Wall Street Journal*, January 31, 1980.

36. "Reagan Assails Carter's Foreign Policy as Weak," *Wall Street Journal*, January 28, 1980.

37. See, for example, Fred Kaplan, *The Wizards of Armageddon* (New York: Simon and Schuster, 1983).

38. Alan Wolfe, *The Rise and Fall of the "Soviet Threat"* (Washington, DC: The Institute for Policy Studies, 1979), especially Chapter 3.

39. See Stanley Kelley Jr., *Interpreting Elections* (Princeton, NJ: Princeton University Press, 1983), Chapter 5.

40. *The Gallup Poll: Public Opinion 1935–1971* (New York: Random House, 1972), p. 1857.

41. Miroslav Nincic, "America's Soviet Policy and the Policy of Opposites," *World Politics*, July 1988, p. 452.

42. See, for example, Paul R. Abramson et al., *Change and Continuity in the 1980 Election* (Washington, DC: Congressional Quarterly Press, 1982).

43. The classic on bureaucratic politics and foreign policy is Graham T. Allison, *The Essence of Decision* (Boston: Little, Brown and Company, 1971); see also Morton H. Halperin, *Bureaucratic Politics and Foreign Policy* (Washington, DC: The Brookings Institution, 1974).

44. Bertram M. Gross, *The Legislative Struggle* (New York: McGraw-Hill, 1953), p. 80.

45. See, for example, "The Doves Capture Control of Trade," *New York Times*, October 23, 1983.

46. Samuel P. Huntington, *The Soldier and the State: The Theory and Politics of Civil Military Relations* (New York, Vintage Books, 1957), Chapter 6.

47. Richard A. Aliano, *American Defense Policy from Eisenhower to Kennedy* (Athens, OH: Ohio University Press, 1975), p. 83.

48. For discussion, see Adam Yarmolinsky, *The Military Establishment: Its Impact on American Society* (New York: Harper and Row, 1971) and Miroslav Nincic, *The Arms Race: the Political Economy of Military Growth* (New York: Praeger, 1982), Chapter 7.

49. C. Wright Mills, *The Power Elite* (New York: Oxford University Press, 1956).

50. Data in this section are from *Statistical Abstract of the United States, 1987* (US Department of Commerce, Bureau of the Census, 1987).

51. Center for Defense Information, "No Business Like War Business," *The Defense Monitor*, XVI no. 3, 1987.

52. See Robert W. DeGrasse Jr., *Military Expansion, Economic Decline,* Rev. Edition (Armonk NY: M. E. Sharpe, 1983); Roger H. Bezdek, "The 1970 Impact—Regional and Occupational—of Compensated Shifts in Defense Spending," *Journal of Regional Science*, XV, 1975, pp. 183–198; same as 48, Nincic, Chapter 3.

53. See "Military PAC's Led Donations in '86 Campaigns," *New York Times*, August 28, 1987.

54. The emergence of the strategic bomber force is described in Norman Polmar, *Strategic Weapons: An Introduction* (New York: Crane, Russack, and Company, 1975), Chapter 2.

55. This subsequently was scaled down to 1,000 Minuteman Is and 54 Titan missiles.

56. A link between difficulty of policy change and exaggerated statements of Soviet threat also is suggested in Nye, same as 21, p. 112.

57. This problem has been developed theoretically by J. David Singer in "Disarmament: the Domestic and Global Context," in John S. Gilbert, ed., *The New Era in American Foreign Policy* (New York: St. Martins Press, 1973).

58. Dean Acheson, *Present at the Creation* (New York: W. W. Norton, 1969), p. 219.

59. Same as 58, p. 219.

60. John Edward Smith, ed., *The Papers of General Lucius Clay: Germany 1945–1949* (Bloomington, IN: Indiana University Press, 1975), pp. 568–569; Daniel Yergin, *Shattered Peace* (Boston: Houghton Mifflin Company, 1978), p. 351.

61. Same as 58, p. 374.

62. For example, Norman Podhoretz, *The Present Danger* (New York: Simon and Schuster, 1980), p. 98.

63. "Lobbying Body to Push Congress for a Nuclear Edge Over Soviet," *New York Times*, January 6, 1981.

64. Quoted in Arthur Macy Cox, *Russian Roulette* (New York: Times Books, 1982), p. 69.
65. Quoted in Center for Defense Information, "Militarism in America," *The Defense Monitor,* XV no. 3, 1985, p. 2.

# CHAPTER FIVE

◆ ◆ ◆ ◆ ◆

# Russia's American Policy and the Structure of Soviet Politics

R ussia's foreign policy is at once simpler and more difficult to account for than America's. On the one hand, Soviet foreign policy has the appearance of consistency, of holding a patient and steady course toward clear-cut objectives. It seems to lack the frequent zig-zagging and ambivalence about ultimate goals that many see in US international behavior. Moreover, Soviet policy often is assumed to be the product of a highly centralized political process—where decisions are made by a narrow elite and faithfully implemented by droves of service subordinates—quite unlike the complex mechanisms and multifarious interests that characterize US democracy. Although these assumptions contain some truth, there are layers of complexity to Soviet foreign policymaking that escape simple dichotomies and that, in addition, are absent from the US approach. This is revealed in two ways. First, the *objectives* driving Moscow's American policy may in fact be more numerous than those guiding Washington's Soviet policy. Secondly, the *rules* of foreign-policy decision making have been less stable in the Soviet Union than in the United States. These differences, together with the obvious discrepancies in the two political systems and the fact that much less information is available on Soviet politics, make it difficult to draw direct parallels between the sources of our policies toward each other. Nevertheless, as we will see, a number of similarities are apparent.

## ELEMENTS OF COMPLEXITY

### The Complexity of Objectives

Whereas both the United States and the Soviet Union pursue several parallel objectives in the context of their rivalry, there are certain objectives Washington does not share with Moscow. Both countries seek to enhance their security and to gain geopolitical, diplomatic, and strategic advantages at each other's expense. In addition, however, the Soviet Union's US policy is driven by the pursuit of international *prestige* and by a need to be recognized, as closely

as possible, as America's equal. There is nothing comparable on the US side. Undisputed power and wealth, a culture
widely imitated in other societies, and a sense of standing
for lofty moral and political values have made the United
States one of the most self-confident nations on earth. Despite an occasional need to be reassured of the international
deference their country commands, the US public and its
leaders have never displayed the slightest sense of inferiority
vis-à-vis the Soviet Union nor craved national recognition
from that quarter.

Russia's feelings of inferiority date back at least to the
era of Peter the Great, when the reality of a major technological lag behind the West first sunk in, and to the reign of
Catherine the Great, who strove to bring her court within
Europe's cultural orbit. But the need to prove that Russia is
the West's, and specifically America's, equal may never have
been quite as strong as in the postwar period. This need has
been manifested in constant Soviet fears that its prestige might
be slighted and in its obvious gratification when Russia has
been treated with the respect it so badly desires. This concern with self-esteem is often displayed in apparently minor
ways. When, for instance, Khrushchev and Bulganin trav-
eled to Geneva for their first postwar meeting with Western
leaders, they were painfully embarrassed at arriving in a two-
engine aircraft rather than the sleeker four-engined aircraft
of other leaders.[1] And when Eisenhower invited Khrushchev to the United States in 1959, the Soviet leadership
worried repeatedly that the Americans might use the
opportunity to undermine Soviet dignity.[2] Nevertheless, the 1959 meeting was a reasonable success, and
Khrushchev exulted:

> If the President of the United States himself invites the Chair-
> man of the Council of Ministers of the USSR, then you know
> conditions have changed. We'd come a long way from the
> time when the United States wouldn't even grant us diplo-
> matic recognition. We felt pride in our country, our Party,
> our people, and the victories they had achieved.[3]

In a similar vein, Kissinger reports in his memoirs that
Brezhnev often had to be reassured that he and his country

were not considered second best. His "major concern seemed to be whether he would be treated as an equal," and he exhibited a "relentless insistence on status and a doubt that it would be conceded."[4] Thus the need for recognition of its superpower position and equal bargaining power are important objectives of Russia's American policy, objectives with no parallels in the US. The Soviet Union also seeks to derive maximum *economic* benefit from the United States and from other Western industrialized nations, a policy that has enhanced asymmetry inasmuch as such interests have had only a minor influence on Washington's attitudes toward the Soviet Union since the Cold War began.

Ideological differences notwithstanding, Soviet leadership has always respected America's material and technological achievements and wished to benefit from them. Although Stalin's pathological fear of Western contamination made him slight this aspect of Russia's American policy, both Lenin before him and successors since have welcomed the prospect of profitable economic ties with the United States. Khrushchev reported that a major goal of his 1959 trip to the United States was to generate some US business interest in dealing with Russia,[5] and between 1959 and 1961 the Soviets purchased approximately 50 chemical plants from abroad. Even when agricultural failures led to the deflection of considerable Soviet foreign exchange for grain purchases, imports of Western machinery and technology surged again around 1967, at a time when Brezhnev was consolidating his grip on power. In fact the Brezhnev years were marked by a vigorous effort to improve economic relations with the capitalist world. And although commercial relations for the most part collapsed during the Second Cold War, Mikhail Gorbachev's commitment to economic reform again has increased Russia's interest in tapping US markets and technology.

Thus the motivational structure behind the Soviet Union's behavior toward the United States appears more complicated than that behind America's behavior toward Russia, and Moscow's quest for status and economic gain has significantly affected the shaping of its US policy.

## Shifting Rules of the Game

There is a second major difference between the two countries. Although political decision making in the United States reflects a multiplicity of interests, the process by which policy is made has been quite stable. The distribution of power and interests shifts occasionally but never appreciably, and, most importantly, the rules of the game have remained fairly constant. The same cannot be said of the Soviet Union.

The most obvious distinction in the Russian case separates Joseph Stalin's rule from that of his successors. At least as much as any notorious despot, Stalin ruled through an absolute and capricious dictatorship. No institution and no individuals were able to challenge Stalin's decisions or offset his influence. His personal paranoia, which reached clinical proportions during the last years of his rule, allowed for virtually no other inputs to major foreign policy decisions. Even Stalin's Foreign Minister, the faithful Vyacheslav Molotov, came under suspicion as a Western agent, and Khrushchev has revealed that no other leaders were privy to crucial military and national-security information.[6] As we pursue the connection between Soviet political structure and Soviet attitudes toward the United States, we must understand that Stalin towered above political structures that were overshadowed by his personal goals, whims, perceptions, and phobias. He had a pivotal impact on US–Soviet relations, but he was a nonrecurring phenomenon. Thus the Stalinist era, in terms of the rules by which Soviet foreign policy is made, must stand apart from every phase of Soviet foreign policy making that followed the dictator's death in 1953.

The other three major periods in USSR postwar history are distinguished by the specific rules of foreign policy making that they produced. In the early years of his rule, Nikita Khrushchev regularly consulted his colleagues within the Soviet leadership, but he became increasingly independent as the years went by. His methods never remotely resembled Stalin's; yet major decisions—such as the emplacement of medium-range missiles in Cuba—did not benefit from extensive discussion with other members of the Presidium (as the Politburo was then called). In fact, Khrushchev's autonomy and voluntarism on major issues of foreign and domestic (especially agricultural) policy were the primary causes of his ultimate political undoing.

This approach contrasted with the collegial don't-rock-the-boat style preferred by Leonid Brezhnev, whose hallmark emphasized consensual decision making within the Politburo (as opposed to the practice of seeking simple majorities on important issues). Because of this, Soviet foreign policy displayed greater constancy during the Brezhnev years than under those of his predecessors. Another difference surfaced as well. Because Stalin's frequent and abrupt personnel changes at various levels of leadership meant that strong institutional loyalties and perspectives never managed to take root, bureaucratic policy perspectives were nowhere near as prevalent as they have since become. And even though greater personnel stability characterized the Khrushchev years, security of tenure ("stability of cadres") reached its peak under Brezhnev. Policymakers having thus developed stronger ties to the institutions they served,[7] one may assume they increasingly acquired the motivational mind-set and perceptual blinders associated with organizational roles in other societies, including the United States.

Gorbachev combines methods preferred by his post-Stalinist predecessors with elements uniquely his own. From Khrushchev he has adopted a boldness of policy initiative, a distaste for excessive repression, and a concern with the lot of the average Soviet citizen. Far more than Khrushchev, however, Gorbachev recognizes the need for building a leadership consensus around the broad themes of national policy, and he is not politically rash. On the whole, Gorbachev has developed thus far a distinctive approach to foreign policy making.

However, important aspects of Russia have not changed over the decades—the primacy of Communist Party rule, the option of ultimate resort to coercion—and other non-democratic policies have been and remain features of Soviet politics. Yet, from the narrower perspective of how Russia's American policy is structured, there are meaningful differences between regimes.

Significantly, the nondemocratic nature of Soviet politics has not precluded the active play of political rewards and punishments. Again, the Stalinist era was exceptional in this respect as well. Personal dictatorship means that the dictator is responsible to no one and that his subordinates are responsible to him alone. Consequently, what political reward structure exists applies only to those subordinates and flows exclusively from his personal preferences. Plainly this does not describe the Khrushchev, Brezhnev, or Gorbachev eras. To varying degrees, each of these three leaders has been responsible primarily to his peers within the Politburo (which, though nominally subordinate to the Central Committee, has acted as the ultimate instance of authority in the Soviet Union[8]) and it is here too that they must answer for their policies toward the United States. And although the broader pattern of interests to which the Politburo responds is somewhat nebulous, the important considerations are that interests within the Soviet elite are not homogenous and that, although substantially muted, cleavages characterize Kremlin politics as they do the politics of democratic regimes—and some of these cleavages bear on the Soviet Union's US policy.

A survey of Russia's US policy over the past several decades yields two broad conclusions. First, the survey reveals a link between an essentially conservative political reward structure and a cautiously hostile policy toward the United States. Secondly, it suggests that fluctuations in foreign policy are due largely to shifts in domestic politics. Most significantly, a relaxation of tensions with the United States impacts the interests and values of each social and political group differently, and changes in their relative positions affect the content of Soviet foreign policy. Conservative inertia and reformist urges have been a permanent part of the postwar pattern of Soviet politics, and the point of equilibrium between the two tendencies has had, and will continue to have, implications for East–West relations. Similarly, because bureaucratic and economic interests are not uniform, certain groups are more likely to benefit from a relaxation of tensions between the two superpowers than others.

As there is less information on the link between domestic politics and external behavior in the Soviet Union than in the United States, we must proceed more inductively than in previous chapters. We next examine the three major phases of Soviet postwar history and follow the threads of domestic interests, beliefs, and power fluctuations in an attempt to discern how they have affected the overall tenor of its policies vis-à-vis the United States and the occasional shifts this policy has displayed.

## THE REGIMES: DOMESTIC POLITICS AND FOREIGN POLICY

### Policy Reversals and the Khrushchev Era

THE CONSOLIDATION OF POWER When Stalin died in March 1953, the Soviet Union's political situation was precarious: a deep chill had engulfed superpower relations and the question of Stalin's successor was not immediately resolved. The dictator's apparent choice had been Georgy Malenkov who, in addition to heading the Communist Party Central Committee, became prime minister upon Stalin's death. But the idea of one-man rule did not sit well with certain other leaders, primarily Chief of Soviet Secret Police Lavrenti Beria and former Foreign Minister Vyacheslav Molotov. Malenkov was made to relinquish command of the party organization (retaining the post of prime minister), and Nikita Khrushchev was invited to become first secretary of the Communist Party Central Committee. Beria was appointed head of the KGB and Molotov given the ranks of first deputy prime minister and minister of foreign affairs. Thus an uneasy system of collective leadership was established. Beria, who made the earliest and least subtle bid for supremacy, was soon ousted and executed, leaving Malenkov and Khrushchev to contend for supreme power.

The Malenkov-Khrushchev rivalry expressed itself in differences on major issues of domestic and foreign policy. Malenkov, virtually alone among his peers on the Communist Party Presidium, took a position against the traditional bias in favor of heavy industry. He argued that light industry should be allowed to grow at a comparable rate, so as to ensure a faster rise in the production of consumer goods and, hence, in the Soviet public's living standards. The major obstacle to such a shift of domestic economic emphasis was that because heavy industry provided the foundation for military production, reduced defense outlays seemed incompatible with the international tensions of the time and with the assumption of an ineluctable struggle with the West. Realizing this, Malenkov attempted to move toward a redefinition of relations with the United States, arguing for a lessening of East–West tensions. Malenkov did not base his argument on a reassessment of the nature of capitalism or on a position that it was less aggressive than the Kremlin routinely claimed it to be, but on the need to reduce the risks of nuclear war that in a departure from established positions, he claimed would result in the "destruction of world civilization."[9]

Khrushchev, by contrast, championed a strong defense and expanded agricultural production, both of which required a foundation in heavy industry. He challenged the notion that nuclear war would mean the destruction of civilization; in Khrushchev's opinion, it would merely mean the destruction of capitalism. He portrayed Malenkov's foreign policy as "weak-nerved," and he favored taking a much stronger attitude toward the United States. On New Year's Day 1955, Malenkov declared that Russia's acquisition of hydrogen bombs made peaceful coexistence both "necessary and possible"; Khrushchev responded that the prime minister was trying to "intimidate" the proletarian revolution with nuclear weapons.[10] Presidium hardliners such as Molotov and World War II hero Marshal Zhukov flocked to Khrushchev's side and, on February 8, Malenkov's resignation as prime minister was demanded and offered. Traditional values, especially the primacy of defense, emerged victorious.

DE-STALINIZATION, ECONOMIC REFORM, AND PEACEFUL
COEXISTENCE  With Malenkov's removal, Khrushchev's grip
on power became increasingly firm, and freedom from immediate political challenge produced a shift in his policies.
The reversal was sufficiently abrupt to suggest that his earlier positions had been tailored to the claims of factional politics and to the imperatives of the political reward structure.
In any case, Khrushchev's tone on East–West matters changed
almost immediately. By this time Washington's own anti-
Soviet rhetoric had reached something of a plateau, and the
Soviet leader's earlier pugnacity yielded to a prudent search
for coexistence with the West.

In mid-May 1955, the Austrian State Treaty was signed
whereby Moscow agreed to withdraw its troops from Austria and to recognize that country's neutrality. In an even
more symbolically important move, a meeting between
Khrushchev and the Western leaders was arranged to be held
in Geneva in July. Although the event produced few tangible breakthroughs and even foundered on the question of
Germany's future, it also reflected a declining USSR paranoia and suggested the possibility of a future relationship
based on dialogue rather than military confrontation. Unfortunately, the Spirit of Geneva did not last long, but was
the first encouraging movement in US–Soviet relations since
the Cold War began.

The connection between détente and domestic reform
was becoming increasingly apparent. Khrushchev's predilection for agriculture was given full reign in 1954 when he
launched his "virgin lands" project, designed to increase food
production by cultivating vast new tracts of land in eastern
Russia and Kazakhstan. In a move toward political liberalization, Khrushchev also oversaw the release of throngs of
imprisoned victims of Stalin's arbitrary repression. His most
momentous initiative, however, was the "secret speech" delivered to the Twentieth Party Congress in 1956, at which
he presented his famous indictment of Stalinist terror. Although he stopped short of implicating Stalin's associates
within the Soviet leadership and was careful to recognize
certain of the late dictator's achievements, Khrushchev's

speech was the most significant step taken in several decades to challenge the legitimacy of massive coercion as a tool of state policy. This step implied a relaxation of the Soviet Union's traditional crisis mentality and an undermining of the proposition that permanent foreign threats justified any level of internal repression. Accordingly, the Soviet leader pressed the view that war was not inevitable and that, as "capitalist encirclement" had come to an end, peaceful coexistence was both desirable and possible. The link between internal reform and relaxation of East–West tensions became the foundation for much of Khrushchev's behavior.

The new political course had its opponents. Although Khrushchev had appointed many of his supporters to the Central Committee, several powerful Presidium members were unhappy with the new emphasis on consumer needs at the expense of heavy industry and were uneasy with the notion of coexistence with the capitalist world as opposed to armed vigilance and international militance. One such member was Malenkov who, although ousted as prime minister, had retained his seat on the Presidium and who reversed his own earlier pro-consumer feelings. Another such member was Molotov, whose hard-line past made him rebel against the new leader's perceived softness in international affairs.

Nevertheless, Khrushchev's concern with the lot of the Soviet consumer became increasingly pronounced. In 1957 he decreed, somewhat unrealistically, that the Soviet Union must overtake the United States in the production of meat, milk, and butter within three to four years. This dramatic shift from defense toward consumer interests is said to have been the final straw as far as the opposition was concerned;[11] Malenkov and Molotov, together with Voroshilov and Kaganovich (both of whom shared the more traditional Stalinist set of values) began to plan Khrushchev's removal. The group made its move in June 1957, but the plot backfired. The conspirators mustered a Presidium majority in favor of Khrushchev's ouster. But with the support of Defense Minister Mashal Zhukov, Khrushchev managed to convene a full meeting of the Central Committee, which overturned the Presidium's decisions. The plotters (subsequently referred to as the "anti-Party" group) were banished to minor jobs, and Khrushchev emerged as the undisputed leader of the Soviet Union.

Enjoying temporary freedom from political challenge, Khrushchev injected new energy into his dual policies of peaceful coexistence and internal reform. He continued pressing for ambitious, but not altogether successful, agricultural programs and voicing the opinion that excessive defense spending was incompatible with domestic goals. The blend of adventuristic militarism and prudence that has always characterized Soviet foreign policy increasingly stressed caution over assertiveness. For example, the Kremlin's response to the 1958 US intervention in Lebanon was surprisingly mild and, during that same year, Russia failed to support Communist China in the "offshore island" dispute with Taiwan. Soviet pressure was exerted on Berlin in 1958, but even in the midst of the crisis atmosphere Khrushchev was busily preparing his détente-reform platform for presentation to the Twenty-First Communist Party Congress. The culmination of the search for limited accommodation came with Khrushchev's 1959 trip to the United States and the Spirit of Camp David that it produced.

One benefit the Soviet leader sought from reduced tensions with the West was the freedom to concentrate on improving agriculture and consumer welfare at home; Khrushchev understood that his economic programs could not be financed adequately if military spending was not reduced. In this spirit he proposed a major revision in Soviet strategic doctrine that, from his point of view, also would have paid welcome economic dividends. The idea was to deemphasize conventional forces in favor of strategic-nuclear weapons, thus pursuing the goal (related in economic intent to Dulles's notion of "massive retaliation") of a "bigger bang for the buck." To the dismay of many military leaders, in January 1960 Khrushchev proposed reductions in ground forces and decreased emphases on naval development as well as on conventional military aircraft, in favor of increased reliance on strategic rocketry.

DOMESTIC STRUGGLES AND KHRUSHCHEV'S US POLICY

Opposition to Khrushchev's new programs continued to simmer and, once again, the Soviet leader found himself fending off challenges to his policies from such conservatives as Mikhail Suslov, a leading guardian of Communist orthodoxy, and Frol Kozlov, a Presidium member with extremely traditional priorities. Unexpectedly, the opposition's hand was strengthened by the United States. In May 1960 an American U-2 spy plane was brought down over the Soviet Union, and the pilot (Francis Gary Powers) was captured and made to confess his espionage mission. Most Soviet leaders already knew that Khrushchev had engaged in lavish bluffing in recent years—making vastly exaggerated claims about USSR missile power—and they now realized that the U-2 overflights must have exposed the bluff. The violation of Soviet airspace was taken not only as further evidence of US aggressive malevolence, but as a blow to Russia's prestige, and Khrushchev's complacency was widely held responsible for the affront.

The Paris summit meeting planned for that May—which was to bring together US, Russian, British, and French leaders—collapsed before it managed to get underway. Khrushchev later explained that he "became more and more convinced that our pride and dignity would be damaged if we went ahead with the meeting as though nothing had happened. Our prestige would suffer, especially in the Third World."[12] The tone of East–West relations deteriorated swiftly, and so did Khrushchev's internal position, as the episode coincided with several leadership changes to the detriment of his supporters. Whatever the U-2's diplomatic consequences, it was an unexpected stroke of luck for Kremlin hard-liners; even *Pravda* began publishing thinly veiled criticisms of Khrushchev's conciliatory gestures toward the United States.[13]

Still, the Soviet leader continued to press his programs, complaining about the opposition of "some comrades" to his pro-consumer initiatives. In November, Kozlov responded that "everyone knows" steel production is a "basic" indicator of a "country's economic strength." And

Kozlov's speeches further betrayed a pronounced preference for heavy industry and military growth over consumer welfare. In January 1961, Khrushchev retorted by announcing an agricultural revolution in favor of the consumer, criticizing the "metal eaters" who would detract from the needs of the Soviet public. By the fall of 1961, Khrushchev indicated that beyond domestic economic priorities, the controversy involved basic issues of foreign policy as well. It became apparent that the major cleavage was between men like Suslov and the politically resilient Molotov, who stressed the need for a militant pursuit of the international class struggle, and those who, like Khrushchev, preferred accommodation with the West.

Here we encounter what may well be the central paradox, not only of the Khrushchev era, but of the Soviet Union's relations with the United States in general. Given that economic reform requires a lessening of East–West tensions, if US and Soviet policies toward each other amounted to no more than a process of reciprocal adjustment, Khrushchev's pursuit of détente would have evoked the cooperative US responses needed to undermine the positions of the opponents of domestic reform. All of this should have encouraged further détente initiatives on the Soviet side, producing a self-perpetuating cycle of decreasing tension. However, this course was obstructed by the occasional bursts of bellicose behavior required on both sides by political, bureaucratic, and other internal interests. Thus, in the wake of the U-2 incident, the success of Khrushchev's domestic programs required evidence that he had not, in fact, drifted into a state of naive complacency vis-à-vis the United States—particularly given the rhetoric associated with the recent US election and the Kennedy Administration's military buildup.

In any event, Khrushchev retreated from his plans for troop reduction and embraced the "combined-arms" policy preferred by his opponents, a strategy that assigned a full complement of missions to the ground, naval, and air forces while nourishing the role of long-range nuclear weaponry. Of course, Russia's military spending expanded accordingly. At the same time, Khrushchev launched a reinvigorated program of nuclear testing, unilaterally abandoning the Soviet Union's moratorium on such tests. It has also been suggested that Khrushchev's confrontational behavior in the summer of 1961, including the decision to erect the Berlin Wall, arose from a need to outflank those critics who sought to depict him as weak-kneed in dealing with the capitalist world.[14]

Nevertheless, Khrushchev planned a major attack on the remnants of Stalinism for the Twenty-Second Communist Party Congress in October 1961, on which occasion he embarked on a renewed denunciation of the late dictator's crimes. For the first time, living Soviet politicians—including Voroshilov, Kaganovich, and Malenkov—were implicated in these crimes. Molotov too came under attack, especially for his resistance to Khrushchev's coexistence policies. But the conservatives were not easily brought to heel, and by the end of 1961 the Soviet leader faced a stalemate on his domestic programs, while his pursuit of coexistence foundered on a lukewarm US response and on resistance from Kremlin champions of military growth and heavy industry.

It may have been this impasse, more than anything else, that impelled Khrushchev to attempt the emplacement of medium- and intermediate-range missiles in Cuba. Strategic considerations militated in favor of the move: America's advantage in intercontinental ballistic missiles, as well as in forward-based weaponry, must have made the notion of an off-setting missile presence in Cuba very appealing. This emplacement also could have provided the added strategic leverage needed to bolster Soviet pressure on Berlin, as well as a bargaining chip with which to seek the removal of US Jupiter missiles from Turkey. Most importantly, however, it could have been a masterstroke in terms of domestic politics. As Carl Linden has cogently argued:

> [Khrushchev] undoubtedly saw the venture as a way of cutting the Gordian knot that entangled his strategy of détente and reform following the U-2 episode. The argument of the defenders of traditional policy that guns and steel could not be sacrificed to butter in the face of a more powerful enemy would have lost force, while Khrushchev's own concept of

the   inexpensive   rocket   deterrent   would   have gained plausibility.[15]

But Khrushchev's gambit failed miserably. Brought to the brink of nuclear war, he was forced to withdraw the missiles with no significant US concessions to show for his efforts. Certainly the military must have been irate and increasingly unwilling to stand behind the Soviet leader "who had caused such embarrassment."[16] The conservative opposition, it can be safely assumed, was delighted. In retrospect, it seems that Khrushchev's decline became virtually inevitable.

From this point forward, Khrushchev no longer explicitly linked military spending and economic goals. Although he maintained a commitment to the long-term improvement of consumer satisfaction—and although Kozlov's physical incapacitation in 1963, as well as successful progress toward the Partial Test Ban Treaty with the United States, added renewed wind to his sails—the estrangement of major domestic interests was perhaps irreversible.[17] However, it should not be assumed that foreign policy was the sole cause of disaffection with Khrushchev; complaints ranged from the failure of numerous agricultural experiments to the unpopular administrative reforms. In October 1964, Nikita Khrushchev was ousted from office and a major era in Russia's postwar history came to an end.

One reason for the Khrushchev era's significance is that, for the first time in its postrevolutionary history, an authentic Soviet structure of political rewards, punishments, and expectations—distilled from the whims of an absolute dictator—was allowed to crystallize. It also was demonstrated during this period that, as in the United States, it is politically safer and more effective to attack an incumbent from hawkish and conservative positions than as a champion of superpower conciliation and policy reform. Khrushchev benefited from this strategy in his efforts to displace Malenkov, and was a victim of the same tactic when he himself was ousted. As leaders could err either by underestimating or by overestimating the threat from the West and the required response, and because the two kinds of errors carried unequal penalties, a bias in favor of toughness at times of unsettled political ascendancy was apparent. Furthermore, it also was demonstrated that freedom from the pressures of domestic political competition makes it considerably easier to act on whatever conciliatory inclination a leader may prefer to pursue. A similar pattern of pressures operating in the United States must be considered a political bias affecting the course of East–West relations.

The events of this period further indicated that Soviet satisfaction or displeasure with the United States can be amplified by the implications of US policy for Soviet prestige. But this is not surprising. Emerging from the role of international pariah that defined it during most of the Stalinist period, the Soviet Union began venturing onto the world stage as a full-fledged participant in great power politics and began seeking the international respect habitually due a major power. It is likely also that, as its reliance on massive repression lessened, the need to build a more stable foundation of legitimacy presented itself more urgently than in Stalin's time. International respect and recognition may have been one of the measures of governmental success that, it was hoped, would favorably impress politically relevant strata of Soviet society.

Although policy moved along a narrower band during the Brezhnev years, a number of similar features revealed themselves, and links between foreign policy and domestic politics became even more apparent.

### Brezhnev and the Narrowing Consensus

The substantive differences between Khrushchev's and Brezhnev's foreign policies were reflected in the disparate domestic contexts within which they were forged. Khrushchev was a reformist, with pronounced positions on major issues. His policies, chosen more with regard to pure policy objectives than to prevailing Presidium inclinations, were often pursued in the face of personal political risks. Brezhnev's policies, defensive rather than reformist, were set within narrow margins determined by establishment consensus. The direction of Brezhnev's policy was less important than the fact that it was the product of decisions that never strayed very far from the least common denominator of the oligarchs' preferences. Still, this dominant consensus was both domestically and externally conservative. In terms of the United States, Brezhnev's policy eschewed excessive conciliation more readily than vigorous competition, while it balanced the interests of national security and military strength against the prestige and economic dividends desired from détente.

Similarly discrepant interests—the civilian versus the military economy, foreign adventurism versus détente, de-Stalinization versus neo-Stalinism—revealed themselves in the course of both men's regimes. Khrushchev's downfall did not end the post-Stalin tension between reformist and reactionary factions within the Kremlin. The major difference was that, under Khrushchev, each side thought it possible to prevail at the other's expense. During Brezhnev's rule, a middle road, albeit one tilting in a conservative direction, provided the fulcrum on which policy rested. Freed of the drama of the Khrushchev years, the political system's natural inclinations were even more clearly displayed.

THE EMERGING NATURE OF THE POLITICAL SYSTEM   Almost immediately upon Khrushchev's ouster the new leadership moved to steer Soviet policy along paths that, from the regime's point of view, seemed more traditional and predictable. The emphasis on de-Stalinization was abandoned rapidly: the dictator was never fully rehabilitated, but it became permissible to recognize his role in Russia's rapid industrialization and wartime victory, and denunciations of his terror became muted and infrequent. As during previous transitions, personal rule yielded to collective leadership, whereby the principal reins of power were held initially by Brezhnev, Kosygin, Podgorny, and Suslov. The movement toward economic reform was replaced by a renewed emphasis on the necessity of centralized management, the regime's priorities leaning away once again from the consumer and toward military growth. Khrushchevite policies at times did find their defenders, but they were, invariably and without much difficulty, checked by the new and more conservative consensus.

An early instance of apparent deviance involved Nikolay Podgorny, who appeared especially intent on identifying with the Soviet consumer. In a speech delivered in May 1965, Podgorny declared that the time when the Soviet people had to accept "material restrictions" had ceded to a time when this was no longer justified by the claims of heavy industry, or even by *defense needs*.[18] In many ways his views were reminiscent of Malenkov's, and they carried the same implications for détente. The conservatives counterattacked in a speech by Suslov wherein it was proclaimed that "the imperialist powers are pursuing the arms race and unleashing military aggression first in one then another part of the world." Accordingly, international reality required "considerable material sacrifices from the Soviet people and the appropriation of a major part of the National Revenue for defense."[19] Notwithstanding, Podgorny's apostasy called for a response. In December 1965, Brezhnev arranged for his transfer to the largely ceremonial position of Chairman of the Supreme Soviet and, at the Twenty-Third Communist Party Congress in April 1966, Podgorny was dropped from the Party Secretariat (though he retained his Politburo membership).

Khrushchev's successors quickly moved to reverse his earlier attempts to erode military spending. The 1965 Soviet state budget, the last prepared under Khrushchev, aimed at paring official defense outlays by some 500 million rubles. By contrast, the new leadership programmed a 600-billion ruble *increase* into declared defense expenditures for 1966, and additional increases followed in subsequent years.[20] At the same time, the Brezhnev regime abandoned all talk of favoring strategic rocket forces at the expense of traditional military services. This did not mean that nuclear missiles would be slighted in future planning, merely that all facets of military growth would be attended to simultaneously.

The ground forces—at which Khrushchev's budget-cutting axe had been aimed most intently—were an immediate beneficiary as were, in the longer run, Soviet naval forces. Although US involvement in Vietnam made it easier to argue for comprehensive military growth, the major impetus came from the new leadership's altered values and the manner in which it defined the system's interests. The renewed attentiveness to military interests was at first facilitated by economic conditions. During its first years at the nation's helm, the Brezhnev Politburo benefited from a reasonably vigorous economy, which allowed the regime to postpone difficult choices. In addition to expanded military programs, the Eighth Five-Year Plan (1966–1970) sought to promote growth in all sectors; this was the first and conceivably the last time the Soviet regime would be able to satisfy virtually all those who claimed a share of the country's resources. Had Brezhnev been compelled to face hard choices, it is likely the military sector alone would have been favored. Podgorny had been pretty much neutralized, and such conservatives as Kirilenko and Suslov emerged as staunch advocates of growing military power. Yet because economic needs could be addressed along a wide front, the scope for political infighting was correspondingly reduced. By the end of the decade, however, it became clear that the free lunch was over, and the trade-offs that were eventually established revealed the bias embodied in the Soviet political structure—a bias with obvious implications for Russia's US policy.

When work began on the Ninth Five-Year Plan (1971–1975) in the late sixties, certain points of friction developed. This time around, Kosygin emerged as the champion of the Soviet consumer and of nontraditional economic priorities. In December 1967 Kosygin called for the accelerated development of light industry and food production; two months later he urged that the public be provided with an "uninterrupted and varied supply of foodstuffs,, clothing, and other consumer goods."[21] Against this, Brezhnev argued for "preserving the accelerated development of heavy industry as the basis of our military might."[22] In December 1968 the

Soviet Ministry of Defense joined the fray by praising heavy industry as "the bedrock" of socialist power.

As the SALT negotiations were about to get underway, the position of the defense industry in the Soviet system of national priorities became the focus of controversy. Kremlin conservatives clamored for vigilance against the "imperialist" enemy, emphasizing the importance of military strength in protecting the interests of the Soviet Union and of international Socialism. In light of the emerging conservative consensus, no Soviet leader could go very far toward easing US-Soviet tensions; accordingly, President Johnson's 1967 and 1968 overtures toward the Soviet Union were generally rebuffed.

It should be noted that although the new regime leaned considerably further toward conservatism and military interests than its predecessor, *extremes* in that direction were not countenanced. Alexander Shelepin, chairman of the Soviet Party-state Control Commission and former KGB chief, embarked on an early, but unsuccessful, campaign to outflank Brezhnev on the political right[23] as did, even more persistently, Petr Shelest, the Ukrainian party leader. During the late sixties, Shelest identified closely with the economic interests of the defense establishment and pressed for a more assertive attitude toward Western Europe. He opposed normalization with West Germany and showed far more enthusiasm for an ideologically militant foreign policy than was compatible with improved East–West relations. However, such views did not prevail. Displaying his preference for a conservative yet essentially centrist position, Brezhnev resisted the arguments of the ideologues who "struggled tirelessly against those who wished to blur the image of a world divided between socialist good and imperialist evil."[24] Progressively, the Brezhnev regime gravitated toward détente.

THE POLITICS OF DÉTENTE   By 1970, accommodation with the West unexpectedly became the cornerstone of Soviet foreign policy, its appeal rooted in expectations of both external and domestic benefits. China's emergence as Russia's most immediate adversary made it more urgent than earlier to minimize security threats from the West; it was hoped that détente with the United States would discourage the Nixon Administration from strengthening its ties to Beijing (Peking). It must also have occurred to the Kremlin that normalized relations with the industrialized democracies might weaken military and political bonds within the Western world itself, further reducing overall Soviet fears.

Although Soviet foreign policy objectives were an important reason for seeking détente, anticipated domestic payoffs should not be slighted. Moscow's interest in improved East–West relations coincided with signs of a Soviet economic slowdown and a growing realization that future growth would benefit from access to Western goods and technology. The average rate of Soviet economic growth during the 1950s had been right at six percent, but this dropped to about five percent in the 1960s and to below four percent in the early seventies.[25] 1969 was especially disappointing as food production on the one hand, and iron and steel production on the other hand, fell considerably short of expectations. It became clear that growth rates could not be maintained, much less improved, without significant increases in economic productivity—itself dependent on access to improved technology. As early as 1966, Kosygin had been arguing for increased technological imports but, initially at least, Brezhnev deferred to the sensibilities of the leaders who most feared dependence on the capitalist world. However, as the new economic reality sunk in, a Politburo consensus emerged in favor of expanded commercial dealings with the West and, for the first time since the Cold War's outbreak, the traditional Soviet biases were temporarily offset by economic necessity.

Indeed, in the early seventies it seemed that bilateral trade might get off the ground. In 1972 a commercial agreement was signed whereby a number of major machinery orders were placed by the Soviets, and Russia's purchase of US grain amounted to one-quarter of American grain production for that year. Yet despite its promising beginnings, economic cooperation did not manage to surmount the political obstacles placed in its path.[26] Some of these obstacles originated in the United States, where strong domestic pressures militated for continued confrontation. Such pressures yielded the Jackson Amendment to the 1974 Trade Act—linking *most-favored nation status* to increased emigration of Soviet Jews—and produced the Stevenson Amendment to the 1974 Trade Act—significantly restricting the use to which the Soviets were allowed to put US export credits. Although these initiatives were rooted in domestic political conditions, they had a predictably damaging effect on superpower relations. Irked by what they viewed as gratuitous barbs, and aware they were being denied some of the major economic rewards they had expected from détente, the Soviet leaders abrogated the 1972 trade agreement with the United States.

It is interesting to speculate on the course events would have taken had commercial relations managed to get off the ground, but their collapse altered the configuration of domestic forces that had made détente politically acceptable within the Soviet Union. The political advantage to those urging cooperation with the capitalist world had always been precarious and, by the mid-seventies, those who had taken a dim view of economic cooperation felt vindicated—especially since it also became apparent that Soviet hopes of driving a wedge between the United States and China had been disappointed as well.

US attitudes aside, détente as a foreign policy goal never managed to rise above the pursuit of narrowly instrumental benefits throughout the Brezhnev era, which in turn had much to do with the ideological inclinations, and the pattern of interests, shaping the Politburo consensus. Politburo conservatism largely was rooted in the type of leaders comprising its membership. Almost without exception these were men who rose through the power structure during Stalin's rule,[27] and who owed their current positions to active participation in, or at least passive concurrence with, Khrushchev's ouster.

The regime's predilection for hefty military outlays and opportunistic international militancy also may have been related to the links between military and foreign policy-making elites that had congealed during the Brezhnev years. In his quest for expanded power at the expense of others within the collective leadership, Brezhnev sought a closer alliance with military elites than his predecessors had thought appropriate. Brezhnev's links to Marshal Grechko and Admiral Gorshkov were in many ways politically beneficial, and he cultivated an image as sponsor of military interests by promoting himself first to Army General and then to Marshal of the Soviet Union.[28] The military found that it enjoyed greater institutional autonomy,[29] and that it was integrated more closely into the upper echelons of political decision making than ever before.

In 1973, Brezhnev sought to increase the weight of the regime's foreign policy consensus by elevating the heads of the three principal national security bureaucracies—Foreign Minister Gromyko, Defense Minister Grechko, and KGB Chief Andropov—to full Politburo membership. In addition, national-security decision making increasingly was vested in a Defense Council that included senior military and Politburo figures and that answered to the Politburo. Brezhnev's action brought together the principal institutional interests within the defense establishment and bestowed on major decisions in this area sufficient authority to immunize them against criticism from elsewhere within the Soviet elite.

Political power thus was concentrated in the hands of those whose interests and beliefs were associated with domestic conservatism and an assertive international posture. This outcome, combined with the internal resistance to cooperation that had emerged within the United States, ultimately proved incompatible with détente. Although the Kremlin continued to press for agreements that would endow the rivalry with controlled predictability, it did not estimate the likely rewards from moderation to be sufficiently high to merit restraint in the Third World or to deprive itself of the benefits of military growth. By this time too, Brezhnev seems to have muted any significant source of opposition to his policies that might have come from a reformist direction. In the spring of 1977, Podgorny was definitively purged from the leadership and stripped of his position as Chairman of the Presidium of the Supreme Soviet. Though Kosygin continued to press for consumer interests and improved agricultural productivity, by the mid-seventies his influence was insufficient to threaten Brezhnev's priorities—which included a continued emphasis on heavy industry, referred to as "the foundation of the economy,"[30] a priority that was reaffirmed in the Eleventh Five-Year Plan (1981–1985).

Thus, in the late 1970s, a firmly rooted conservatism combined with the pragmatic pursuit of external gain came to dominate Soviet policy. Significant challenges to established methods and priorities became inconceivable, as demonstrated in Brezhnev's insistence that détente did not imply a relaxation of the "international class struggle" and that fundamental differences between US and Soviet foreign policy objectives had by no means vanished. Although détente was meant to reduce the risk of nuclear war, Brezhnev explained that it ultimately would place the Soviet Union in an even stronger position to confront the "imperialist" powers, recognizing that "we make no secret of the fact that we see détente as the way to create more favorable conditions for peaceful socialist and communist construction."[31] The domestic political structure cultivated by Brezhnev clearly was not geared to promoting a fundamental reassessment of Russia's US policy in the absence of dire necessity or major American incentives.

## Gorbachev and the Politics of Reform

By the time General Secretary Gorbachev came to power in 1985, the prospects for meaningful change had improved considerably. To begin with, the Soviet Union's foreign and domestic problems had become more serious. Matching President Reagan's massive rearmament program strained the country's resources, but was essential if Russia were to maintain the rough strategic parity with the United States it had attained during the seventies. Moreover, the Kremlin's attempts to create discord between the United States and its Western European allies over the issue of medium-range nuclear force deployments had failed. And difficulties with the West were compounded by losses in the Third World. Russia's influence in the developing regions was slipping: attempts to reinject itself into Middle Eastern politics were going nowhere, and most of the influence and respect it had once enjoyed elsewhere in the Third World were already lost. Finally, and despite certain continuing irritants, relations between the United States and China showed no signs of fraying—heightening Russia's sense of hostile encirclement. Traditional Soviet foreign policies simply were not serving the Soviet Union's international objectives, and there was no reason to think that the situation would improve without a radical change of course.

Domestically, the sense of lethargy and the reality of stagnation no longer could be ignored, especially within the economy. Andropov already had criticized the country's industrial and agricultural performance, and by stressing improved labor discipline had encouraged a five-percent growth in industrial production during the early part of 1983.[32] But these gains were almost immediately lost under Chernenko and, when Gorbachev came to power, it had become evident that minor tinkering with the economic mechanism would not shake it out of its torpor. At the same time, political apathy and cynicism had deepened even further, becoming the dominant attitude of the Soviet public. The joint impact that consumer dissatisfaction and political alienation had produced in Poland must have impressed the Kremlin as a consequence it too might face in the absence of decisive reforms.

Not only was the need for change more urgent than before, but the regime had become more willing to tackle its problems—a willingness facilitated by the generational turnover at the uppermost levels of leadership. Several major holdovers from the Stalinist era had departed in the years preceding Gorbachev's accession to power: since 1982, the Politburo had lost seven members (Suslov, Kirilenko,

Brezhnev, Pel'she, Andropov, Ustinov, and Chernenko); whereas during this time, only two new members (Aliyev and Solomontsev) had joined it. Moreover, Gorbachev himself had achieved a political career entirely in the post-Stalinist period. As Archie Brown has pointed out, a "Soviet political leader who began his full-time political career in 1955 had a better chance of retaining or acquiring a relatively open mind than one who had first set his foot on the bottom rung of the ladder 20 years earlier."[33] Thus, by 1985, the prospects for major reform in the Soviet Union were exceptionally good.

THE NEW LEADERSHIP    Gorbachev understandably devoted most of his first months in office to consolidating his position—removing from office as many of the remnants of the Brezhnev era as possible and replacing them with politicians who, while not necessarily Gorbachev's clients, shared his dynamic attitude toward national policy. Within his first six weeks as party chief, five new members—three full members and two candidates—were added to the Politburo[34] and by the end of 1985, Grigorii Romanov, Leningrad's former party boss, and Victor Grishin, Moscow's party chief, were ousted. Both had been conservative hardliners and both were regarded as Gorbachev's leading political rivals. During his first year in office, he also appointed 30 new ministers (out of a total of 80).

At the 27th Communist Party Congress in February 1986, Gorbachev again took on the Brezhnev Old Guard—replacing almost half the Central Committee and much of the Secretariat with younger members. Although resistance was not neutralized, these personnel changes created a critical mass within the leadership on which the new leader could call in support of his reform programs. By 1987, Gorbachev's actions had crystallized into as explicit and radical a set of policies as the Soviet Union had witnessed in decades. The emerging tension has pitted an entrenched structure of political and economic interests, as well as of established habits, against the requirements of the system's own welfare.

THE THRUST OF INTERNAL REFORM   By the end of Gorbachev's second year at the helm, domestic reform crystallized around two foci. The first, *glasnost* (openness) involves the nation's overall political and cultural climate. The second, *perestroika,* addresses the economic, and to some extent political, structure of the Soviet Union. The two are related, since the Soviet government's ability to restructure the economy will depend on the society's readiness to shake off its lethargy and cynical indifference to national policy. In turn, the government must relax its traditional shackles on thought and expression.

Conspicuous instances of glasnost include the release of prominent critics of the Soviet regime. In February 1987, dissident Andrei Sakharov was freed from forced internal exile in the town of Gorky. Sakharov's release was preceded by that of other major dissidents, such as Anatolii Scharansky and Yuri Orlov. During the same month, 140 political prisoners were freed and press censorship was lighter than it had ever been since the heyday of Khrushchevian liberalism. Stalin's terror again drew official denunciation. Georgian director Tengiz Abuladze's film "Repentance," which dealt with the moral consequences of Stalinist terror, received the regime's tacit endorsement. Anatoly Rybakov's novel, *Children of the Arbat,* detailing the mass repression of the Stalinist period, was excerpted in a Soviet weekly magazine 20 years after it had been written, and Boris Pasternak's *Doctor Zhivago* was removed from the list of proscribed publications. Major national problems were aired in the media, including such sensitive matters as organized ethnic unrest in non-Russian republics.[35] A series of articles in *Pravda* even exposed the misconduct of several KGB officials charged with illegally arresting a reporter who had uncovered corruption in a coal-mining region of the Ukraine. Everything is relative—but freedom of expression in the Soviet Union had never attained such heights.

Although the program of economic reform took longer to congeal, it ultimately proved to be more radical than expected. The costs of entering the twenty-first century with the existing economic machinery appeared intolerable,and

Soviet economists were encouraged to develop new ideas for revamping its increasingly creaky mechanisms. Limited operational scope was permitted for individual small businesses, and farmers were allowed to sell more goods at market prices. Most importantly, a new economic program was presented to the country at a meeting of the party's Central Committee in June 1987;[36] its proposals were almost as radical as Lenin's New Economic Policy of the 1920s. The program's core comprised a partial dismantling of the two linchpins of Soviet economy: rigid central planning and subsidized pricing.

Planning mechanisms were not to be abandoned, but their role would be reduced by granting greater autonomy to the enterprises themselves. The state planning agency, *Gosplan,* no longer would decree the minutiae of national economic activity but would, henceforth, merely provide overall guidelines and broad strategic plans (and ensure that the military had sufficient resources), while the enterprises would fill in the details. At the same time, Gorbachev called for a "radical reform" of the elaborate system of controlled, and often heavily subsidized, pricing, by which prices of more than 200,000 goods were set by the government. The Gorbachev plan envisaged the development of direct links between enterprises (e.g., a manufacturing plant and a supplier of raw materials) that would negotiate prices at the wholesale level between themselves. In this way, elements of price determination by supply and demand would be introduced. The same Central Committee meeting (at which three new full members and Gorbachev allies were added to the Politburo) decided that the New Economic Mechanism, an apparent reference to Lenin's New Economic Policy, would be implemented fully by the Thirteenth Five-Year Plan beginning in 1991. In January 1988, enterprises producing 60 percent of the country's industrial goods were placed under a system that permitted bankruptcy for unprofitable enterprises; by 1990, the system is to include virtually all Soviet industry.

In his book *Perestroika,* Gorbachev hinted at a significantly greater future role for market mechanisms.

"Enterprises," he explained, "must be put in such conditions as to encourage economic competition for the best satisfaction of consumer demands and employees' incomes must strictly depend on end production results, on profits."[37] Whereas a reformer previously could have been considered someone favoring consumption and investment over military needs, along with minor tinkering to improve the economy's efficiency, now the very cornerstones of socialist economics were to be ground down.

As might have been expected, glasnost and economic reforms were accompanied by attempts to alter important features of the Soviet Union's political system. By 1988 it became accepted officially that "civic" organizations, including non-Communist groups, could play an active role in Soviet political affairs. At the same time, Gorbachev called for a "major reform of our courts," to grant them greater independence from political pressure and to protect the rights of defendants. In a major departure from Communist political practice, an extraordinary party conference in June 1988 (the first since 1941) decided that, henceforth, competitive elections and the secret ballot would be used to elect party and government officials, and that their tenure would be limited to two consecutive five-year terms—eliminating the ossification of leadership that previously had characterized Soviet politics. At the same conference, delegates agreed to transfer significant power previously exercised by the Communist party to the national legislature and to a head of state entrusted with broad powers over both domestic and foreign policy.

Never within living memory has so much happened so fast within the Soviet Union. Because foreign policy is, as argued consistently, largely a product of domestic political structure, it is natural for the Gorbachev reforms to be associated with radical movement on the international front as well.

THE REVIVAL OF FOREIGN POLICY   The first signs of the new Soviet diplomacy orientation were apparent by the middle of 1986. In attempting to allay European fears about its intentions, the new Soviet administration avoided crude propaganda in favor of frank summitry and bold arms-control initiatives. Although relations with China have resisted significant improvement, medium-level negotiations on various aspects of functional cooperation got underway and the tone of Sino-Soviet rivalry lost much of its earlier stridency. Moreover, the Soviet Union abandoned its heavy-handed attitude toward the Third World in favor of a more flexible, and ultimately more successful, diplomacy.

The altered Soviet diplomacy was especially apparent regarding the Persian Gulf. A decade before Gorbachev's assumption of power, the Russians had been effectively shut out of the Middle East: Kissinger's diplomacy had succeeded in drawing most of the Arab world away from the Soviet Union and, by the time of Carter's Camp David agreement, the Kremlin was playing no major role in Arab-Israeli politics. Russia's consistent support of the communist side in internal struggles in South Yemen and in Oman further estranged moderate Arab governments, and the invasion of Afghanistan even further alienated the Muslim world. Gorbachev, however, moved to shore up his country's position in the Middle East, and did so in a generally restrained and skillful manner. He managed to create a foundation of low-level diplomatic contacts with Iran, making it less likely that Teheran would strive to export Islamic fundamentalism to the USSR Central Asian republics, and making it harder for the United States to recover its former influence over Iran. At the same time, Moscow continued to arm Iraq, thus acquiring some potential leverage over the course of the Gulf war between these two countries. The Kremlin also established diplomatic ties with Oman and the United Arab Emirates, and chartered several tankers, together with a modest amount of naval protection, to Kuwait whose own vessels were under Iranian attack in the Gulf (prompting the United States to establish a naval presence in the Persian Gulf). The Soviet Union also took tentative steps toward normalizing relations with Israel. All in all, the Gorbachev regime has conveyed a solid preference for diplomacy over gunboats, and has projected an image of restraint and caution.

Gorbachev's most dramatic initiatives concerned relations with the United States and, most specifically, arms control. The collapse of SALT II left the Soviets with an adversary economically and technologically better equipped to conduct an all-out arms race, and President Reagan's early arms-control proposals seemed designed primarily to ensure their rejection by the Kremlin. The most prominent among such Reagan proposals was the so-called "zero-zero" option on medium-range nuclear missiles of November 1981, the crux of which was that each side should eliminate all its medium-range missiles in Europe. Although superficially a reasonable offer, it actually was far less than balanced: the Soviet Union already had deployed a substantial arsenal of such weapons, whereas the United States cruise missile and Pershing IIs would be deployed only if political opposition within the host countries could be overcome. Moreover, the proposal would still leave the Soviets facing British and French medium-range missiles, while none of its allies had an independent nuclear force with which to confront the West.

Ultimately, however, the Soviet Union's concessions led the way to a version of the zero-zero arrangement and, although Western Europe's decision to accept the American missiles affected Russia's trade-offs, the decisive factor was Gorbachev's readiness to compromise. At first the Kremlin sought to link a medium-range missile agreement to substantial curbs on the US Strategic Defense Initiative (Star Wars) program—as during the impromptu summit in Reykjavik in October 1986—but Washington would not budge. The Soviet leadership then agreed to de-link the two issues, but continued to insist on concessions regarding British and French missiles, and preferred to retain 100 medium-range missiles in Asia (while allowing the United States to keep the same number on US territory). But the West stood firm and, on this issue too, Moscow gave in. Suddenly the United States was faced with the prospect of having to accept what amounted to its own earlier proposal. However, Washington hardliners demurred, and the United States responded that a bargain would have to include USSR *short-range* missiles as well. To the Administration's astonishment, the Soviets agreed to this demand as well, making a "double zero" arrangement (i.e., one including the removal of both medium- and short-range missiles) possible. Russia's unprecedented flexibility cleared the way toward the first significant *arms-reduction* treaty between the superpowers, which was signed by Reagan and Gorbachev in December 1987.

Within the next several months, the Kremlin also sought to move toward an agreement on conventional-force reductions in Europe. Responding to a long-term Western concern about the Soviet Union's nonnuclear armament superiority in Central Europe, Moscow agreed to accept asymmetrically large cuts in its own forces, urging that both the NATO and Warsaw Pact alliances alter their military postures in the region—from one stressing *offensive* capacity to one emphasizing *defensive* forces.

Although rapid progress on nuclear arms control was the most apparent expression of Russia's newly forthcoming attitude, other bits of evidence pointed in the same direction. For example, as the Central American peace process gained momentum in the summer of 1987, the Soviet Union decided to restrict its aid to Nicaragua's Sandinista government, mainly in the form of reduced oil shipments—the idea being, in all likelihood, to make it easier for Washington to downgrade the level of US support for the Contras. When Libya appeared ready to supply Iran with mines for possible use against US naval forces in the Persian Gulf, Moscow joined Washington in dissuading the Libyans.[38] In response to American concerns that a large Soviet radar station at Krasnoyarsk, Siberia, might represent a violation of existing arms control agreements, the Soviets invited a delegation of US congressmen to visit the installation.[39] While there the visitors took over 1,000 pictures of the radar installation—something that would have been fantastically inconceivable at any previous time.

In February 1988, the Kremlin announced plans to pull

out of Afghanistan in the course of a year—without insisting on the maintenance of a pro-Soviet government. And by August, on schedule, fully half of Russian forces had returned home. Actually, there remained little reason to doubt that the character of USSR policy had changed. All this did not mean that the Soviet Union had abandoned its role as superpower, with all the implications for opportunistic action that this carries. But it was becoming evident that the pursuit of diplomatic position had displaced the search for ubiquitous military advantage, and that controlling the arms race and decreasing the risks of superpower war had come to dominate Russia's foreign policy priorities.

POLICY OPTIONS AND DOMESTIC CONSTRAINTS   Gorbachev's departure from his predecessors' foreign policies is connected closely to the process of domestic reform—a link he has candidly recognized. In a speech delivered in February 1987, Gorbachev declared that Russia would have to seek international stability so as to be able to concentrate on solving its domestic problems: "Our international policy is more than ever determined by domestic policy, by our interest in concentrating on constructive endeavors to improve our country."[40] And although such statements may be designed partly to portray the Soviet Union in a nonthreatening light to the outside world, they also reflect an objective reality and must, therefore, be taken seriously.

The reallocation of economic resources within the Soviet Union requires not only economic cooperation with the capitalist West, but the sort of international climate unlikely to skew national priorities toward external militancy (hence high rates of military spending) and ideological rigidity. Even though Gorbachev's efforts and the generational succession have altered the Soviet leadership's composition, the beliefs and interests of political elites cannot be expected to change overnight. Existing patterns of political rewards and established habits of thought continue to constrain the regime's foreign policy latitude. Nevertheless, successful political and economic reform may encourage the development of a structure of interests and power decisively favoring reform over stagnation. Nonetheless, it is inconceivable that such a transition could be accomplished without substantial domestic resistance from the multitude of entrenched interests that represent the legacy of neo-Stalinism in Soviet politics.

Gorbachev described the situation as "an acute, uncompromising struggle of ideas,"[41] and all indications point to a protracted conflict within the Soviet polity. Thus far, opposition to the reforms has been rooted in various levels of society. In spite of the fact that the composition of the Politburo did not, as of 1987, favor the Brezhnevite Old Guard, it was not Gorbachev's passive instrument either. At least two men have surfaced as sources of conservative opposition within this body. The first is Vladimir Shcherbitsky, party chief of the Ukraine, and a politician in the old mold—distrustful of economic reform, détente with the West, and internal liberalization. The second is Yegor Ligachev, the chief ideologue and number-two man in the party hierarchy. Ligachev seems to empathize with the need for economic restructuring while feeling that liberalization and criticism of past practices is going too far.[42] His major concern, and of like-minded Soviet leaders, is a fear of undermining the Communist system's legitimacy by discrediting too much of its past.

Despite potential pockets of resistance within the Politburo, it is probable that the main body of opposition to glasnost and perestroika is located at lower levels of the political structure: from the Central Committee and governmental ministries to the factory manager, to the grass roots of Soviet society.[43] To a large extent the resistance involves entrenched interests—people adapted to and benefiting from the traditional way of doing things: the ministerial bureaucrat whose authority is challenged by reform, the party professional whose position is subjected to the uncertainties of intra-Party elections, the factory manager who must face the rigors of increased market competition, the worker who fears an increased workload and possible unemployment. And values and habits, as well as vested interests, create resistance to change: the military officer or ideologue who views accommodation with the West as a compact with the devil, the citizen whose previous pattern of expectations and values is being shattered.

Gorbachev's proposals at the June 1988 party conference to transfer significant power from the Communist party to a head of state with vastly increased responsibilities and to the legislature suggests that, in the search for political backing for reform, it is easier to boost the power of less refractory governmental bodies than to expect significant change within the party itself, where conservatism is most firmly entrenched.

Generally, however, organized opposition to Gorbachev is not expected. The more likely scenario involves subtle and passive resistance that erodes the pace of progress or discredits reforms by making them appear ineffective or counterproductive. The future of Gorbachev's initiatives, both domestic and external, will remain uncertain for some time to come; their significance for our purposes is that they represent the first attempt since Stalin's death to introduce meaningful political and economic change in Soviet politics that carries inevitable consequences for Russia's foreign policy as well.

## THE DOMESTIC ROOTS OF FOREIGN POLICY

The stretch of historical experience surveyed thus far reveals that in the Soviet Union, as in the United States, there exists an interplay between domestic politics and foreign policy, making the latter comprehensible only in terms of the former. No Soviet leader since Stalin has been able to ignore the pressures and constraints that existing patterns of interests and beliefs, and the configuration of domestic political power, have placed before him. The political reward structure that has evolved in the Soviet Union has, for the most part, encouraged distrustful interpretations of America's intentions as well as cautiously assertive behavior. At crucial junctures in superpower relations, this evolution has led the Kremlin to neglect genuine opportunities for improved relations. Hesitant Soviet attempts at altering the traditional course of foreign policy occasionally have been attempted, but were usually the temporary outcome of a power shift at the pinnacle of the political system. Because such attempts were never associated with meaningful changes in the over-all *structure* of power, the impact on foreign policy has always been ephemeral.

For our purposes the most striking and abiding similarity between the two superpowers is that, within both, the punishments for erring on the side of unwarranted conciliation have consistently been greater than those meted out for erring on the side of unjustified hostility—and it has never been apparent that the rewards for legitimate cooperativeness would be any greater than those for justifiable toughness. Accordingly, and with only occasional exceptions, national leaders have found it politically wiser to tilt their policies toward confrontation whenever there was any ambiguity about the other side's intentions and capabilities. For the Soviet Union, as for the United States, this bias has been the product of dominant patterns of interest, beliefs, and power.

## The Functions of Conservative Ideology

When examining the domestic sources of America's Soviet policy we noted the role played by goals of *pure policy,* namely those linked to political beliefs rather than vested interests. Such goals have affected Russia's policy toward the United States as well. Although we are not (as explained in Chapter 2) dealing with a strictly ideological society, a rudimentary system of Marxist belief, and a set of widely repeated clichés and slogans, are part of the official framework of ideological reference and have shaped the general contours of national political priorities. Articles of official political faith are adhered to for several reasons: they may be found attractive and compelling in the abstract, they may provide a convenient rationalization for a situation from which one derives a personal benefit—and very often both circumstances apply. Whatever the grounds for political beliefs, ideological precepts that consecrate an existing distribution of benefits are, necessarily, conservative precepts. Accordingly, the central ideological cleavage in the Soviet Union is not between communism and democracy but between *conservatism* (which strives to replicate the past in the present) and *reformism* (which seeks to transcend both past and present). Reformism has been most closely associated with Khrushchev and Gorbachev; conservatism with Stalin, Brezhnev, and the lower tiers of the political structure. Of the two, conservatism has been the indisputably dominant tendency of the Soviet Union's postwar history.

The most effective form of political organization in the conservative perspective is one that concentrates power at the apex of the Party-state. In turn, this concentration implies that there is a single truth, a single set of valid priorities, and that the goal is not to fashion optimal polices through the confrontation of ideas and interests but to implement without challenge those polices known to be "correct" by the reigning oligarchy. The economic corollary is rigid central planning. Neither the marketplace nor those directly responsible for production (the enterprises, agricultural producers) best understand what should be done and how— this understanding is the sole prerogative of the bureaucratic pinnacle. Moreover, inasmuch as tradition has emphasized certain sectors (e.g., heavy industry) and not others (e.g., consumer goods), this must have been the correct emphasis; arguing otherwise would challenge the elemental wisdom of the Party-state. A natural implication of this thinking is that dissent is illegitimate; it cannot strengthen the social fabric or contribute to effective policy because there are no recesses of doubt within which it can operate validly. Dissent is simply pernicious—and must be repressed.

Such are the tenets of conservative Soviet orthodoxy; and they were, to a varying but always substantial extent, part of the priorities of such people as Beria, Kaganovich, Molotov, and Kozlov during the Khrushchev years, most members of the Brezhnev Politburo (especially men like Shelepin and Shelest), and such conservative opponents of the Gorbachev reforms as Shcherbitsky and, to some extent, Ligachev. These tenets also run below the top levels of leadership and permeate most strata of the political system.[44]

Foreign policy consequences flow naturally from conservative assumptions. A regime that invariably is right naturally will be considered threatening by political systems that, being very different, are necessarily wrong and are fighting the flow of history. Accordingly, military force is required to discourage capitalism's predatory intentions, and the secrecy of a closed society is required to thwart its more subversive designs. Support for the military establishment and the security police is the natural inclination of Soviet conservatives, for these are the services "that guard order against change, native tradition against 'alien' influences, the present against the future."[45] To the extent that the interests of such institutions are connected to some level of international tension, the result of their association with the dominant ideological conservatism is a strict limitation on permissible conciliation with foreign adversaries.

Brezhnev was a conservative closely associated with détente. But this was not inconsistent for, from Brezhnev's point of view, the underlying purpose was to make it easier to postpone meaningful internal change. Foreign technology would provide a respite for the ailing Soviet economy, and the regime's legitimacy would be strengthened by its acceptance as an equal by the United States. Thus, for Brezhnev, accommodation with the West never had more than a shallow and instrumental value, and its failure was predictable in retrospect.

Conservative ideology is therefore a central determinant of a political reward structure that traditionally has limited permissible cooperation with the United States. It cannot, however, be disentangled from the pattern of *interests* that has dominated Soviet life.

### Vested Interests and Foreign Policy

We cannot assess the degree to which conservatism reflects disinterested beliefs as opposed to cynical rationalization of the social and political rewards enjoyed by certain social strata. Still, several segments of Soviet society derive direct professional and personal benefits from a political system organized around conservative precepts. That these precepts should come to dominate their thinking, and that they may be genuinely believed, is not really surprising; nevertheless, it is necessary to identify, as closely as possible, the nature of the interests that stand to profit from the established pattern of political and other rewards and, especially, from some measure of East–West tension.

It is a widely held, and considerably oversimplified, view that the Soviet ruling elite (the so-called *nomenklatura*) is driven to expansionism by self-serving interests. Yale's Wolfgang Leonhard, for example, maintains that "the nomenklatura is by its very nature expansionist. It knows that it can keep and consolidate its power inside the Soviet Union only if it can point to foreign policy successes."[46] Other students of Soviet behavior draw a more nuanced picture by recognizing that the Soviet elite is not monolithic and that certain vested interests are in fact better served by successful détente than by militant confrontation.[47] It even has been suggested that a political party that has monopolized power is likely to have *more* internal diversity (albeit below the surface) than a party in a multiparty system—since there is no organized alternative outside the Party-state—[48] and that no single foreign policy goal can be imputed to heterogenous interests.

Several lines of fission course through the Soviet power elite and society (we shall address certain of these); however, there is little doubt that the dominant pattern of interests during the past several decades, like the dominant pattern of values, has been fundamentally conservative. A political elite that brooks no active opposition is likely to encourage, albeit incrementally, a system of political, social, and economic rewards that preferentially benefits its members—either in terms of their personal or their organizational interests—and its conservative predilections are, partly at least, linked to a desire to maintain the system thus created.

A traditional party bureaucrat or government administrator cannot lay a strong claim to power and its perquisites unless it is accepted that power must indeed be concentrated within the Party-state, an assumption that has been easier to justify in Russian history under threatening international circumstances. Accordingly, there probably has been a level of conciliation with the West beyond which many Soviet leaders were not willing to go—because of calculated self-interest as much as for purely ideological reasons. Some interests, moreover, are linked to superpower rivalry in a very specific, though not invariably simple, manner.

By many criteria, US-Soviet relations impinge most powerfully on the fortunes of the Soviet *military* establishment, and its role should be examined in some detail. Two questions in particular suggest themselves: What are the natural inclinations of the Soviet military on matters of East–West policy? and, Is the Soviet defense establishment in a position to actually influence the foreign policy decisions of the civilian leadership?

Like their US counterparts, Soviet military leaders are not generally active champions of East–West détente. Never reckless, they nevertheless have usually favored an assertive foreign policy, having adopted a dim view of chances for long-term accommodation with the United States. Military officers frequently have stressed the pitfalls of arms control agreements, and have pressed energetically for adequate concessions from the West. As Timothy Colton has observed, some of the most outspoken statements on the dangers of détente during the Brezhnev years came from the Main Political Administration (MPA), an arm of the military bureaucracy. This body, which has been referred to as one of the "centers of neo-Stalinist sentiment,"[49] is entrusted with overseeing political indoctrination in the armed forces and with monitoring the military's adherence to party policy.[50] Most fatefully for détente, the military was in the forefront of those arguing for the adoption of a globalist and interventionist foreign policy in the seventies, the very policy that turned many Americans against the idea of cooperation with the Soviets. In 1974, Marshal Grechko, the Soviet defense minister, explained:

> At the present stage the historic function of the Soviet Armed Forces is not restricted to their function in defending our Motherland and the other socialist countries. In its foreign policy activity the Soviet Union purposefully opposes the export of counter-revolution and the policy of oppression,

supports the struggle for national liberation, and resolutely resists imperialist aggression in whatever distant region of our planet it may appear.[51]

This assertion of an "equal right to meddle in Third Areas"[52] may have reflected ideological conviction, but it probably had even more to do with organizational interests since, in an era of nuclear stalemate, the expansion of the military's resources and missions—the essence of any bureaucracy's concerns—depends extensively on an activist foreign policy, especially with regard to the developing regions of the world. A basically cautious but nevertheless forceful approach to dealing with the United States is the natural preference of the Soviet armed forces, a policy that is no more conducive to superpower accommodation than are the inclinations of the US military. Nevertheless, we must ask how great an impact the Soviet defense establishment can hope to have on the foreign policy decisions of the Party-state?

Although sustained dissent from the civilian leadership's policies is not tolerated, leading military officers are not simply passive executors of the civilian will. Within certain bounds they *are* in a position to affect national security policy and the Kremlin's US policy, and their ability to do so flows from several sources.

To begin with, the Soviet military establishment is able to influence the *selection* of political leaders at times when civilian authorities are divided; therefore, their policy preferences cannot be ignored by prudent politicians. In 1957, for example, Nikita Khrushchev's position was saved through the assistance of his defense minister. The Presidium, at the instance of the "anti-Party" group, had agreed to oust Khrushchev; however, Khrushchev did not meekly comply, being helped by Defense Minister Marshal Zhukov who provided air-force planes to convene the Central Committee that, when assembled in Moscow, overturned the Presidium's decision.[53] We have also seen how Brezhnev thought it useful to secure military support as a way of bolstering his political position. And when Brezhnev died in 1982, Marshal Dmitri Ustinov, defense minister and a full member of the Politburo, provided the decisive support that ensured Andropov's rise to power over Konstantin Chernenko.[54] Thus the specter of the Soviet defense establishment's power can never be dismissed entirely, as its role has often been decisive during power struggles. Accordingly, one assumes that Soviet politicians cannot afford the luxury of ignoring the military's views on major foreign-policy issues.

A second, and perhaps as significant, source of Soviet military influence springs from the close identification of civilian authorities, as well as of Soviet society as a whole, with the values and goals of the armed forces. Russian political culture simply is less averse than the political culture of many other countries to seeing things from the military's point of view. Many leaders of the pre-Gorbachev generation were active participants in World War II. Moreover, even as war memories fade it must be expected that a history so strongly shaped by warfare and armed resistance would make both civilian and military leaders sensitive to the need for military preparedness and wary of the external world.

Soviet armed forces have been well-placed to influence the course of defense procurement, and thus the course of US-Soviet military rivalry, in another way as well. Far more than in America, the Soviet military has guarded a jealous monopoly on sensitive military information and knowledge not easily available to the civilian leadership.[55] The Kremlin has no equivalent of the civilian defense intellectuals and think-tanks available to US political leaders (e.g., the Brookings Institution, the Rand Corporation, the Congressional Research Service, and the Office of Technology Assessment), and thus has been less able to second-guess military interpretations of security needs and of foreign threats.[56] Although it is difficult to trace the impact this quasi-monopoly on information has had at various junctures of the Cold War and détente, because the defense establishment ordinarily does not harm its organization interests by understating the US threat, the impact is far more likely to have had an exacerbating than a mellowing effect on the rivalry between the two superpowers.

The Soviet military, unlike its US counterpart, lacks the ability to influence policy by creating alliances with other sources of political power (such as the legislative branch or public opinion); nevertheless, this does not mean it is without domestic allies. Not surprisingly, its most important support has come from heavy industry and, especially, from those segments of heavy industry primarily engaged in military production. The interests of the two are in many ways symbiotic and, while the exact forms of their interaction are not known by Western observers,[57] the institutional contexts that bring them together are easier to identify.

Soviet defense production has been the responsibility of several industrial ministries, a number of which work almost exclusively for the military sector.[58] These various industrial ministries respond to orders placed by the Ministry of Defense, and are associated with a variety of research and development institutes whose principal task is to design weapons systems (see Table 5-1). The integration of Soviet industrial ministries into the political process is ensured in several ways.

Ministerial heads are members of the Council of Ministers that, according to the Soviet constitution, is "the highest executive and administrative organ of state power."

## Table 5-1
### Principal Defense Ministries in the Soviet Union*

| Ministry of | Major product |
| --- | --- |
| Defense (industry) | Conventional arms and equipment |
| Aviation (industry) | Aircraft |
| Shipbuilding (industry) | Naval vessels |
| Radio (industry) | Electronic systems and radiotechnical equipment |
| Electronics (industry) | Electronic components for other ministries |
| General machine building | Ballistic missiles and space systems |
| Medium machine building | Nuclear weapons |
| Machine building | Ammunition |

Source: *In 1985–1986—in an effort to streamline the system of ministries—Gorbachev grouped them within a number of closely related complexes, placing over them a superministerial body headed by a deputy prime minister. See Ed A. Hewett, *Reforming the Soviet Economy: Equality versus Efficiency* (Washington, DC: The Brookings Institution, 1988), pp. 335–337.

Further, they are members of the Communist Party of the Soviet Union's Central Committee. The Military Industrial Commission traditionally has been an especially important institution in the area of military industry.[59] Its task is to supervise the work of defense producers, and it functions as an interface between central political authorities (in this case the Politburo and the Defense Council) and the ministries responsible for defense production. The Commission also appears to have some say in matters of national security policy, as suggested by the fact that its officials have "figured prominently" in US-Soviet strategic-arms limitation talks.[60]

Scholars disagree on whether one can speak advisedly of a Soviet military-industrial complex. On the one hand it has been observed rightly by David Holloway, an expert of Soviet military politics, that neither the defense industry nor the armed forces have been in a position to *dictate* governmental policy and that they do not have an independent power base.[61] On the other hand, these are rather restrictive qualifications for a military-industrial complex (in these terms, one would not exist in the United States either), and a looser conception might be more useful.

Vernon Aspaturian, another student of Soviet politics, argued in an earlier study that if a military-industrial complex is thought of as a "symbiotic sharing of interests" between military, industrial, and high-ranking political figures whose collective influence often allows them to shape policy in accordance with their joint interests, then such a complex does indeed exist in the Soviet Union.[62] But according to Aspaturian:

> What converts the functional role of the military establishment and the defense industries—the core of the Soviet military-industrial complex—into a political role is the support they receive from and, in return, give to heavy industry and *the conservative wing of the party apparatus* (emphasis added).[63]

Thus there is reason to believe in the existence of a tripartite alliance between the military, heavy industry, and party conservatives who together benefit from a national perception of external threat, the maintenance of tight controls over domestic dissent, and the suppression of consumer interests. Although some disagreement is inevitable within the ranks (party conservatives might desire greater political control of the armed forces, whereas officers dislike civilian meddling in military affairs), in all likelihood a strong core of common interests does exist.

According to Aspaturian there is little doubt that "the military, heavy industry, and the apparatus have benefited immensely from policies justified by perceptions of external danger."[64] Generally too, these group interests have been on the side of domestic conservatism rather than reform. And this circumstance should come as no surprise. After all, a relaxation of domestic political controls would be hard to reconcile with the crisis mentality on which their group interests depend, and a greater emphasis on producing consumer goods would jeopardize their own resources.

## THE SHIFTING IMPACT

A generally conservative set of ideological tenets and a comparably conservative set of vested interests—revolving around the preferences of party professionals, the military establishment, and some sectors of the economy—have decisively impacted on Soviet policy, and their influence has affected foreign as well as domestic policy.

We established earlier that the political reward structure of the United States has nudged America's Soviet policy in a hostile direction; yet we also identified several recurring circumstances that have made this policy, at times, either particularly bellicose or unusually accommodating. Recurring political rhythms are less likely to characterize authoritarian systems, where change tends to be linear (if the regime is enlightened) or discontinuous and crisis-induced (if it is not). Nevertheless, some regularities are apparent on the Soviet side as well. Post-World War II history suggests that the circumstance weighing most heavily in favor of a more conciliatory Soviet stance toward the United States has been the emergence of a leader whose domestic priorities deemphasize heavy industry, rigid planning, and safeguarding the privileges of an ossified Party-state bureaucracy in favor of attempts to decentralize political and economic authority and to do more for the Soviet consumer. Although Khrushchev and Gorbachev are the best examples of such leaders, Gorbachev's tenure by Soviet standards is in its infancy and Khrushchev's experience demonstrates that conciliatory foreign policies are domestically riskiest when the leader's position is being challenged, and vice versa. Thus the political security of a leader with progressive domestic priorities portends a future of cooperative Soviet external behavior.

But even a conservative leadership may favor limited détente under certain conditions—in anticipation of economic benefits from cooperation with the West, for example. This was certainly the major boon that Brezhnev expected from the thaw in Soviet-American relations during the late sixties and early seventies. Khrushchev too hoped that one payoff of the "spirit of Camp David" might be heightened US interest in trade with Russia, and better economic relations certainly have been on Gorbachev's mind as well. By the same token, Brezhnev's disenchantment with détente, and his consequent unwillingness to subordinate Russia's geopolitical interests to its pursuit, resulted partly from the failure of economic cooperation to get underway.

We must again appreciate the extent to which a craving for prestige, especially for international recognition as America's equal, has molded Soviet attitudes toward the United States. Soviet dignity and status were almost an obsession with Khrushchev and Brezhnev; both leaders exulted in the implications of equal status conveyed by US-Soviet summitry. And it is likely that Jimmy Carter's criticism of Russia's human rights policy offended the Kremlin as much by its impression of patronizing superiority as by its challenge to the political practices of Soviet communism. As Stephen Cohen has accurately observed:

> [The] prestige factor can cause them to postpone, or even jettison, international relations that they otherwise desire. . . .
> On the other hand, when they perceive a ratification of Soviet prestige it can lead them to join in international agreements that included provisions not to their liking. . . .[65]

At the same time, a number of circumstances have accounted for the ephemeral quality of the Soviet Union's cooperative gestures toward the West. To some extent, this has resulted from a US foreign policy that, rooted in America's internal political conditions, often has made it difficult for American leaders to take major conciliatory steps. For example, resistance within the United States to granting the USSR credits and "most-favored nation" status meant that the Soviets would not receive the economic payoffs they desired from détente, and strengthened the hand of those in the Kremlin who consistently had opposed extensive dealings with the capitalist world. Similarly, the U-2 incident—a boost to Kremlin hardliners—made it harder for Khrushchev to garner political support for his domestic reforms and for a policy of coexistence with the United States.

Ultimately, however, it is the pattern of rewards and punishments traditionally running through Soviet politics that has been the major obstacle to restraint in foreign affairs. The pattern is rooted in the power enjoyed by those interests and beliefs that have regarded conciliation with disfavor; however, it must be remembered that the Soviet political system has never been characterized by a uniform system of preferences. And when discrepant interests are associated with an altered structure of domestic political power, changes in the Soviet Union's external priorities become likely.

Alexander Yanov has distinguished between three potential clusters of interest within the Soviet Union. The first is a conservative, Brezhnev-style, coalition that includes party professionals, the military-industrial complex, and the central economic bureaucracy. These are the group interests that have been politically dominant during the past several decades—and they bear much of the responsibility for the stagnation that afflicted the Soviet Union during the sixties and seventies. The second cluster of interests and beliefs is of a reformist bent, encompassing labor and metropolitan elites, the intelligentsia and professional class, as well as certain factions within the national leadership. It is this second coalition that has been most willing to back meaningful reform and détente with the West. The third—and possibly the most disturbing—coalition is a reactionary alliance that includes a religious and Great-Russian movement within the national leadership, the military-industrial complex, and unskilled workers and peasants. According to Yanov, this extreme right-wing coalition would pursue an anti-Western and anti-semitic policy in the guise of a return to "traditional" (i.e., prerevolutionary) Russian values.[66]

Divergent interests can be found within the *state* itself. Were the Soviet Union a democracy in the Western mold, interest groups would emerge at various levels of society: some might exist within the network of institutions that comprise the government, whereas others would originate outside its ambit, in what is referred to as *civil society*. Because in Russia the scope of civil society is very restricted, most policy factions are nested in the state, especially within the bureaucracies—the natural repositories of vast and structured interests. When these factional interests collide, and in Russia they often do, the result is a system of "institutional pluralism,"[67] wherein policy is shaped by the pull of organizations and interests within the Party-state. Given that Russia lacks an autonomous civil society, the regime is nondemocratic; nevertheless, because policy is frequently the outcome of a struggle of interests within the state, it is not the classical dictatorship of an individual or of a homogenous and cohesive oligarchy. Moreover, these plural interests are affected by, and in turn influence, the Soviet Union's US policy.

Institutional pluralism is sometimes reflected within the very center of the bureaucratic apparatus. For example, it has been argued that in 1968 different parts of the foreign policy establishment took contrasting positions on the issue of invading Czechoslovakia to crush the mildly liberal Dubcek regime.[68] Party bureaucrats charged with indoctrination and maintenance of ideological orthodoxy, as well as KGB officials—fearing that the Czech "disease" would pose a problem to the containment of domestic dissent, thus impeding their own organization's mission—generally supported military intervention. Decision makers responsible for foreign affairs, mainly officials of the Foreign Ministry, and

even those in the Central Committee responsible for relations with Western communist parties—fearing that an invasion would complicate their jobs by alienating foreign
countries—were not inclined to support the idea.

Occasionally, these institutional cleavages reflect more
than the parochial interests and perspectives of bureaucratic
groups—involving, for example, the conflicting economic
interests of the military establishment and the consumer, or
of light industry and heavy industry. The point is that institutional cleavages do exist, and that a coalition of interests
preferring cooperation to confrontation with the West and
pressing for a restructured set of domestic priorities can be
identified. Such coalitions, having tentatively emerged in the
past, have always been at a disadvantage in the overall Soviet power structure, and attempts to reorient State policy
have always been short-lived. One of the objectives of the
concluding chapter is to suggest the conditions under which
this scenario may no longer be as true in the future.

## NOTES

1. Nikita S. Khrushchev, *Khrushchev Remembers* (Boston: Little Brown,
   1970), p. 395.

2. For example, when preparing for the trip to the United States, the
   Soviet delegation was informed that a stay of a few days at Camp
   David had been scheduled. Neither Khrushchev, nor the Soviet em-
   bassy in Washington, nor the Ministry of Foreign Affairs had the
   slightest idea what or where Camp David was. Khrushchev recalled
   in his memoires:

   > One reason I was suspicious was that I remembered in the early
   > days after the Revolution, when contacts were first being estab-
   > lished with the bourgeois world, a Soviet delegation was invited
   > to a meeting held someplace called the Prince's Islands. It came
   > out in the newspapers that it was to these islands that stray dogs
   > were sent to die. In other words, the Soviet delegation was being
   > discriminated against by being invited there. In those days the
   > capitalists never missed a chance to embarrass or offend the Soviet
   > Union. I was afraid maybe this Camp David was the same sort
   > of place, where people who were mistrusted could be kept
   > in quarantine.

   *Khrushchev Remembers: The Last Testament* (Boston: Little Brown, 1974),
   p. 371.

3. Same as 2, p. 374.

4. Henry A. Kissinger, *Years of Upheaval* (Boston: Little Brown, 1982), p. 231.

5. Same as 2, pp. 382–383.

6. Same as 2, p. 361.

7. On this point, see Dimitri K. Simes, "Soviet Policy Toward the United States," in Jospeh S. Nye Jr., *The Making of America's Soviet Policy* (New Haven: Yale University Press, 1984), p. 299.

8. The most comprehensive treatment of the Politburo is provided by John Loewenhardt in *The Soviet Politburo* (New York: St. Martin's Press, 1982).

9. *Pravda,* March 13, 1954.

10. Myron Rush, *Political Succession in the USSR* (New York: Columbia University Press, 1965), p. 60.

11. See Roy Medvedev and Zhores Medvedev, *Khrushchev: The Years in Power* (New York: Norton, 1977), p. 75.

12. Same as 2, p. 451.

13. *Pravda,* May 18, 1960. The politics surrounding this episode are described in Michel Tatu, *Power in the Kremlin* (New York: Viking Press, 1967), pp. 63–68.

14. Carl A. Linden, *Khrushchev and the Soviet Leadership, 1957–1964* (Baltimore: The Johns Hopkins Press, 1966), p. 114.

15. Same as 14, p. 152.

16. Same as 13, Tatu, p. 273.

17. As George Breslauer pointed out, "Even at the height of his counteroffensive, the First Secretary's pronouncements sounded like those of a politician who was on the defensive politically." *Khrushchev and Brezhnev as Leaders: Building Authority in Soviet Politics* (London: George Allen & Unwin, 1982), p. 108.

18. *Pravda,* May 22, 1965.

19. *Pravda,* June 5, 1965.

20. Sidney Ploss, "Politics in the Kremlin," *Problems of Communism,* May–June 1970, pp. 5–6.

21. Same as 20, p. 8.

22. Same as 20, p. 8.

23. In response to the Jackson Amendment to the US-Soviet Trade Bill, Shelepin apparently had urged, as a retaliatory measure, that the Politburo send "volunteers" to Portugal on the model of the Soviet Union's support for the Republican forces during the Spanish Civil War. The purpose was to benefit from possible instabilities following the collapse of the Caetano dictatorship. On this, see Arthur Macy Cox, *Russian Roulette: the Superpower Game* (New York: Times Books, 1982), p. 34.

24. Harry Gelman, *The Brezhnev Politburo and the Decline of Détente* (Ithaca, NY: Cornell University Press), p. 88.

25. U.S. Congress, Joint Economic Committee, *USSR: Measures of Economic Growth 1950–1980* (Washington, DC: U.S. Government Printing Office, 1982), p. 15.

26. There were nonpolitical obstacles to expanded economic cooperation as well. The nonconvertibility of the ruble was one obvious problem, and the structural incompatibilities between a market economy and a rigidly planned one was another.

27. See, for example, Seweryn Bialer, *Stalin's Successors: Leadership, Stability, and Change in the Soviet Union* (Cambridge: Cambridge University Press, 1980), Chapter 5.

28. Same as 24, pp. 92–95 and 105.

29. See Dimitri K. Simes, "The Military and Militarism in Soviet Society," *International Security*, Winter 1981–82, pp. 123–143.

30. Same as 17, p. 222.

31. Keynote address at the Twenty-fifth Congress of the CPSU, Moscow, February 25, 1976.

32. Zhores A. Medvedev, *Gorbachev* (New York: Norton, 1986), p. 90.

33. Archie Brown, "Gorbachev: New Man in the Kremlin," *Problems of Communism*, May–June 1985, p. 5.

34. The three new full members were Yegor Ligachev, Nikolay Ryzhkov, and Viktor Chebrikov. Ligachev, as we shall see, has emerged as a potential opponent of Gorbachev.

35. See, for example, "Soviet Ethnic Minorities Take Glasnost Into the Streets," *New York Times*, August 30, 1987; "Soviet Reports Major Unrest in Armenian Areas in South," *New York Times*, February 24, 1988.

36. For the text of Gorbachev's speech outlining the program, see *The Current Digest of the Soviet Press*, July 29, 1987. A good analysis of some of the obstacles to radical economic reform is found in Alec Nove, " 'Radical Reform:' Problems and Prospects," *Soviet Studies*, July 1987, pp. 452–467.

37. Mikhail Gorbachev, *Perestroika: New Thinking for Our Country and the World* (New York: Harper and Row, 1987), p. 86.

38. "U.S. and Soviet Protest to Libya Over Iran Mines," *New York Times*, September 11, 1987.

39. "Soviet Eyes on Sky: Questions of Trust," *New York Times*, September 20, 1987.

40. "Gorbachev Avows a Need for Peace to Pursue Reform," *New York Times*, February 17, 1987.

41. See Radio Free Europe/Radio Liberty, "Broad Resistance to Restructuring Gorbachev Favors Reported in Press," *Soviet, East Europe Report*, February 20, 1987.

42. See "No. 2 Soviet Official Puts in a Bad Word Against 'Glasnost,' " *New York Times*, September 24, 1987.

43. See Seweryn Bialer, "Gorbachev's Move," *Foreign Policy*, Fall 1987, pp. 59–87.

44. On the conservatism of Soviet society and its link with overall political conservatism, see Stephen F. Cohen, *Rethinking the Soviet Experience: Politics and History Since 1917* (New York: Oxford University Press, 1985), Chapter 5.

45. Same as 44, p. 132.

46. Wolfgang Leonhard, *The Kremlin and the West: A Realistic Approach* (New York: Norton, 1986), p. 80.

47. For example, Alexander Yanov, *Détente After Brezhnev: The Domestic Roots of Soviet Foreign Policy* (Berkeley, CA: Institute of International Studies, 1977).

48. Stephen F. Cohen, "Soviet Domestic Politics and Foreign Policy," in Fred Warner Neal, ed., *Détente or Debacle: Common Sense in U.S.-Soviet Relations* (New York: Norton, 1979), p. 15.

49. Same as 59, Holloway, p. 167.

50. A concise description of the MPA's functions is provided in Timothy J. Colton, "The Impact of the Military on Soviet Society," in Seweryn Bialer, ed., *The Domestic Context of Soviet Foreign Policy* (Boulder, CO: Westview Press, 1981), pp. 119–138.

51. Marshal A. A. Grechko, "Rukovodyashchaya Rol 'KPSS v Stroitel' stve Armii Razvitogo Sotsialisticheskogo Obshchestva," *Voprosy Istorii KPSS*, May 1974, p. 39.

52. The words are those of a Soviet official quoted in Alexander Dallin, "The Road to Kabul: Soviet Perceptions of World Affairs and the Afghan Crisis," *The Soviet Invasion of Afghanistan*, ACIS Working Paper No. 27, Center for International and Strategic Affairs, University of California at Los Angeles, September 1980, p. 57.

53. Fearing that Zhukov might feel that his assistance entitled him to a greater role in political decision making, Khrushchev fired his erstwhile supporter several months later.

54. Same as 32, p. 108.

55. This is also discussed in Miroslav Nincic, *The Arms Race* (New York: Praeger, 1982), p. 67.

56. See, for example, Condoleeza Rice, "The Party, the Military, and Decision Authority in the Soviet Union," *World Politics*, October 1987, pp. 55–81.

57. Some thoughts on the *economic* relation between the two is provided in George G. Weickhardt, "The Soviet Military-Industrial Complex and Economic Reform," *The Soviet Economy*, July–September 1986, pp. 193–217.

58. A description of military production arrangements is provided in Arthur Alexander, "Decisionmaking in Soviet Weapons Procurement,"

*Adelphi Paper No. 148,* International Institute of Strategic Studies, London, 1978; Mikhail Augursky and Hannes Admoeit, "The Soviet Military-Industrial Complex, *Survey,* Spring 1979, pp. 106–132; and same as 59, Holloway, Chapter 6.

59. The Military Industrial Commission is described in David Holloway, "Technology and Political Decision in Soviet Armaments Policy," *Journal of Peace Research,* XI, 1974, pp. 259–260 and in Jerry Hough and Merle Fainsod, *How the Soviet Union Is Governed* (Cambridge, MA: Harvard University Press, 1979), pp. 382–383.

60. Ellen Jones, "Defense R & D Policymaking in the USSR"; same as 68, p. 126.

61. David Holloway, *The Soviet Union and the Arms Race* (New Haven: Yale University Press, 1983), p. 159.

62. Vernon Aspaturian, "The Soviet Military-Industrial Complex— Does It Exist?" *Journal of International Affairs,* XXVI, no. 1, 1972, pp. 1–28.

63. Same as 62, p. 20.

64. Same as 62, p. 25.

65. Stephen C. Cohen, "The Friends and Foes of Change: Soviet Reformism and Conservatism," in Stephen C. Cohen, *Rethinking the Soviet Experience: Politics and History Since 1917* (New York: Oxford University Press, 1985), p. 132.

66. Alexander Yanov, *The Russian Challenge and the Year 2000* (New York: Basil Blackwell, 1987), Chapter 20 and p. 296.

67. The term is from Jerry Hough, "The Soviet System: Petrification or Pluralism," in Jerry Hough, *The Soviet Union and Social Science Theory* (Cambridge: Harvard University Press, 1977), pp. 19–48.

68. See Jiri Valenta, "Soviet Decisionmaking on Czechoslovakia, 1968," in Jiri Valenta and William Potter, *Soviet Decisionmaking for National Security* (London: George Allen & Unwin, 1984).

# CHAPTER SIX

◆　◆　◆　◆　◆

# The Implications

# THE ROOTS OF RIVALRY

We have seen the impracticality of equating the circumstances that accounted for the onset of Soviet-American animosity with those by which it subsequently has been driven. The history of Soviet-American relations was tempestuous long before the Bolshevik Revolution, and US willingness to think ill of Russia preceded the ideological cleavage that emerged in 1917. Against this background, and because communism has always stood for so much that is antithetical to US beliefs and values, it is not surprising that relations should have been as frayed as they were in the interwar period. And in the mid-forties, behavior by both sides provided additional fuel for their developing antagonism. Since then, however, forces of a different nature have controlled the rivalry.

Given that the course of Soviet-American relations has been as much determined by circumstances operating within the superpowers as by their reactions to each other's foreign policies, this does not imply that either side has been unwilling to respond to the rival's outright provocations. However, both the United States and the Soviet Union are much less likely to acknowledge signs of conciliatory intent. Moreover, since each country's behavior usually can be accounted for in more ways than one, interpretations are chosen largely on the basis of internal political inducements to view such behavior in either a threatening or benign light. In fact, an appreciation of how patterns of domestic incentives and disincentives shape US and Soviet foreign policies probably sheds more light on the rivalry than any of the three approaches surveyed in Chapter 1.

The demonological perspective establishes a direct link between domestic policies deemed repugnant and predatory external behavior considered their natural extension. This perspective is deeply ingrained in the American definition of its international situation, and it plays a large part in how many Soviet ideologues view the United States. Unfortunately, the demonological perspective provides no guidelines to improved relations (other than the collapse of the adversary's political system) and misses the more prosaic realities of how national foreign policies actually are formed—policies that are far more compatible with incremental adjustment to changing circumstances than with the grand strategies demonologists impute to the other side. The demonological perspective may be emotionally gratifying—and it requires minimal analytical exertion—but it is misguided as analysis and dangerous as a foundation for policy.

Starting from very different assumptions, realpolitik makes no specific assumptions about the incompatibilities that can propel nations into conflict, but merely presumes that such conflict usually happens in an anarchic world. Consequently, the pursuit of power is the goal of all countries, and foreign policies are as ambitious as relative power positions permit. Political realism is not inconsistent with demonological views, for the latter might assume that other nations are driven by malevolent designs and that they will do as much evil as their international power permits. Yet there is no *logical* link between the two approaches, for political realists—as long as they do not regard power as an end in itself—rarely have much to say about the motivational patterns that ultimately attend foreign policy. Accordingly, the contribution of the two perspectives to explaining the superpower rivalry has been modest, and we are impelled to search elsewhere for an explanation of why the United States and the Soviet Union should regard each other as adversaries.

Although similar judgments apply to game theory, game theoretic approaches have the virtue of clarifying the choices available to actors in situations of interdependent decision making and of demonstrating how suboptimal outcomes can be reached via decisions that individually are quite rational. With regard to US-Soviet relations, the prisoner's dilemma shows how the two superpowers—distrusting each other and considering their interests at least partly incompatible—fail to take cooperative steps that would benefit them both. Game theory may account therefore for the self-sustaining character of the rivalry, but sheds no light on the matter of where the assumption of incompatible interests and the mutual mistrust originates. In other words, the approach takes for granted that which most needs explaining. There have been efforts at integrating game-theoretic analyses of specific situations with attempts to account for the context that produced the game's payoff matrix,[1] but not much of this is directly applicable to superpower relations.

Because neither realpolitik nor game theory tells us where the rivalry originates—merely how it is likely to be conducted—our task has been to discover why the two sides have defined each other as adversaries in the first place, and to account for the upswings and downswings that their hostility has subsequently displayed. The process has been one of elimination, starting with the most apparent explanations and working toward those that are considered less often. The case for objective conflicts of interest proved fragile, for there are few plausible instances of situations where something desired in its own right by either side could be attained only at the other's expense. The most compelling incompatibilities involved the pursuit of the *means* with which to pursue the competition. However, since this approach assumes that a rivalry already exists, it cannot be its major cause. Thus we are left with the question of how derivative incompatibilities are sustained so effectively.

Psychological dynamics provide valuable clues but by no means a complete answer. Images define a level beyond which either side cannot easily take its cooperative gestures. And perceptual bias can substantially increase the amount of evidence needed to establish the rival's conciliatory intent compared to what is required when perceptual lenses are less tainted. But psychological explanations do not carry us far enough. Individuals can, and often do, overcome misperceptions through learning: Kennedy and Kissinger displayed an ability to bend with the evidence, and even President Reagan's perceptions of the Soviet Union evolved over the course of his two terms. Brezhnev's learning curve was flat and lifeless, but both Khrushchev and Gorbachev could adjust their views when stirred by experience. Not only can statesmen learn, but they can navigate around their perceptions if there is good enough reason for doing so. For example, the Cuban Missile Crisis convinced both sides that some level of accommodation was necessary, even though they continued to think ill of each other. In the absence of objective conflicts of interests, it is tempting to place most of the burden on images—but there is considerably more to the rivalry than an unfortunate pattern of mutual misperception.

By the late forties both nations had undergone a variety of *internal adaptations* to hostility; the Cold War encouraged the development of values and interests built around the rivalry, and the configurations of domestic political power in which they were imbedded. As a result, a bias emerged in favor of continued hostility within the political reward structures of both countries. As we have seen, political punishments for unjustifiable accommodation have been far greater than those meted out for unjustified hostility, whereas rewards for warranted accommodation have not been more substantial than those for warranted hostility. Accordingly, uncertainty regarding the most appropriate behavior generally has been resolved by slanting policy toward the confrontational side of the spectrum.

An important corollary is that challenges to political incumbency have been mounted more effectively from hawkish than from dovish positions. Eisenhower's campaign criticized Truman's Soviet policy for its insufficient assertiveness; Kennedy's campaign criticized Eisenhower's alleged willingness to let America's military strength slip relative to Russia's; and a cornerstone of Reagan's challenge to Carter was his denunciation of détente and call for increased anti–Soviet toughness. Similarly, Khrushchev's challenge to Malenkov included an indictment of peaceful coexistence; yet, when Khrushchev later espoused this very policy, he too fell victim to those who thought him insufficiently attentive to the US threat. Although Brezhnev never went so far as to invite serious political attack, those who oppose Gorbachev's foreign policy do so more often from hawkish than from pro-détente positions. Accordingly, beleaguered incumbents often seek to disarm their challengers by moving toward the confrontational end of the continuum. By extension, the most conciliatory steps toward the adversary are taken by leaders whose position is secure or appears to be increasingly secure.

The bias in favor of continued hostility is produced by several forces. The kinds of *values* at issue matter considerably and, because of the preeminent position that security has achieved over most other national values, an unwillingness to pursue a military edge is considered grossly irresponsible and punishable accordingly. At the same time, the values with which accommodation is associated are perceived more vaguely and diffusely; consequently, rewards for conciliatory behavior are tenuous, and political prudence encourages statesmen to err on the side of strength and assertiveness. Moreover, the interests of assorted groups within both countries depend on continued hostility, and traditionally their political power has exceeded that of groups whose interests are harmed by US-Soviet antagonism. Since policy ultimately reflects the relative power behind the various interests that it affects, the tilt toward continued confrontation is understandable. Under the circumstances, and within both nations, the underlying conflict no longer requires precise definition—especially when, as here, a generalized "image of the enemy" helps blur the distinction between the means and the ends of the contest. All this certainly applies to both the United States and the Soviet Union, but several differences must be noted as well.

The patterned regularity that democratic elections impart to US political contests is absent in Russia. Accordingly, while America's Soviet policy has developed a rhythm of sorts, the Soviet Union's policy toward the United States— to the extent it is affected by the competition between challengers and incumbents—displays this effect with no discernible periodicity. Because the rules of foreign-policy decision making are less stable in the Soviet Union, unpredictability is particularly pronounced. And because the implications of American actions for Soviet prestige matter so much to the Kremlin, the amplitude of the swings in Russia's US policy may be especially large.

At the same time, overreactions to Soviet behavior that

coincide with the development of major new weapons systems in the United States and that seem intended to foster a climate receptive to their procurement and deployment have had no parallel in the USSR. No doubt this is because the United States—the scientific and economic top dog between the two—has originated most of the military technologies in the superpowers' arsenals. Consequently, a strong case for counterprocurement can be made within the Kremlin on the basis of external evidence alone, lessening the need to mobilize support for the new system through an *internally* generated sense of imminent threat. Should the Soviet Union become the original developer of major military systems in the future, the logic of mobilizational overreaction could make its debut there as well.

Great differences between the two countries notwithstanding, the political reward structures underlying their East–West policies are cut along similar lines and have produced similar consequences for their relations with each other. One consequence, as we have seen, is that ambiguous evidence about the other side often is interpreted in unnecessarily threatening terms. Stalin's belief that the West's early appeasement of Hitler was meant to encourage the German dictator's designs on the Soviet Union is an example of warped interpretation. Moscow's conviction that the West's delay in opening the Second Front was intended to permit Germany and Russia to bleed each other dry is another example. There are, as well, many examples of biased US interpretations of Soviet behavior: Russian intentions in Turkey and Iran in 1946, Russian involvement in Cuban activities in Africa during the seventies. Although any explanation for the American bias is partly psychological, in all likelihood it was due also to US domestic politics.

In the same vein, authentic opportunities to move off the confrontational track were frequently not acted upon, and internal constraints on cooperation must bear some of the onus. America's hesitant responses to Khrushchev's overtures must be counted as one of the major missed opportunities for an early détente. Khrushchev's drive to reorient the Soviet Union's domestic priorities toward the consumer, agriculture, and light industry required an easing of superpower hostility, and the Spirit of Camp David held out a fleeting promise that this could be achieved. But by the end of the decade this hope had evaporated, largely because of US recalcitrance, which almost certainly had something to do with the 1960 presidential election. Accordingly, conservative pressures within Russia, especially following the U-2 incident, drove Khrushchev to harden his attitude and created internal conditions that may have made emplacement of missiles in Cuba seem like the solution to many of the Soviet leader's problems.

Throughout the seventies, détente was hobbled by the inability of both superpowers to place cooperation high enough on their hierarchy of objectives—a failing with many domestic roots. US unwillingness to grant the commercial concessions the Soviets had expected from détente, and the increasing assertiveness of anti-détente interests and hard-line values within the United States, diminished the utility of cooperation from the Russian standpoint. Geopolitical concessions could not be justified domestically, and arguments for military restraints must have had a hollow ring in the Kremlin's councils. By the same token, the lethargic ethos of the Brezhnev years—and the need to deal with arch-conservatives of the ilk of Shelepin and Shelest—meant that no more than instrumental value could be assigned safely to détente by the Soviet leadership, and this was insufficient to induce Soviet restraint when it most mattered to the United States. Likewise, the political pressures within America, which were part of the Second Cold-War mentality, made it hard for President Carter not to deal confrontationally with the Russians. Given the weight of domestic obstacles, cooperation could never have progressed very far, and the return to Cold War status seems unsurprising in retrospect.

The conventional view is that Soviet and US leadership react directly to each other's behavior. But the process is indirect as well. For political leaders respond just as strongly to their domestic political conditions, which, in turn, are often shaped by the other side's behavior. In game-theoretic terms, foreign-policy decision makers are engaged in two games. The first (presumably a prisoner's dilemma) is played with the other superpower; the second is played with the decision maker and his domestic political setting, where the payoff matrix of the second game is largely shaped by the course of the first.

To discuss the most effective ways of addressing the obstacles to Soviet-American cooperation, we must decide first just how ambitious we wish to be. Given that perfect harmony is too elusive a goal, the realistic aim, perhaps, is to achieve a stable state of constructive tolerance, wherein the cooperative elements of the relationship significantly outweigh its confrontational components. The danger of nuclear war through miscalculation, preemptive strike, or escalation from conventional conflict should shrink to trivial proportions, with the probability of a nonnuclear clash becoming negligible. The share of national resources that each superpower devotes to confronting the other should dwindle to a fraction of what it is now. Commercial and other exchanges, and an occasional willingness to tackle joint problems, should become part of the normal pattern of relations—although the two countries would matter less to one another than they currently do.

Of course, some things would not necessarily change. The distribution of international power is not easily altered, and the bipolarity that has characterized the international system during the past several decades might not, and need not, be replaced with a multipolar arrangement. In addition, genuine warmth of feeling between the two countries would not be a necessary part of the new arrangement. Even so, the suggested objectives would suffice to close the post-World-War II chapter in Soviet-American relations and to launch a new era in world politics. Notwithstanding that these are substantial objectives and that they may not be soon attained, it useful to identify the paths by which they could be pursued in principle.

Not every empirical conclusion yields useful policy guidelines; the primary purpose of scientific study is to identify the mechanisms that account for important phenomena. Generally we are satisfied to discover close associations between cause and effect, even when the most powerful causal levers may be those that, when identified, are the most difficult to move. Thus, policies that would produce the greatest impact if pursued are sometimes least likely to be selected. The purpose of this study then is to identify what is most important, not what is most malleable, and to target objectives that may not be attainable as well as policies that are more immediately feasible.

In principle, policy could be directed toward any or all three directions: toward the stakes of the rivalry, toward the psychological mechanisms that help sustain it, toward the domestic pressures that, if we are correct, are its major driving force. We shall consider each in turn.

## ADDRESSING THE STAKES

Plainly, US–Soviet antagonism cannot be divorced from its international context. Regional struggles in the developing world, a race in strategic weaponry, and rival positions in Europe provide the concrete stakes over which the two superpowers clash. It is significant that these clashes tend to be issues connected to derivative conflicts of interest, and of a predominantly military character. Military rivalry constitutes an authentic conflict of interest in that either side's gain is considered the other side's loss: every additional missile added to the other side's arsenal appears to create a dangerous vulnerability; every new client of one side is viewed as a threat to the other side's geopolitical position. In and of itself, however, military competition cannot be a primary source of antagonism unless a fair amount of hostility already exists for such things to matter. For example, Belgium does not feel threatened by Holland's military power nor does Norway worry much about Canada's. Nevertheless, superpower competition over relative military strength sharpens the antagonism by giving it a seemingly objective substance; by providing something over which to vie, the antagonism often is confused with its primal determinant.

Thus, derivative conflicts of interest help fuel a competition of which they are not the actual cause.

Acting on the *stakes* of confrontation is the approach to conflict resolution with the longest history. If two nations quarrel over some payoff (a piece of land, a commercial concession, a military ally), the solution may be to deal directly with the conflict in a way that will satisfy, or at least placate, the antagonists. This approach applies to stakes in both objective and derivative conflicts of interest.

A frequent solution to such a conflict is to divide the prize so that although no party gets all it desires, no party is sufficiently aggrieved to instigate a confrontation. During the wave of colonial expansion that focused on Africa between 1870 and 1914, the expanding European powers often found it necessary to carve out interest zones. For example, in 1885 the Germans negotiated spheres of influence with the French regarding the West Coast of Africa. Germany then reached similar agreements with Britain for those parts of Africa where "the interests of the two countries might conflict."[2] Within Europe, Poland was partitioned between contending powers on several occasions. The most recent example is the sundering of Europe into Soviet and US spheres of influence along lines drawn at Yalta. However, Germany and Korea present even more graphic instances of this approach to conflict resolution.

An alternative to carving up the prize is to compensate the party not acquiring it with some sort of "side payment." In 1911, for example, Germany was incensed at France's pretensions toward and obvious intention of annexing Morocco. The Germans protested, sending a gunboat to Agadir and encouraging Moroccan resistance to the French. The crisis was resolved finally by agreement to a French takeover of Morocco in exchange for a German extension of Cameroon in equatorial Africa (which may have been what Germany wanted all along). In a more recent but different example, the SALT I talks found Moscow initially insisting that any agreement should include US forward-deployed aircraft which, from their bases in Europe, could deliver nuclear payloads to Soviet territory. The Soviets thought this only equitable since the USSR had no comparable weapons within reach of US territory. The United States refused, insisting that only systems with an intercontinental range be included in the talks. In compensation for the Kremlin's willingness to drop its insistence on including forward-based systems (as well as for America's lead in number of warheads on certain categories of long-range missiles), the Soviet Union was allowed a larger number of strategic delivery vehicles.

A third solution is to remove certain stakes from the competition altogether. Although this cannot be achieved easily in a conflict over something regarded as desirable in and of itself, it can work in situations where both sides pursue the prize simply to stop the other from acquiring it. A foreign military installation or an ally, sought by parties already locked in conflict, are examples of stakes that contestants might be willing to renounce by mutual agreement. Traditionally this has been achieved by neutralizing disputed states and territories. Typically, a neutralized territory cannot be part of the other side's war effort nor can it join a military alliance, thus helping "to protect the weak from the strong but especially to protect the strong from themselves."[3] Examples include the neutralization of Switzerland by the Congress of Vienna in 1815 and the creation of a neutral Belgium in 1831. The decisions to establish the neutrality of Austria in 1955 and of Laos in 1961 are more recent applications of this method of conflict resolution.

Remedies with an established historical pedigree have a powerful attraction—their logic is easily understood and they have often been successful. Yet, we probably would not get far by making these the primary focus of efforts to change the course of Soviet-American relations. To begin with, many instances where such approaches have worked involved rivalries centered around conflicts of interest. On such occasions the value of even a share of the spoils, or of a compensatory side payment, was probably sufficiently attractive to make sustained antagonism pointless. Unfortunately, where the international stakes of the rivalry are dwarfed by their domestic roots, traditional modes of conflict resolution are less useful.

Solutions that fail to address the primary sources of hostility are unstable: they do not preclude the emergence of new, and possibly even more serious, issues over which to quarrel. Neutralizing Laos did little to check East–West tensions elsewhere in Southeast Asia; the division of Germany accompanied massive force deployments on either side of the common border; SALT I's ceiling on strategic missiles did not stop either side from increasing the number of warheads deployed on each individual missile, or of deploying new types of weapons not covered by the treaty (e.g., cruise missiles). Nevertheless, in the absence of a cure the value of a remedy cannot be minimized, and diplomatic efforts at resolving individual bones of contention should not be discarded. Such efforts tackle conflicts of interest, particularly those of a derivative nature, head-on, and make it less likely that the confrontation will be escalated further. Certain sore points provide a convenient handle for groups with a vested interest in sustaining hostility; if the sore points are eliminated, such groups have less to grab onto. Moreover, each spectacle of US–Soviet sparring nourishes hostile images and increases opportunities for dangerous misperceptions. Although particularly contentious issues may be symptoms of much deeper problems, many are nevertheless self-amplifying, and present a danger that neither US nor Soviet diplomacy can ignore.

## THE PSYCHOLOGICAL SUBSTRATUM

US-Soviet misperceptions probably are not the primary causal force behind the rivalry; they are, however, not irrelevant, and relations might be improved if certain psychological snares were avoided. An early example of a psychologically based prescription for ending the East–West confrontation was provided in the sixties by Charles Osgood, a social psychologist interested in international affairs. If, as Osgood reasoned, tensions are caused primarily by a chain of reciprocally hostile actions that flow from and amplify threat perceptions, the obvious aim is to *reverse* the process. To engineer such a reversal, one side must adopt a series of *unilateral* initiatives, yielding what Osgood termed Graduated Reciprocation in Tension-Reduction (GRIT).[4]

The idea is that rewards for acts that dampen hostility are more effective tools of perception modification than punishments for those that increase it. Accordingly, the side initiating GRIT undertakes a series of conciliatory moves toward its adversary. Although such moves should never seriously jeopardize national security, they should amount to more than merely cosmetic gestures. In addition, the moves should be unambiguously friendly and appear entirely voluntary (to avoid being attributed to duress). Moreover, the gestures should be made without regard to reciprocity—an unmistakable demonstration of sincerity is the object, not an immediate *quid pro quo*. Eventually, both sides revise their opinion of the other, threat perceptions are reduced, and appraisals of the other's actions become more objective and rational.

This proposal rests on an intuitively appealing logic: if the hostility-creating process can operate in one direction, why not simply turn things around and make it operate in reverse? Nevertheless, there are grounds for skepticism. To begin with, it is not clear that cooperation between rivals is best encouraged by unilaterally extended conciliatory moves. Robert Axelrod has argued that a tit-for-tat strategy—where one always reciprocates both hostile and friendly acts but avoids an unreciprocated form of either—may be the most effective way to engender cooperation in relations at least partly conflictive.[5] In other words, one does not advance cooperative relations by appearing too nice. Even if the GRIT principle is based on correct psychological assumptions, it may nevertheless be undermined by domestic politics. It is likely that the nation taking the first cooperative steps would have a considerably more restricted idea of what is required to establish sincerity than its rival would. Although the initiator might believe it had done more than enough to establish its good faith, the recipient might regard such gestures as tricks designed to lull it into misguided complacency, and thus require much longer to become convinced than political pressures within the initiating country will permit.

A dangerously counterproductive situation arises if the recipient nation interprets the conciliatory moves as a sign of weakness (as Dulles was prone to do regarding the Soviet Union) and hastened to adopt a more implacable line of its own. Even if this situation does not develop, it remains that when conciliatory moves are taken by national leaders

> the probabilities are all too high that the competence, courage or patriotism of one or both sets of elites will be challenged by a "hard line" domestic opposition, be it a legitimate political party in a democratic system or a less institutionalized faction in a more autocratic system.[6]

A major barrier to the policies proposed by Osgood may be the domestic political risks they entail.

Robert Jervis has addressed the typical psychological problems in a more direct manner. If striving to reduce cognitive dissonance and a need to make incoming information compatible with existing beliefs distort perceptions of others and our understanding of the best way to deal with them, then we must simply learn how to avoid such traps. The thrust of Jervis' prescription is that decision makers should become more self-consciously aware of the perceptual errors they commonly make and should be more sensitive to the full range of possible explanations for the other side's behavior.[7] For example, if American leaders doubted Soviet readiness to comply with its arms control obligations, and if this suspicion flowed from a need to maintain cognitive consistency in the face of American dislike of Russia's political system, then an awareness of the basis for American distrust might demonstrate, to their satisfaction, that the suspicion is unwarranted. According to Jervis the first step is to compel decision makers to scrutinize the reasoning behind their policies by making their assumptions more explicit.

Because institutional blinders shape images of the outside world, Jervis argues that leaders should not permit organizational identity to influence answers to questions that should be decided on empirical and logical grounds alone. He further urges decision makers to ensure that conflicting policy preferences among their subordinates are heard and that a variety of analysts, with different perceptual predilections, are asked to tackle the evidence. In fact, "devil's advocates" should be encouraged as a matter of explicit policy.[8] In this manner options are not foreclosed by what social psychologist Irving Janis has called "groupthink,"[9] and decision makers can improve their ability to recognize the perceptual distortions to which they may fall victim.

What are we to think of these prescriptions? On the one hand, Jervis is right to believe that perceptual distortions are avoided most effectively by improved awareness of the mechanisms of reasoning and image formation. If all that he prescribes were implemented successfully, images probably would be more accurate, means would be related to ends more sensibly, and frictions in US-Soviet relations would be reduced. But Jervis is asking decision makers to annul their psychological machinery, and that is asking much indeed.

The assumption is that a conscious desire to reduce perceptual bias can be made more powerful than the deeply imbedded psychological mechanisms by which it is created—but it is difficult to act against human nature through the medium of human nature. For example, the suggestion that devil's advocates be encouraged may be unrealistic, as Jervis himself recognizes.[10] Pressures for compliance with group thinking are extremely powerful, and only the most committed devil's advocate is likely to take that role beyond its minimal requirements. In addition, the opinions of someone cast in the role of devil's advocate are not likely to be considered seriously, inasmuch as such opinions probably would be attributed to the assigned role rather than to authentic beliefs. Finally, if the role is of a pro-forma nature, the practice may serve actually to reinforce bias: the decision makers ultimately may claim that their opinions remained unchanged despite their willingness to listen to opposing points of view—which only goes to prove how valid these opinions must be.

An awareness of the ways in which perceptions can be warped and information twisted to conform with preexisting beliefs should be promoted whenever possible; and although it is difficult to act against one's psychological inclinations, this sometimes can be done. As we have seen, statesmen can learn from experience, and may even act contrary to their perceptions when their interests so dictate. The problem is that in US-Soviet relations, political calculations generally do not so dictate—quite the contrary. Soviet and American leaders typically have acted confrontationally toward each other, not just because of the psychological difficulty of doing otherwise, but also because of the political risks and costs of cooperative behavior. As domestic pressures represent hostility's first layer of causality that, if left untouched, ensures that most policies produce but ephemeral benefits, then the road toward meaningful improvement in US-Soviet relations begins *within* each country's political system.

## ADJUSTMENTS FROM WITHIN—A FIRST GLANCE

The paramount question is whether the structure of domestic inducements can be modified so as to balance, from the perspective of each nation's leaders, the political rewards of confrontational and conciliatory policies or, even better, whether the rewards of accommodation can be made to exceed those of hostility. In either case a harmful bias would be eliminated, and US-Soviet relations could develop more easily on the basis of objective issues that are not deeply conflictive and that ordinarily could be resolved through diplomatic mechanisms of conflict resolution. Although hostile perceptions might continue to exercise a drag on East–West conciliation, there would be fewer obstacles to effective learning and the political costs of *ignoring* negative images when mutual interests so demand would be reduced. As we have seen, political reward structures are determined by a combination of values and interests of politically significant groups, and any effort to modify such structures must take these values and interests as a point of departure.

### Values and East–West Confrontation

The punishments for misguided accommodation toward the other side arc greater than those for misplaced hostility largely because the superpowers, as indeed most other nations, place national security at or near the pinnacle of their hierarchy of values. Generally, security is defined as the absence of threats to those interests that, as a nation, we care about most—especially the physical well-being of our population, the integrity of the normative order, and the health of the economy. Because all such values can be assaulted from abroad, the primacy of national security is understandable; what is less apparent is why national security is viewed almost exclusively in *military* terms or why its enhancement is defined so single-mindedly as the amassing of armed might. Thus a natural inclination, when addressing the issue of value modification, is to urge a more nuanced, and less militarized, conception of national security.

For example, it can be observed that the very things theoretically protected by military power can also be harmed through the process of its acquisition. Most obviously, much of the hardware and technology acquired through the pursuit of military strength may augment the destructiveness of conflict, should it occur, and hence increase the damage to population, normative order, and economy. Given that the destructiveness of potential conflict should be brought into the equation more explicitly, even this is only part of the picture. When we speak of enhancing national security, we imply that both of two benefits are obtained: an improved ability to prevail over an aggressor and a decreased likelihood that aggression will occur. But this second desideratum is, at best, related ambiguously to the process of augmenting one's military power.

On the one hand it appears that the stronger one is, the lesser the likelihood of foreign aggression. On the other hand, the likelihood also depends on the aggressor's assessment of the need to act militarily against an adversary. This need may be particularly acute when relations are tense, and arms races necessarily generate tension through the mutual threat perceptions they kindle. Moreover, some military systems undermine rather than enhance deterrence. The danger is that either side may acquire the ability to undertake a disabling first strike against the other; if relations deteriorate far enough, each side may see an advantage to making the first strike— and may act accordingly.

Military growth and security are not necessarily incompatible, but the relationship is complex and can work both ways. Theoretically it is conceivable that a more comprehensive and nuanced view of superpower relations would encourage both countries to place the value of armed force in a different perspective; a flawed concept of national security might, then, no longer sustain US-Soviet hostility. But not too much should be expected in this regard: even if the debate on national security became more sophisticated, other values, as well as concrete interests, would continue to militate against conciliation.

In significant pockets of both societies, hostility has become a value in and of itself: toughness toward the rival has achieved the status of an elevated moral principle, proving fealty to the values for which one's own nation is supposed to stand. Any mellowing of attitude toward the adversary renders one's loyalty to domestic principles suspect; therefore, hostility should never falter. Such positions are not associated merely with right-wing purists in the United States or neo-Stalinist ideologues in the Soviet Union. American moderates, and even liberals, often display implacably Cold-War attitudes similar to those of arch-conservatives. Moreover, in the USSR pugnacity toward the West is not solely a product of *communist* ideology, but also of a New Right that has emerged recently as a nonmarginal political force whose hallmarks are a reverence for Russia's historical roots (including the Orthodox church), a belief in communal

Russian values, anti-Semitism, and a dogmatic and virulent anti-Westernism.[11] Accordingly, tension cannot be mitigated merely by promoting an extended conception of security, since hostility often appears as a value in its own right, not just as an appendage to national security.

The manner in which core values and beliefs can be addressed most effectively depends on their source. Beliefs are not necessarily the result of considered reflection; sometimes beliefs derive from intellectual habits, and frequently they correspond to a specific pattern of interests. As history teaches major societal actors which values are most congruent with advantages they wish to acquire or maintain, these values come to permeate a society's belief system. Although individuals or organizations may not consciously articulate the relation between their personal or institutional interests and foreign policy, the link is often there; when it is activated, foreign policies register the impact. Perhaps then the most effective way of addressing values is via the interests from which they flow, for by acting on interests one is acting at two levels simultaneously—the interests themselves and the values they yield.

### Addressing Interests

Under Mikhail Gorbachev the Soviet Union has made significant moves toward a more conciliatory international stance; nevertheless, many established interests within the country would have difficulty adapting to a world with no tension. Claims to power by party professionals would be frail indeed if the need to maintain ideological orthodoxy in a hostile world were not taken seriously. The authority of government officials would slip without a need to regiment society in the face of a quasi-permanent state of emergency. The military establishment would be harder-pressed to justify its position within the bureaucratic hierarchy and the demand it places on economic resources if the capitalist world seemed much less menacing.

Vested interests are tied to Cold-War attitudes in the United States as well. US national-security bureaucracies promote their institutional weal as vigorously as their Soviet counterparts, and they too would founder in placid international waters. When such bureaucratic needs so dictate— as when new military systems clamor for justification—they are prepared to encourage a perception of heightened external threat. And powerful economic interests also are connected to the arms race. Athough society would almost certainly benefit from a demilitarized economy, several major industries would feel the immediate shocks of authentic arms control, certain regions would suffer the loss of defense contracts, and segments of the labor force would experience the pains of unemployment. Thus we cannot expect the beneficiaries of hostility to be advocates of cooperation.

Despite contrasts between the United States and the Soviet Union, the foreign policy preferences of their national-security bureaucracies, and the position they occupy within their respective governmental structures, are not very different. These bureaucracies are situated strategically within both political systems, and they are responsible for assessing the very foreign threats upon which their growth and position depend. The potential for self-serving assessments is enormous. Moreover, the paradoxical nature of the relationship between US and Soviet national-security bureaucracies is quite interesting. While their mission is to struggle against each other, in fact they also are mutually dependent: without a threatening rival neither could find the arguments with which to justify its domestic position. Political leaders have sometimes commented on this bond. Norman Cousins reports that on President Kennedy's behalf he visited Khrushchev in 1963, in an attempt to clarify the US position on a nuclear test-ban treaty. Cousins recounts that Khrushchev described the pressure he was under from his military establishment, explaining that:

> Hardly a week passes without my generals coming to me with all sorts of terrifying stories—presented with all sorts of secret documents—saying that the Soviet Union is far behind the United States in the development of this or that weapon. They tell me that they cannot be responsible for the security of our country unless they get more rubles—billions of rubles—for

protecting us against your schemes to get ahead of us. I know the same thing is happening in your country. The generals need each other. That is the best way they have of strengthening their positions and making themselves important.[12]

When Cousins related this conversation to Kennedy, the president agreed with the Soviet leader's diagnosis. "Khrushchev has the system down pat," he said.[13]

However understandable the priorities of national-security bureaucracies may be, they should not be permitted to jeopardize a national security that depends at least as much on the absence of foreign adversaries as on an ability to confront them with force. National-security bureaucracies should not be allowed to fuel tension because their corporate interests call for a new piece of hardware, an increased slice of the budgetary pie, or expanded missions. In short, the growth of national-security bureaucracies should not be a product of their own *internal* needs but only of genuine threats from the other side.

However, it cannot be expected that national-security bureaucracies would bring their objectives into line with the long-term national interest when the two happen to conflict. Much as it is difficult to modify human nature through the vehicle of human nature, so it is naive to hope that entrenched organizations would readily renounce the pursuits upon which their position and resources hinge. Occasionally it may be possible to alter the nature of an organization's mission, while preserving its institutional interests, by channeling its resources into related but politically or socially more beneficial activities. For example, an arm of a military bureaucracy devoted to developing space-based weapons could be charged with developing space-based systems for monitoring arms control agreements—but such possibilities are quite limited. The realistic judgment is that national security organizations will continue to define their interests in terms of acquiring more missions or weapons and, wittingly or unwittingly, of encouraging the sort of international climate that this requires. Remedial pressure must therefore come from outside these organizations.

We know that government bureaucracies are extremely resilient. A study conducted by Herbert Kaufman of the Brookings Institution shows that of a sample of 175 US governmental organizations extant in 1923, fully 148 (85 percent) were still functioning 50 years later.[14] But an organization's influence is not necessarily constant, and there are ways in which it can be checked. The most direct approach is to reduce the bureaucracy's legal authority and the resources at its disposal. While there is some scope for this approach in all political systems, it is more easily accomplished under an authoritarian than a democratic regime. For example, and as already pointed out (Chapter 4), the US military establishment is in a unique position to create powerful alliances with members of the legislative branch or to appeal directly to public opinion via the news media. None of these options have been available to its Soviet counterpart, which cannot as easily sidle around central political authority.

The defense establishment's influence could be curtailed indirectly as well, by promoting the countervailing power of organizations with opposite interests. For example, the goal of offsetting the views and influence of the US Department of Defense likely was behind President Kennedy's decision to create the Arms Control and Disarmament Agency (ACDA) in 1961. This agency was to be the premier institution charged with planning for and pursuing arms control, but ACDA has not lived up to its promise. Instead, ACDA has had a minor influence on decisions regarding major military acquisitions and its directors have not always been chosen on the basis of their commitment to arms control. Lacking "both institutional weight and a public constituency,"[15] ACDA can hardly be considered a success; however, there is no other plausible example of an attempt to offset the power of a bureaucratic beneficiary of international tension by fostering an institution with competing interests.

Countervailing power need not always require the emergence of *new* institutions, since there are established governmental organizations whose interests are better served by conciliation than confrontation. The Department of Commerce in the United States and a variety of economic ministries in the Soviet Union are examples. To some extent the US Department of State and the USSR Ministry of Foreign Affairs may fall into this category as well. Under very special circumstances the aggregate power of these institutions could offset that of the national-security bureaucracies, but this too would require significant central governmental initiative and support.

These are ambitious propositions, and normally one would doubt that much could be achieved along these lines: it is difficult to tackle values directly and bureaucratic interests are resilient to change through explicit governmental action. Moreover, the economic interests that underpin the arms race also must be taken into account. The different nature of the superpower economic systems implies that although the defense effort carries virtually nothing but costs in the Soviet case, certain economic interests do benefit from military growth in the United States. Even though a demilitarized US economy is likely to benefit all Americans in the long term, it is the short-term costs that would matter most to the firms that lose lucrative military contracts, to unions whose members see defense-related jobs slipping away, to mayors whose cities are threatened by the closing of military-industrial facilities, and so forth. Naturally enough, political authorities would fear being held accountable for the short-term economic dislocations caused by reining in an arms race whose justification is lost as the Cold War unravels. So we must ask just how serious and unavoidable these dislocations would be?

Some research has been conducted on the conversion of military to civilian production, and a reasonably clear picture of the problems has emerged.[16] To begin with, the two sectors place different requirements on their members. Defense production, because of the nature of the missions it involves, imposes extremely high standards of performance and tolerance on designers and producers. On the other hand, questions of cost are of secondary importance for several reasons including the size of the Pentagon's budget, a general lack of competition among military producers, and the fact that pricing (and profit) are calculated on a cost-plus basis. On the other hand, in the civilian sector performance requirements are loose but cost is of paramount importance: here most products can find a market at the right price, no matter how shoddy their quality. Defense-industry managers and engineers thus would have to adapt to markets with very different demands. One such difference comes from the fact that in the military market one is dealing with a single customer. Whereas in the civilian market there are myriad customers who are not always easily identifiable in advance, and for whose business producers must constantly compete. Accordingly, deftness at bureaucratic lobbying would have to be replaced by expertise at commercial marketing—skills that are hardly similar.

Although certain problems are inevitable and some costs would have to be absorbed, they need not be extensive. One econometric study covering the period 1975–1980 assumed a hypothetical reduction in the Pentagon's budget of 30 percent, to be compensated for by an equivalent *increase* in the budgets for education, health, public assistance, and environmental programs. On the basis of a comprehensive model of the US economy, the study calculated that net output and employment would *rise* by 2.1 percent above the level otherwise expected.[17] In other words, no losses would be experienced *if* the cut in military outlays was associated with a simultaneous increase in public spending for civilian needs. In principle this is reassuring, but the key assumption of a compensatory increase is heroic. Despite its obvious desirability, spending on environmental protection, housing, or public health is just not the sort of stuff that kindles political ardor to the extent that defense against an ignoble enemy does—and it is not dealt with in as favorable a fashion by the political reward structure.

The practical challenges are not unmanageable, and the experience of communities affected by a loss of defense-related activity has been encouraging.[18] The problem is not of a technical but of a political character, and most of the impediments stem from the interests linked to military growth.

It is seldom acknowledged that military spending provides US governments with a useful tool of macroeconomic policy. In particular, increased military spending seems to be used in a Keynesian mode to offset the economic effects of sluggish consumer and investment spending. It is thus an instrument of countercyclical economic stabilization that would not be readily relinquished.[19] This difficulty is compounded in election and preelection years by the governmental practice of stimulating the economy in recognition of the US electorate's responsiveness to changing economic conditions.[20] Accordingly, adjustments in military spending may respond to electoral, as well as economic, cycles. If this strikes you as farfetched, the recollection of then Vice President Richard Nixon should prove enlightening. Apparently Arthur Burns, Eisenhower's economic adviser, visited Nixon in March 1960 and

> expressed great concern about the way the economy was then acting. . . . Burns' conclusion was that unless some decisive governmental action was taken, and taken soon, we were heading for another dip, which would hit its low in October, just before the elections. He urged strongly that everything be done to avert this development. He urgently recommended that two steps be taken immediately: by loosening up credit and, where justifiable, by *increasing spending for national security* (emphasis added).[21]

Thus, indirectly at least, defense spending provides a means of addressing the US public's economic desires to the government's political advantage. The political utility governments derive from military budgets, the fear of short-term dislocations if they are reduced significantly, and the difficulty of generating compensatory public spending in what is an essentially conservative society indicate that a substantial political will is required at the pinnacle of the political system before major steps toward accommodation can be taken.

What is called for is a significant reappraisal of national priorities by at least *one* of the superpowers, a reappraisal that would encourage moves to restrain those interests that militate against a revision of traditional priorities. The expectation is that this would then induce the *other* superpower to reciprocate and encourage it to overcome domestic resistance to accommodation. Ordinarily—and for all the reasons given—the scenario would be so implausible as to make this an idle line of inquiry, but post-Brezhnev developments in the Soviet Union offer the historically unique possibility that a path toward superpower conciliation might actually be developed in this manner.

## ADJUSTMENTS FROM WITHIN—AN OPTIMISTIC SCENARIO AND ITS LIMITS

### The Soviet Dilemma

The challenges facing the Soviet Union are great, and successful reforms will require a tranquil international environment. The regime's continued legitimacy will call for increased democratization and a redistribution of political power to those whose expertise will be most needed—but this cannot be accomplished in the face of external threats. At least as important, economic problems cannot be tackled successfully under conditions of East–West tension and an unrestrained arms race with the United States. In fact, Soviet economic problems may present the condition that, assuming appropriate US responses, could set in motion a chain of events ultimately leading to significantly improved relations between the two countries. The scenario is optimistic, but perhaps not unreasonably so.

Most of the problems stem directly from the Soviet economy's basic design. A system of rigid and comprehensive planning, associated with a measure of political coercion, may be the most effective way of realizing the capital accumulation needed when industrialization is launched initially, or when an economy must recover from the ravages of war. Soon, however, the efficient allocation of resources, individual motivation, and even technological creativity require the stimulus and discipline of the marketplace[22]—even if its vagaries are tempered in diverse ways. The problems of an inappropriate and run-down Soviet economic structure have been compounded further by the costs of East–West tension, which have assumed two principal forms.

To begin with, there is the problem of foregone trade with the United States. Restrictive US legislation—born of a political aversion to doing anything that might strengthen Russia's economy and power—and the rigidities of Soviet planning have hampered commerce between the two countries. During the past two decades the volume of Soviet trade with the United States has fluctuated between $2 and $4 billion, out of a volume of total trade with the developed world that has hovered in the vicinity of $40 to $50 billion.[23] In 1984, the year before Gorbachev came to power, exports to the United States accounted for only four percent of total USSR hard-currency exports. During the same year, however, imports from the United States represented twelve percent of the total USSR hard-currency imports,[24] which, although not a great deal, is nevertheless a meaningful amount. Grain purchases are a large part of these Soviet imports, but technologically advanced capital goods are much desired as well, and their importance to the Soviet economy probably exceeds their dollar value. The transition from extensive to intensive growth demands improved productivity, and it is less expensive to purchase the needed technology from abroad than to absorb the entire research and development costs. Even though sophisticated machinery and production-facility imports are rarely used by the Soviets as efficiently as they should be,[25] their economic value typically surpasses that of domestically available products and facilities. Access to US technology was a major carrot luring Brezhnev along the path to détente—and it matters to Gorbachev as well—but expanded trade demands cooperative Soviet-American relations, which in and of itself provides a strong incentive for the Kremlin to act accordingly.

Secondly, superpower rivalry continues to undermine the Soviet economy by the direct burden the arms race places upon it.[26] Because the Soviet economy is supply driven, growth is determined by the amount of goods and services that can be produced, which itself depends on the quality and availability of requisite factors of production. In principle, although industrial facilities constructed for civilian needs are unavailable for defense production (and vice versa), this does not present an immediate problem. Major investments in defense plants and industrial facilities were made in the seventies, and weapons produced through the early nineties will be manufactured in plants already built.[27] Accordingly, a steady pace of military production will not preclude an expansion of facilities for civilian production, at least not in the short term. However, competition between the military-industrial and civilian sectors could be fiercer in other ways. They could vie for limited supplies of raw materials—especially iron, steel, and certain chemicals as well.[28] There also could be considerable competition for energy and, most importantly, for skilled labor. For example, defense production and modern civilian industry require computer technicians and software engineers—both of which the Soviet Union lacks in sufficient numbers.

A lighter defense load would not create an immediate surge in economic growth—the decreased military burden would have to be substantial and sustained—but it could hasten the expansion of *consumption* levels,[29] which would be a major political boon for the regime. By bolstering public support for additional reform, improved consumption would create a domestic climate that could make long-term change politically feasible. Moreover, a reduction in East–West tensions would encourage increased social and cultural freedoms that, in turn, would release some of the country's long-suppressed creative energies and reduce the general cynicism that afflicts Soviet society.

All these potential benefits certainly have occurred to Gorbachev, and have played a significant part in Moscow's numerous conciliatory gestures during the first years of his incumbency. The desire for a placid international climate almost certainly inspired the Soviet leader to declare in a February 1988 speech primarily devoted to the virtues of economic reform and the need to "unshackle grass-roots initiatives," that international conditions had entered a "new phase" marked by a decrease in the expansionist threat posed by capitalism.[30] The link between domestic needs and international conditions has never been as evident.

Although political and bureaucratic opposition ultimately may thwart Gorbachev's reforms, it will be harder to muster conservative resistance to change than it was in previous decades. For example, until quite recently it could be claimed that the military represented "one of the forces opposing any significant change in the Soviet Union,"[31] including any shift away from heavy industry—yet the Soviet defense establishment is not myopic. It is perfectly capable of taking a long-term view of its own needs and of understanding that the economy's predicament does not bode well for its ability to sustain major levels of military procurement in the future. Thus, it is reasonable to think that the defense establishment would not be entirely hostile to reforms likely to improve productivity, boost scientific and technological innovation, and, more generally, improve the economic base from which its own resources spring. To this extent then, the defense establishment might be less inclined to see eye-to-eye with guardians of Party orthodoxy who oppose meaningful economic change, and relations with traditional heavy-industry interests could become more ambiguous than in the past. Moreover, realizing that the United States is economically and scientifically better equipped to pursue long-term competition in high-technology weapons, the Soviet military is likely to welcome arms control agreements that soften this reality.

These conditions reflect the changing nature of choices. For many decades, the question was who among several claimants would get a bigger slice of the budgetary pie. Would it be industry or agriculture? Consumption or investment? Guns or butter? But the emerging trade-offs are no longer between current claims on resources, but between the *present* and the *future*. A few sectors of Soviet society may not benefit from reform, and some will cling with bovine singlemindedness to the status quo; many, however, will understand grim reality and accept the short-term risks and difficulties of adapting to a new set of rules.

It also must be recognized that power eventually devolves to those groups, organizations, and individuals who hold the keys to society's effective operation (e.g., the business and legal professions in the United States). Accordingly, the Soviet system would no longer favor persons capable of protecting the status quo from challenge, but those best able to accomplish objectives involving change in the face of opposition born of inertia and entrenched interests. Authority might progressively shift from planners, professional ideologues, and policemen to managers, economists, and administrators. The power structures created by Stalin, unsuccessfully challenged by Khrushchev, and nursed along by Brezhnev might finally be transcended.

The result certainly would not be a Jeffersonian democracy, but the product of a long history finally adapted to the realities of the late-twentieth century. Although lip-service might still be paid to ideological goals, more effort would be devoted to rationalizing their practical neglect than to ensuring their successful pursuit. Expanded commercial relations with the West may raise fears of external economic dependence but, with declining threat perception, their credibility would lessen. More importantly, the political clout of those most prone to fan such fears would shrink and no longer merit constant deference by leaders concerned with their political future.

### A US Response

If the structure of its domestic political rewards and punishments has been primarily responsible for Moscow's US policy, then the fact that this structure is undergoing radical change must have major implications for superpower relations. A confluence of political and economic crises has created a genuine Soviet need for accommodation with the West; the central question is whether the United States will grasp this opportunity. Although no definitive answer is possible, it is difficult to assume with reasonable confidence that the opportunity will be seized. Even if the USSR does marshal the consensus needed to ensure steady progress toward conciliation, ultimately the United States may fail to reciprocate, thus undercutting the Kremlin's ability to persevere in this direction.

The Soviet Union is responding to a crisis caused by the inadequacy of its internal political and economic arrangements—the United States is not. Although US society would no doubt also benefit from various reforms—reduced economic reliance on the military sector, for example—and even though some of these reforms require a relaxation of East–West tensions, the problems here are not nearly as pressing as in Russia. Moreover, the Soviet need for improved access to American technology has no reciprocal parallel; likewise, the Soviet craving for the prestige that treatment as America's equal would confer upon it has no parallel US equivalent.

Given that incentives in the US are less pronounced, domestic difficulties may be greater. It is at once the major strength and the principal weakness of democracy that governmental freedom of action is circumscribed by the special needs and preferences of many different vested interests operating both within the state and within civil society. At times the power of such groups is disproportionate to their size (e.g., the National Rifle Association); nevertheless, the clarity with which they define their interests and their numerous points of access to power create both practical obstacles and political risks for a government attempting to oppose them.

Consequently, the US government may not marshal the political will needed to offset domestic resistance to improved Soviet relations. The motivation may not exist and, even if it does, the political risks of major strides in this direction may seem too great. National political values may, on balance, militate against a display of too much goodwill toward Moscow. Although to some extent American values flow from established interests, even if such interests are altered, Cold-War beliefs derive from a specific set of historical experiences as well—beliefs sustained by a variety of psychological and cultural mechanisms, none of which is easily molded to fit the requirements of specific policies.

These problems are, however, balanced somewhat by an apparent mellowing of American public opinion toward the USSR, a development reflected in its attitude toward the Soviet leader. In December 1987, just before the Washington summit that produced the agreement eliminating medium-range nuclear missiles in Europe, the American public was asked to evaluate Gorbachev. Thirty-eight percent of respondents reported a favorable opinion, whereas less than half as many (16 percent) reported an unfavorable impression (45 percent had not formed an opinion).[32] The significance of these figures is reflected in the fact that Gorbachev received a higher approval rating than any declared US presidential candidate at the time except George Bush (who received a 39-percent positive rating that was, however, balanced by a 25-percent negative rating). Earlier surveys conducted by the Gallup Poll reported even higher favorable ratings for Gorbachev compared to substantially less favorable ratings for the Soviet Union's other major reformer, Nikita Khrushchev (Table 6-1).

Although total pessimism is not justified, political realism cautions against unbridled optimism; the scenario outlined earlier may have assumed too much. The recent changes in the Soviet Union may yet be reversed and, even if they are not, the United States may not respond fully to the conciliatory moves that are their logical consequence. If so, no

**Table 6-1**
US Public Rates Gorbachev and Khrushchev*

|  | Gorbachev | | | Khrushchev | |
|  | Favorable | Unfavorable |  | Favorable | Unfavorable |
|---|---|---|---|---|---|
| 1987 (July) | 54% | 28% | 1957 | 7% | 61% |
| 1987 (October) | 44% | 47% | 1963 | 5% | 91% |
|  |  |  | 1964 | 10% | 82% |

*Source: "Gallup Report," No. 263, August 1987, p. 30.

more may be attainable—despite the changes in the Soviet Union—than détente of the sort effected by Nixon and Brezhnev. Even this would be better than what usually characterizes superpower relations, but considerably less than what might have been. From the Soviet perspective, such limited cooperation would focus on acquiring whatever economic benefit could be had; for the United States, the primary benefit would be to strengthen US leverage over Russian behavior. And the arms race might stabilize, but military arsenals would not be meaningfully reduced. The superpower relationship would still be dominated by its confrontational components and, were its equilibrium to be disturbed, the most likely outcome would be a return to the Cold War. If the political resources necessary to go beyond this state are not mustered, it may be that genuine improvements would be ushered in only by fear born of a near brush with mutual destruction.

## THE ROLE OF FEAR

Dread before the consequences of inaction often overcome resistance and inertia; before the fright, however, they seem nearly intractable. As the federal budget deficit expanded enormously during the Reagan presidency, the Administration and Congress were unable to devise a way of controlling it; yet the President stood firm against the obvious remedy of a tax increase. Enter the stock-market crash of October 19, 1987, which sent the Dow Jones Industrial Averages into its greatest tailspin in history, amid disquieting comparisons with 1929. Within a few days conferees from the executive and legislative branches met to discuss deficit reduction, and the President let it be known that he was softening his opposition to revenue enhancement. The Cuban Missile Crisis during the Kennedy administration provides an even more vivid illustration of the galvanizing effect of intense fear. Despite lengthy efforts, the United States and the Soviet Union had been unable to agree on a treaty limiting nuclear tests; negotiations foundered on issues of verification and the number of tests permitted each side. But the brief glimpse into the abyss permitted by the missile crisis shook the superpowers into the frame of mind that led to the Partial Test Ban Treaty of 1963 and the Hot Line Agreement of 1962, which launched the negotiations that eventually led to the SALT I and SALT II agreements.

The motivating power of fear is widely exploited. In the Soviet Union, fear has long been the foundation of political conformism and control; in the United States it takes various forms. In America fear is a pillar of the advertising industry that, for example, skillfully plays on the dread of social stigma attached to dandruff—which can be avoided only by using a recommended shampoo—or of leaving one's family destitute if a certain company's life insurance policy is not purchased. To a limited but not insignificant extent, scare tactics also are useful in US political life where politicians rouse fears of the consequences (e.g., new taxes or rampant inflation) of electing an opponent or of failing to support certain legislation. We also have seen how efforts to jar the US public into a heightened state of anti-Soviet sentiment relied, in the early fifties and late seventies, on conscious overstatements of the Russian threat.

Although fear has received considerable attention from psychologists studying motivation it has played only a minor role in the traditional focus of political scientists. With the exception of analyses on nuclear deterrence, fear has not been studied systematically as an originator of political activity or as a basis for policy decisions. Yet, where necessary action is hobbled by short-term calculations and assorted vested interests, fear may be the most effective way of breaking the logjam of parochial resistance. Nevertheless, the potential for abuse is enormous when fear is promoted as a matter of policy. However, fear can originate from circumstances not explicitly sought—as evidenced by the stock-market crash of 1987 and the Cuban Missile Crisis of 1962.

One advantage, if it may be considered as such, of intense dread as a motivator is that it can permeate society in a roughly uniform fashion. In a manner of speaking, dread functions economically. Policies targeted directly at various special interests require as many strands as there are separate interests; different groups clamor for varying forms of satisfaction, and a considerable number must be appeased or restrained. Although interests may be manifold, fear, for its part, can operate uniformly—across the board, so to speak. A major benefit of fear produced by a near collision between superpowers is that war avoidance is moved closer to the top of the national system of values, thus addressing the issue of values directly rather than by way of special interests. Even at the brink of disaster, different people assign different probabilities to its occurrence and, ultimately, destruction may not matter as much to everyone. Nevertheless, the most likely thrust of a society's response to near catastrophe is the firm resolve never again to be driven so close to the precipice.

Fear, however, is a complex emotion, and its motivational qualities depend on various circumstances. One must distinguish, as psychologists often do, between neurotic anxiety and realistic fear.[33] The former involves no reality testing to determine if the fear is well-founded; as such, it encourages suppression of thoughts about the danger rather than efforts to deal with it. By contrast, the latter usually leads to realistic action to eliminate or avoid the threat. The distinction is important but not directly relevant to the sort of situation considered here, for we are assuming a fear that is grounded in an authentic and intense sense of peril caused by a brush with nuclear disaster. Perhaps a more relevant question is whether the fear is numbing or galvanizing, for a numbing fear is, at best, a pointless experience.

Robert Lifton, in his widely read book entitled *The Broken Connection,* argues that the anxiety evoked by nuclear threat, and the associated possibility of total loss, produces a form of emotional dulling that "undermines the most fundamental psychic processes."[34] If the price of fright is the creation of emotional vegetables, it could hardly be productive; yet in the nuclear context at least, the evidence points in the opposite direction. Certain more recent experimental research has found that people who engage in antinuclear activism tend to be especially concerned about nuclear war and to consider it a more imminent threat than do others.[35] Another study found that activists' images of nuclear war are more immediate and concrete than those of nonactivists.[36] The implication is that a decision to do something about a threat is linked to the extent of the perceived peril and that, therefore, a dramatically intensified threat is more likely to have a galvanizing than a numbing effect. But, what makes fear a risky proposition—even assuming that destruction does not occur—is that fear can be attributed to either the rival or the relationship itself.

When rival parties become frightened, they may be responding to either of two types of fear. They may be afraid of the consequences that the antagonism could yield or they may be especially afraid of their adversary. For example, rival local retailers, each of whom is trying to undercut the other's prices, are linked by an adversarial relationship. Each may be afraid that the downward pressure on prices caused by the competition will eliminate his (or her) profit margins, in which case the anxiety is produced by the relationship itself. But each party may be even more afraid of the other, anticipating that the rival will capture a sufficient market share to drive the adversary out of business. The importance of the distinction is that the two sources of fear are likely to have entirely different consequences. As a general rule it seems that if the primary source of fear is the relationship itself, steps are taken to make it more cooperative; but if anxiety is directed primarily toward the rival, intensified antagonism ensues. If mutually afraid of the relationship, the two retailers would try to make it cooperative (e.g., through duopolistic price fixing); if primarily afraid of each other, each would seek to make the rival break first under the strain of the price war.

The analogy applies to US-Soviet relations. If the overriding fear concerns the consequences of the superpower rivalry (e.g., mutual destruction), the two countries may take steps to set their relations on a less perilous tack. If each is more afraid of the rival's power or intentions, the competition is likely to be spurred by a determination to overtake (or outmaneuver) the adversary. In the Cuban Missile Crisis, the former was probably the dominant response, although from the Soviet point of view US nuclear superiority aroused elements of overtaking and outmaneuvering as well. Both countries worked to improve their relations and to avoid future crises; the Russians, in addition, sought to catch up with America's missile capacity so as to avoid another humiliation of the sort experienced on that occasion.

The conclusion: If the fright induced by near annihilation is to make both countries rethink the bases of their relationship and to take decisive steps to improve that relationship, certain conditions must be met. Most essentially, the circumstances inducing the fright should appear to each side to have resulted more from circumstances over which neither had much control than from the other's malevolence or assertive power. The most obvious scenario is that situation where both countries are carried on the wave of a runaway crisis toward probable catastrophe but manage, by the skin of their teeth, to avoid disaster. Actual situations could be sketched, but the point is that both sides would be drawn to the very edge of the precipice and manage, only by the most desperate last-ditch efforts, to claw their way back from the brink. The principal consequence might be an intensified sense of dread, a repugnance at the situation they had created for themselves, and a desperate resolve to do better if given the chance.

We have viewed fright as an exogenous condition capable of inducing a change for the better in Soviet-American relations. However, nothing suggests that the apocalypse should be pursued toward this end for, if driven sufficiently close to disaster, the superpowers may well slide into the abyss. A Soviet policy redirected in response to its domestic needs, followed by an American reappraisal of its attitudes, would be a far preferable road toward improved relations. The possibility that the shortest road to conciliation leads through a brush with catastrophe says much about the depth of the rivalry's roots, but not about the strength of its foundations, and better cures can be found only if the sources of the predicament are adequately understood.

In more ways than one, the issues discussed in Chapter

6 involve a struggle between the Old and the New—both within the Soviet Union and in the ways the superpowers deal with each other. If the changes in priorities and in the structure of political and social authority promoted by the Gorbachev regime manage to survive the opposition of vested bureaucratic and other interests and the opposition of those for whom the reforms are ideological anathema, a condition for significant improvement in US-Soviet relations—even in the absence of highly intensified dread—will have been satisfied. If the United States musters the political courage to act on this opportunity, both a necessary and a sufficient condition will have been met. Granted, this may or may not occur—yet an important juncture in international history has assuredly been reached. Neither historical experience nor traditional recipes of political science furnish clear guidelines on how to proceed, but if the reasoning presented in this book is substantially correct, the fundamental solutions and sustained will must come from *within* each superpower.

## NOTES

1. For example, see Robert Axelrod and Robert O. Keohane, "Achieving Cooperation Under Anarchy: Strategies and Institutions," and the other contributions to the special issue devoted to the topic of international cooperation, *World Politics,* October 1985, pp. 226–254.
2. "Crisis Prevention in Nineteenth Century Diplomacy," in Alexander L. George, ed., *Managing the US-Soviet Rivalry: Problems of Crisis Prevention* (Boulder, CO: Westview Press, 1983), p. 45.
3. Same as 2, p. 38.
4. Charles Osgood, *An Alternative to War or Surrender* (Urbana: University of Illinois Press, 1962).
5. Robert Axelrod, *The Evolution of Cooperation* (New York: Basic Books, 1984).
6. J. David Singer, "Disarmament: The Domestic and Global Context," in John H. Gilbert, ed., *The New Era in American Foreign Policy* (New York: St. Martin's Press, 1973), pp. 179–180.
7. Robert Jervis, *Perception and Misperception in International Politics* (Princeton: Princeton University Press, 1976), Chapter 12.
8. The desirability of devil's advocates is also argued in Alexander L. George, "The Case for Multiple Advocacy in Making Foreign Policy," *American Political Science Review,* September 1972, pp. 751–785.
9. Irving Janis, *Victims of Groupthink* (Boston: Houghton Mifflin, 1972).

10. Same as 7, pp. 417–418.

11. See Alexander Yanov, *The Soviet Challenge and the Year 2000* (New York: Basil Blackwell, 1987).

12. Norman Cousins, *The Pathology of Power* (New York: W. W. Norton, 1987), p. 183.

13. Same as 12, p. 184.

14. Herbert Kaufman, *Are Government Organizations Immortal?* (Washington, DC: The Brookings Institution, 1976).

15. Duncan Clarke, *Politics of Arms Control: The Role and Effectiveness of the U.S. Arms Control and Disarmament Agency* (New York: The Free Press, 1979), p. 62.

16. See, for example, Betty G. Lall, *Prosperity Without Guns: The Economic Impact of Reductions in Defense Spending* (New York: Operation Turning Point, Institute for World Order, 1977); Suzanne Gordon and Dave McFadden, eds., *Economic Conversion: Revitalizing America's Economy* (Cambridge, MA:Ballinger, 1984); John E. Lynch, ed., *Economic Adjustment and Conversion of Defense Industries* (Boulder, CO: Westview Press, 1987).

17. Roger H. Bezdek, "The 1980 Economic Impact—Regional and Occupational—of Compensated Shifts in Defense Spending," *Journal of Regional Science,* XV (1975), pp. 183–198.

18. See, for example, The President's Economic Adjustment Committee, *Economic Recovery: Community Response to Defense Decisions to Close Bases* (Washington, DC: Defense Office of Economic Adjustment, 1976) and Thomas P. Ruane, *Federal Responses to Economic Crises: The Case of Defense Economic Adjustment* (Washington, DC: Department of Defense, 1977).

19. As John Kenneth Galbraith has accurately observed:

    If a large sector of the economy, supported by personal and corporate income taxation, is the fulcrum for the regulation of demand, plainly military expenditures are the pivot on which the fulcrum rests.

    *The New Industrial States* (New York: Penguin, 1967), p. 235.

20. See Edward Tufte, *The Political Control of the Economy* (Princeton, NJ: Princeton University Press, 1978) and "The Determinants of the Outcome of Mid-term Congressional Elections," *American Political Science Review,* LXIX, (1975), pp. 812–826. Also, Gerald Kramer, "Short Term Fluctuations in US Voting Behavior, 1896–1964," *American Political Science Review,* LXV, (1971).

21. Richard M. Nixon, *Six Crises* (New York: Doubleday, 1962), p. 309.

22. For a leading exposition of the pervasive utility of markets, see Charles F. Lindblom, *Politics and Markets* (New York: Basic Books, 1977).

23. For quantitative information on the developments in US-Soviet trade, see Hertha W. Heiss, "U.S.-Soviet Trade Trends" and Joan F. McIntyre, "The USSR's Hard Currency Trade and Payments Position,"

both in *Gorbachev's Economic Plans: Study Papers Submitted to the Joint Economic Committee, Congress of the United States* (Washington, DC: U.S. Congress, Joint Economic Committee, 100th Congress, 1st Session, 1987), pp. 450–473 and 474–488.

24. See *Foreign Economic Trends and Their Implications for the United States* (Washington, DC: U.S. Department of Commerce, December 1985).

25. The problems the Soviet Union encounters when trying to apply Western technology are detailed in Marshall I. Goldman, *Gorbachev's Challenge: Economic Reform in the Age of High Technology* (New York: W. W. Norton, 1987), Chapter 5.

26. On this topic, see Miroslav Nincic, *The Arms Race: The Political Economy of Military Growth* (New York: Praeger, 1982), Chapter 3 and Abraham S. Becker, *Sitting on Bayonets: The Soviet Defense Burden and the Slowdown of Soviet Defense Spending,* Rand/UCLA Center for the Study of Soviet International Behavior, JRS-01, December 1985. On a related issue, see Charles Wolf, Jr. et al., *The Costs of Soviet Empire* (Santa Monica, CA: Rand Corporation, R-3073/1-NA, 1983).

27. See Central Intelligence Agency and Defense Intelligence Agency, "The Soviet Economy Under a New Leader," (Washington, DC: Report Presented to the Subcommittee on Economic Resources, Competitiveness, and Security Economics of the Joint Economic Committee, March 19, 1986).

28. Same as 27, p. 21.

29. For reasons why consumption would benefit before overall growth rates accelerated significantly, see, for example, Gregory G. Hildebrandt, "The Dynamic Burden of Soviet Defense Spending," *Soviet Economy in the 1980's: Problems and Prospects* (Washington, DC: Selected Papers Submitted to the Joint Economic Committee, Congress of the United States, December 31, 1982.

30. "Gorbachev Urges Party to Update Communist Theory," *New York Times,* February 19, 1988.

31. Jerry Hough, *Soviet Leadership in Transition* (Washington, DC: The Brookings Institution, 1980), p. 106.

32. "Gorbachev a Hit With the American Public," *New York Times,* December 4, 1987.

33. See, for example, Kenneth L. Higbee, "Fifteen Years of Fear Arousal," *Psychological Bulletin,* LXXII, 1969, pp. 426–444.

34. Robert J. Lifton, *The Broken Connection* (New York: Touchstone Books, 1979).

35. Margaret Garrett Locatelli and Robert R. Holt, "Antinuclear Activism, Psychic Numbing, and Mental Health," *International Journal of Mental Health,* XV, pp. 143–161.

36. S. T. Fiske, F. Pratto, and M. A. Pavlechak, "Citizens' Images of Nuclear War: Content and Consequences," *Journal of Social Issues* XXXIX, 1983, p. 41.

# AFTERWORD

◆ ◆ ◆ ◆ ◆

On December 8, 1988, Mikhail Gorbachev cut short a brief visit to the United States, returning home to supervise Soviet relief efforts in the wake of the catastrophic earthquake that had stricken Armenia the previous day. His brief visit marked the transition from the Reagan era to the presidency of George Bush, and was designed to set the stage for relations during the remainder of the decade and the beginning of the next. The mini-summit differed from most that had preceded it. Unlike the meetings of the fifties and sixties, it was not an exercise in Cold War sparring and self-serving propaganda. Unlike several more recent summits, no one anticipated that a single major breakthrough would propel relations into a new era. Much had already been achieved by December 1988, and the prospect of steady, if incremental, progress on the course charted between 1986 and 1988 was what most observers expected to witness. At the same time, the brief summit and the circumstances that preceded it and surrounded it brought home a number of truths— above all, that the policies of each superpower toward the other reflect, not just its own external and domestic interests, but those operating within the *other* side.

Although the recent US presidential election retained a number of traditional features, a sense of change was nevertheless apparent. Democratic nominee Michael Dukakis initially tried to capitalize on the friendlier public mood toward the Soviet Union, arguing against major new weapons systems and an interventionist foreign policy. Following established formulas, Vice President George Bush moved the debate to more traditional turf—defending the new strategic weapons systems as necessary precautions against the Soviet threat and going so far as to question Dukakis's patriotism. President Reagan joined the fray, vetoing the proposed military budget on grounds of its alleged insufficiency, prompting Senator Lloyd Bentsen—Democratic vice-presidential nominee—to accuse the President of "poisoning defense politics with partisan politics."[1] The anti-Soviet electoral theme had played an even greater role in the Republican Party's primary elections.

Nevertheless, the old convictions seemed somewhat shopworn and, although the traditional political reward structure pierced through the new sobriety in America's attitudes, it did so in a milder, more halting, manner. After the primaries, the need to support steadily improving relations was never seriously questioned, and no major buildups of military force were promised or contemplated.

A number of politically significant events occurred in the Soviet Union during the months preceding the final summit of the Reagan era. Gorbachev's sternest critics within the Politburo, Yegor Ligachev and Viktor Chebrikov, were moved to positions of lesser responsibility within the power structure. Moreover, shortly before the Soviet leader's arrival in New York—in an effort to circumvent the centers of resistance to reform within the party—the Supreme Soviet enacted a government reorganization plan. The plan granted parliament more authority than it had ever had since the 1930s, and it endowed the post of president, which Gorbachev assumed, with significant new powers. Revisions in the penal code were also being hammered out that placed the rule of law on a much firmer footing, largely eliminating political terror and arbitrary exercise of state coercion.

At the same time, several events served to remind all who cared that the new political reality rested on fragile foundations. During his visit to New York, General Secretary Gorbachev delivered an address to the UN General Assembly in which he proposed major unilateral cuts in the USSR's conventional forces. He offered to reduce Soviet troop strength by approximately 500,000 (some ten percent of the total) and to remove 10,000 tanks (of a total of 40,000) from Eastern Europe. As Russia's edge in tanks remained a major source of concern to NATO, the gesture was enthusiastically welcomed in the West—but greeted with less than universal enthusiasm within the USSR. Marshal Sergei Akhromeyev, the Soviet Chief of Staff who was considered one of Gorbachev's close supporters, promptly resigned amid grumbling in several sectors of the military establishment.

By the time of the visit, it was also generally recognized that perestroika had as yet to produce tangible results. This, of course, should have come as no surprise: an economic mechanism as enormous and creaky as that evolved by the USSR cannot be altered and set on a dynamic footing in a few short years. In fact, it may be unreasonable to expect the fruits of economic reform to become apparent until the end of this century, or the beginning of the next. Still, the patience of the Soviet public, and the forbearance of the newly disenfranchised segments of the traditional power elites, have their limits—and if significant challenges to Gorbachev's leadership emerge, they are far more likely to come from a hawkish than a dovish direction. Moreover, by late 1988, the danger of economic discontent in the Soviet Union was compounded by serious ethnic unrest—in Armenia and Azerbaijan in the south, and in the Baltic republics in the north. It became apparent that Gorbachev's ability to deal with the challenges of managing a restive, multinational nation would shape the prospects for glasnost and perestroika as well and, by extension, his ability to sustain the newly cooperative course in foreign policy.

If one is constantly reminded of the fragility of the power structure that, within the Soviet Union, must bear the weight of bold and risky reforms, one must also recognize that its stability will be affected by the responses of the United States—and these, in turn, depend on US domestic political patterns.

As the US President, President-elect, and Soviet leader met over lunch during the mini-summit, the Americans assured their guest that the United States wished his reforms well. Apparently they were responding to Gorbachev's concern that politically powerful US groups desired otherwise. And to some extent, he was right. US conservatives argued that a more economically successful Soviet Union would not be in America's interests, and William Webster, Director of Central Intelligence, observed as late as October that it was "not at all clear" that the West should want Gorbachev to succeed in his domestic effort.[2] Resistance to change by national bureaucracies on both sides was also recognized by each leader over lunch, and President Reagan pointed out that "whether it's a Russian bureaucracy or one of our own, the first rule of bureaucracy is to protect itself."[3]

Thus, as a new US administration assumed office, and as the Gorbachev regime continued to confront its many challenges, we were reminded then, as now, that superpower relations are as much the product of domestic political circumstances as of the interplay of international interests and capabilities. Accordingly, the future of the new détente continues to depend on the balance between confrontation and conciliation produced by the evolving structure of interests, beliefs, and power within the United States and the Soviet Union.

## NOTES

1. "Bentsen Terms Veto of Military Bill Political," *New York Times*, August 7, 1988.
2. "Reagan and Bush Told Gorbachev of Hope for Perestroika Success," *New York Times*, December 10, 1988.
3. Same as 2.

# Suggested Readings

Abel, Elie. *The Missile Crisis* (New York: Bantam Books, 1966).

Axelrod, Robert M. *The Evolution of Cooperation* (New York: Basic Books, 1984).

Bailey, Thomas A. *America Faces Russia: Russian-American Relations from Early Times to Our Days* (Ithaca, NY: Cornell University Press, 1950).

Blacker, Coit. *Reluctant Warriors: The United States, the Soviet Union, and Arms Control* (New York: W. H. Freeman, 1987).

Brams, Steven. *Superpower Games: Applying Game Theory to the Superpower Conflict* (New Haven: Yale University Press, 1985).

Cohen, Stephen. *Rethinking the Soviet Experience* (New York: Oxford University Press, 1985).

Gaddis, John L. *Strategies of Containment: A Critical Appraisal of Postwar American National Security Policy* (New York: Oxford University Press, 1982).

George, Alexander L. *Managing US-Soviet Rivalry: Problems of Crisis Prevention* (Boulder, CO: Westview Press, 1983).

Gorbachev, Mikhail. *Perestroika: New Thinking for Our Country and the World* (New York: Harper and Row, 1987).

Jonson, Christer. *Superpower: Comparing American and Soviet Foreign Policy* (New York: St. Martins Press, 1984).

Kennan, George F. *Russia and the West Under Lenin and Stalin* (Boston: Atlantic Monthly Press, 1960).

Lafeber, Walter. *America, Russia, and the Cold War*, 5th edition (New York: Alfred A. Knopf, 1985).

Lewin, Moshe. *The Gorbachev Phenomenon: A Historical Interpretation* (Berkeley: University of California Press, 1988).

Nincic, Miroslav. *The Arms Race: The Political Economy of Military Growth* (New York: Praeger, 1982).

Nincic, Miroslav. *United States Foreign Policy: Choices and Tradeoffs* (Washington, DC: Congressional Quarterly Press, 1988).

Nixon, Richard M. *1999: Victory Without War* (New York: Simon and Schuster, 1988).

Nye, Joseph S. Jr., ed. *The Making of America's Soviet Policy* (New Haven: Yale University Press, 1984).

Weisberger, Bernard A. *Cold War, Cold Peace* (New York: Houghton Mifflin, 1984).

White, Ralph K. *Fearful Warriors: A Psychological Profile of US-Soviet Relations* (New York: The Free Press, 1984).

Yanov, Alexander. *The Soviet Challenge and the Year 2000* (New York: Basil Blackwell, 1987).

# Index

9486